THE MORNING LIGHT

*Prue Smith was born in Johannesburg in 1923. After studying
at Wits University, she won a scholarship to Oxford.
Her working career began as producer in the talks department
of the BBC's Third Programme. After a spell in Longman's
African division, she was called back to the BBC as
production director for their new Open University productions. Later she worked as a freelance in the cause of
education by radio in Africa and Asia. Prue Smith died in
Oxford on Christmas Eve 1999.*

THE MORNING LIGHT

A South African childhood revalued

Prue Smith

DAVID PHILIP
Cape Town

First published in 2000 by David Philip Publishers (Pty) Ltd,
208 Werdmuller Centre, Claremont 7708, South Africa

© 2000 The estate of Prudence Smith

ISBN 0-86486-461-2

Text design by Sarah-Anne Raynham
Cover design by Sarah-Anne Raynham and Julia Raynham

Printed by Creda Communications, Epping, Cape Town

CONTENTS

PREFACE

This is a book about my childhood in South Africa, long ago, and about what those early years have meant for me in the decades since (as soon as I could) I left the country; and about what its new political freedom, and my ability to return, mean to me. But anyone who looks for clear statements or predictions – for 'opinions', let alone prophecy – will be disappointed. I am not a seer, or a power. I am daily surprised by the enormity of the events and the disclosures which pour forth from so troubled and manifold and now so confessional a land; but I am also, time after time, dumbfounded with wonder and thankfulness at the difference between the now and the then of living there.

My record of these events and experiences lies far beyond the scope of 'opinions'. Opinions are the discarded shells in which hermit crabs hide themselves, trying for a new security or a new identity. What I have put down may be seen as moves towards such a fastness, at least for myself; at any rate, I know that in sometimes minute recollections of my own past I have found ways of thinking and feeling which enliven my view of the present and steady me when I think of the future and of the country's future.

In the years since I have felt able to stay again in South Africa, the warmth and sunshine themselves seem to have lighted the way back to my childhood and to the great ones of my childhood; and that, in turn, to have shown me the directions, or the reasons for them, of the rest of my life. It has been a strange, even miraculous experience, to revisit a past which I had thought was lost. It is not to be compared with the change which political freedom has meant to the black people of South Africa; but for people like me, too – and there are very, very many of us – there have been, in spite of many consequential problems, untold blessings and releases in the Freedom of Mandela.

Cape of Good Hope, 1998

DEDICATION

～⌒～

For Michael
and for our dear children

"As the apple tree among the trees of the wood, so is my beloved
among the sons. I sat down under his shadow with great delight,
and his fruit was sweet to my taste."

— *The Song of Solomon* 2.3

The Morning Light

1 Babur, Boers and a Briton

A few years ago I went to see some of the gardens created in India by the great Moghul emperors of the fifteenth and sixteenth centuries. There is little left today to remind you of the savagery of their warfare, their debauchery, drunkenness and successional murders. What you see are the ruins of their pleasant places and the evidence of exquisite judgement in matters of taste: halls, pavilions and bowers, refuges against the heat and the blinding light of the day; terraces to enjoy the evening and the stars; above all, places for water – pools, basins, channels, fountains. There are few flowers planted there today, but you can see the elaborate provision for curving, geometric beds of them and the channels and wells for their watering.

In the great halls and colonnades and audience chambers, on almost every surface of pillars, walls, dados, balustrades and sills, there is the exquisite inlay work and sometimes carving of tendrils, petals, leaves, calyces and twining stems of minutely observed flowering plants. Their delicate arabesques and intricate patterning of form and colour play like tender music over the massive forms of the architecture; as once, long ago, the elaborate watercourses over the bold forms of the gardens.

Except in Kashmir, there was rarely enough water to sustain these gardens, and there is even less now. Akbar had to leave, after only fourteen years, the beautiful and elaborate city he built at

Fatehpur Sikri. It must be the absence of water which has led to its fine state of preservation so that today you can walk around and admire complete forms of architecture, and streets, façades, gardens, paths, basins and unexpected glimpses, between buildings, of the countryside. You can visit a past lacking only the people who made it – and of course, still lacking water. When I was there I saw in a courtyard, under a stunted tree, a man surrounded by a crowd of gourd-like clay pots; they looked like an attentive audience of little rotund figures listening to the repeated phrases in which, it appeared, he announced that he was selling these oriental pipkins of water to thirsty tourists.

A smaller, sadder, monument to drought and desertification can be seen at Agra where Akbar's grandfather, Babur, laid out the garden he especially loved and in which, in 1530, he died. When he first reached Agra, Babur wrote in his journal, 'One of the great defects of Hindustan being its lack of running waters, it kept coming to my mind that waters should be made to flow by means of wheels erected wherever I might settle down, also that grounds should be laid out in an orderly and symmetrical way.' Babur's Ram Bagh is laid out high on the eastern bank of the Yamuna not far from the Taj Mahal, though almost no one of the millions who visit the Taj ever goes there. I had to steer around a resting cow and clear away mounds of pruned branches and dead leaves before I could even pass through its entrance. The prunings were evidence of basic maintenance and care, even if of public neglect. I came upon two or three men weeding with small knives, sitting on their hunkers in the time-honoured way of Indian gardeners, as you can see in Moghul paintings. I wanted to photograph this position, which is to us, who are used to chairs, so painful; but the young man whose permission I asked insisted on standing up, brushing himself off and stiffly posing; even both rows of his shining teeth came out on parade. It was an interesting clash between a man's historical and professional role (my idea) and his feelings as a human being (his idea). I asked his name so that I might send him his portrait, but he said 'Babur'. Perhaps it was.

In Babur's time water was often taken up from the river by bucket-paddled wheels – 'Persian' water wheels – set in towers which were built into great retaining walls. In the usual fashion it would be taken to high storage tanks and from there controlled to flow down a succession of terraced levels through channels and down chutes into lower tanks and basins, and at length thrown into the air in the release of fountains, in some spot where, after all its work of watering the beds and filling the pools, it could afford to humankind a blessed refreshment at the end of the day.

It happens, however, that on this site Babur changed his mind about the use of Persian wheels for water and resorted instead to a well and storage tanks. When I was there, even this system had become far from operational. As for the great river Yamuna, it had become, at that season, a slimy, shallow stream wandering through wide, flat beds and bordered by shores, the evidence of its former abundance. I stood on Babur's high ramparts and looked down to watch where, on the old river beds, men were working on well-established allotments and women were laying out washing to dry. The Lord Krishna, the powerful blue-skinned flautist, used to graze his cows and flirt with the milkmaids on the banks of the Yamuna. When I was there, children were coaxing the family cows down onto the bed to graze on viridian or emerald patches of algae, or to drink from the shallow, muddy pools.

In Babur's garden, as in the deserted, ghostly city of Fatehpur Sikri and in other ancient Indian gardens, I became aware of a strange, sad sweetness in my mind. Many of us succumb to delicious melancholy among deserted human places – the melancholy, as Shenstone remarked, 'which proceeds from a reflexion on decayed magnificence' – but my sensations were not brought on entirely by historical reflections, or by the ambience of these places. I found my spirits affected by specific instances that were all to do with the water, or lack of it. The storage tanks were dry and dusty, rather smelly, withered debris in their corners; the water chutes which conducted the rills to progressively lower terraces had been in their prime glazed blue and sculpted into the little carved waves which used, I suppose, to make the water flash and twinkle. Now they were dry, of course, whitened, cracked and baking in the blaze of the sun.

I know now that what I was experiencing was a rather pure form of nostalgia – pure because it was unwilled, not brought on by hardship or self-pity; it came of itself and was all of the memory and the senses, and the memory of the senses. It was nostalgia for the country and continent that I had left, my first home, my home garden, my childhood and – part of all these yet more than all – for my father.

It caused me to turn aside from research into the horticultural nature of Paradise, or paradises (the chief conclusion of which was that their imagined features, however holy, are always based upon the gardens of the contemporary rich), to the study, instead, of my own paradise. This is why I sought again, one time more out of many, to trace and to face the memory of my father; for it was he who made our garden, out of the side of a barren, waterless hill of the Highveld, in the outskirts north of Johannesburg.

My father, Leslie Pryce, was an Englishman, tall, handsome and, because in fact half Welsh, dark. He was a loving and humorous man yet in his manner grave, I thought even majestic; a considerate, quiet person. He was utterly methodical, orderly and rather cautious in all he did, but the garden was a monument to his creativity, which must always have been there; brought to flower, perhaps, by my mother's eagerness for beauty and for social renown, and by their common longing for a good place to bring up children. I don't suppose it was an outstandingly happy marriage, for they were by temperament almost precisely opposed; but it was a marvellous conjunction.

I have two albums of photographs which between 1900 and 1902, long before his marriage, my father had sent from South Africa back to his home in England. His sister Olive carefully

Father and daughter

mounted and labelled them according to what his letters said. He
was born and educated in England but had gone to South Africa as
an engineering student aged 17, joining the Electrical Engineers'
Volunteer Corps to fight in what his and my generation (of English
speakers) always called the Boer War but which is now usually
called the South African War. 'Boer' has become a doubly offensive
word, meaning not only a rustic Afrikaner but now, at least in the
parlance of the black majority, any confirmed pro-apartheid
oppressor. The word is showing, in response to changing historical
attitudes, the same lurches of connotation which have marked, in
South Africa, the passage from 'kaffirs' through 'natives' to the
now rejected 'bantu' and 'African' to plain 'black', though I have
heard it's changing again, as it did in Zambia after Independence

where it went through similar changes and has ended up, simplest of all, as 'Zambian'. I don't suppose this excellent and unifying solution is open to us in South Africa – for a while.

My father's second and later album does indeed show evidence of electrical interests: not only some stunning photographs of lightning, cracking the sky or emblazoning the horizon, but also the erection of signalling masts, hospital lighting and, most interesting of all, the lighting of the camp of the peace conference at Vereeniging in May 1902. There are some pictures from Vereeniging marked 'very rare' by Olive, interpreting or copying my father's letters. One of the photographs was taken from just inside the flap of his tent and, I judge, from a crouching or even a prone position, since it has blades of grass sticking up in the foreground. It shows a procession of Boer officers riding into the camp, led by mounted British officers. Perhaps it was 'rare' even at the time because it was a forbidden glimpse, or a forbidden photograph, or perhaps my father was the only photographer in the Electrical Engineers' Volunteer Corps. 'Rare', certainly, because he took this photograph on what he must considered one of the great days of history. He would have supposed, out there in the camp on the veld with the ranks, that the Peace of Vereeniging was solely a matter between Boer and Briton, even though large numbers of blacks were persuaded to join either side; and he would have been in most respects right, for the concord which gave Vereeniging its name was achieved in large part by the agreement to disregard the political rights of blacks – 'to secure', as the treaty document puts it, 'the just predominance of the white races'. I am bound to say that I do not suppose that, if he had known about this limitation, he would have thought it a matter of historic significance. He was a humane, sensitive and sensible man, but entirely of his time, class and country. He had volunteered his young life to go and fight the Boers, not to change the destiny of the 'natives'. It would have seemed self-evident to him that only whites could develop the country in a way which to him seemed progressive and desirable.

But my father's earlier months of that war were spent in quite a different and a lowlier way – as the driver of a large and cumbrous steam traction engine: a long, black, horizontal, tubular tank which housed both the water and the furnace and spared a tiny platform for the driver and his mate. In the pictures it is always drawing a huge bogie for carrying its fuel, and sometimes, behind that, other carriages to take its various loads. Sometimes it was used for moving British artillery to the front, sometimes for the removal of captured Boer weaponry (in one or two of the pictures one senses great excitement about a huge Boer field gun called 'Kruger'), sometimes for roadmaking and sometimes for the transport of electricity poles. It is a useful, multi-purpose engine said to have been one of the technical innovations introduced for the first time in this war by General Buller, an aid towards bridging the gap between the

My father and his traction engine, Anglo-Boer War, 1901

Boer delegates arrive at the Peace Conference, Vereeniging, May 1902

guerrilla warfare of the Boers and the traditional fighting modes of a British army. But even if it made its own roads, it was not ideally suited to a terrain lacking both water and wood, its sole and proper fuels.

It is apparent that all of my father's pictures of that time were taken either by him or by his mate, whose name was Mr Wetherall (as Olive's captions always refer to him), and that they were always alone, just the two of them. Only in one, where the engine appears to have capsized into a ditch, is there any sign of other help or labour: a few ragged black men standing around and considering the problem. So that since one man would be taking the photograph, what I have in my pictures looks always like the poor lot of one, lone soldier, his identity almost wiped out by the surrounding sepia immensity of a parched and featureless veld. The lone soldier is cutting down bushes for fuel (there is no sign of trees), or bent double shovelling twigs into the furnace, or drawing up buckets of water from a ditch, or leaning wearily against the side of the tank. My father was learning the lesson of water in an arid land, a lesson which he never forgot.

A few months ago I was astonished to meet the very blood (or iron) brother of this steam engine. Driving across the Namib Desert in indescribable heat, my friends and I were searching the flat and endless horizons where a dune becomes as exciting as a range of mountains – searching for examples of *Welwitschia mirabilis*. This is indeed the most miraculous of plants, found nowhere else in the world, survivor and adaptor over the millennia from an era when the climate of Africa was entirely different. In evolutionary terms it has performed as many tropes, evasions, attacks, diversions and transmogrifications as Homer's Old Man of the Sea – and it has kept, and displays about its mysterious person, all the weapons and disguises and support systems, alternatives, aids and adjuncts which (so far as we know) it has ever been called upon to use in order to escape extinction. It has no thorns, though. It has, it seems, never needed thorns because no grazing animal can have lived in the climates and conditions which *Welwitschia* to this day has endured.

Each plant displays all this paraphernalia of evolution. It is a wonderful thing to see, and we saw several, and tried to photograph every aspect of its strange collection of forms. But it has to be said that the first sight of a *Welwitschia* is akin to that of a dead octopus, or jellyfish, or any old heap of seaweed lying limp upon the sand. There is one which is particularly famous (to botanists), huge, convoluted, said to be about 1500 years old, which, until you are close enough to marvel at its array of weird evolutionary devices, resembles a heap of discarded old tyres.

The Austrian botanist Friedrich Welwitsch, who discovered his first example in 1859, wrote that he 'knelt on the hot sand and stared at the plant in bewilderment, thinking that his fantasies had taken flight'. This describes very well what I felt – not, however, at my first *Welwitschia*, but when suddenly, in front of the car, nothing else in sight, I saw 'Martin Luther', as the local colonists named it. The old engine (which I photographed as avidly as I had the plants) was instantly recognisable in every detail and proportion as a twin of my father's iron mount. How could I have expected ever to come across such an engine? There it is, stuck in the Namib Desert, grotesque and incongruous, abandoned by the German

'Martin Luther', stranded in the Namib Desert

army which sought to extirpate the Herero people in the savage colonial war of 1903–1907; which is, to the Herero, the War of Liberation that nearly wiped them out. The *Welwitschia* overcame the virtually total absence of rain by contriving, over the centuries and among many other unique adaptations, to develop a system which enabled its leaves to convert into water the fog which sometimes drifts along these barren wastes. The men who left the Martin Luther there, stuck for ever on the sandy, stony plains between Windhoek and Swakopmund, had failed to learn the lessons of a waterless land. '*Hier stehe ich, ich kann nicht anders. Gott helfe mir,*' Martin Luther says, to this day, to anyone who passes this deserted place.

My father returned to England from the Boer War, completed his engineering studies, somewhere adding mining to electrical, and went back to the Transvaal as a fledged mining engineer. He seems to have done well, for there is a posed group picture of him in 1912 when he was 28, given pride of place in Olive's album, as the construction engineer of the City Deep Mine. He is sitting in the middle of the front row, also in pride of place, looking at least half the age of the tough and rough company around him. But he forsook this promising beginning and returned to England on the outbreak of the Great War to serve as a balloonist in the Observer Corps of the force which became, in 1918, the RAF. I have read that balloons, tethered, were first used for observation in the Boer War, so this must be where he got the idea of combining patriotic service with his beloved hobby of photography. There are no Great War pictures from the air in these albums. He would have observed not only the terrain but every jot of the regulations about security. There are a couple of pictures of an unfortunate balloonist stranded at the top of a tree, hanging down like a stowed puppet. It cannot have been my father himself, since he would have had to throw his camera down to a photographer below; and it is inconceivable that so careful a man would have thrown a camera, in any circumstances whatever.

After demobilisation in 1919 he returned to his profession in

My mother at the time of her marriage to my father

Johannesburg, bringing his new wife, who became my mother. He
was still an active photographer, for my mother sent many pictures
home to her family of the garden they were making, the
Mornington garden. She was very proud of its size – eight acres,
she underlines in a note on the back of the first garden picture,
'and all grass!!' She may have hoped to imply that the bare veld
was a spacious lawn; or she may have been unable to use the word
'veld'. For this first picture is of the great sepia slope of the hill;
nothing else, except in the distance an iron windmill and rows of
barbed-wire fencing. The house is invisible, over the crest of the
hill. It seems clear to me that my father took this picture not (for he
was not, very much not, vain or boastful) so that my mother could
send it proudly home to her parents and seven brothers and sisters
in Finsbury Park (where the lawn was about the size of a double
bed), but as his first step in the recording of what they intended to
be their own private Creation – their colony or shaping of their
new world to resemble whatever had been good, or desired, in
the old.

Mornington as it is, and was

That is how it came about that I lived the morning of my life in the garden of a house called 'Mornington'. It really was, and is, called that. I am not inventing spiritual sonorities of the kind that Bunyan's poor Christian had to suffer – Slough of Despond, and so on. But 'Mornington', miraculously, means what it says as well as what I mean it to say: the place or settlement of the morning; so henceforth, even though it is only a modest house in the northern suburbs of Johannesburg, it will lose its inverted commas.

But my morning was long ago, before anything in the northern suburbs became so plush. It is true that the gardens there in those days were very much larger than they are now, but most of the houses were very much smaller and humbler; and the roads were dirt roads with tufts of the veld still struggling through their edges, which were certainly not pavements. As the decades have passed, the gardens have been chopped up into 'lots' (which ought to be called 'littles') and sold, bringing progressively greater profit to the sellers since this district, being as far as possible away from most of the black townships, is where white Johannesburg chose to live. The houses that were built on the 'lots' became higher and mightier so that the parent bungalows, if they have not been demolished, look now like poor relations skulking at the edge of a garden party. The gardens have become smaller not only by subdivision but because what is left of them is increasingly filled up with swimming pools, tennis courts and double garages. As though to compensate for the decline (or changing role) of the gardens, the edges of the roads have blossomed into sometimes exquisite arrangements of flowering shrubs and even little lawns; but hedges and fences have been replaced by forbidding walls.

I grew up in a house as well as a garden – I am not a shrub, or an aloe, or a dog. But my home was, and has always seemed to be, the garden – that garden, the garden of Mornington. I feel affectionate towards the house, a modest bungalow with a corrugated iron roof and many small rooms darkened by shutters against the sun. The only room filled with light was the veranda or *stoep*, which I think was the only Afrikaans word in my parents' vocabulary. William Morris said that a house should have a large room for living in and small rooms for sleeping or sulking in, and that is how it was. Even so I am sure that the house was not designed with any Art Nouveau notions by the person who built it on the bare veld and died before he could start a garden. He was guided, I think, by the need for economy, but at the same time he built (according to my father) with thoroughness and quality, and its style and dimensions were guided by modesty – when I revisit it now, after all these years, I am surprised at its modesty, since we lived well, for those days – and (my father also said) everything was done with practical common sense and making do with the labour and materials that were to hand. Apart from careful maintenance and, in due course, the addition of modern plumbing and sewerage, there were no alterations to the house in our time. The garden, however, which over the years my parents made, was quite another matter.

This book is not *about* that garden; or about, as such, my life. But I have to start at a beginning.

When I lived in it, that garden, to me, was what people meant when they said 'South Africa' or even 'Africa'. And when I came to learn about Eden and Paradise, which are so close to each other, I already knew, from our garden, their attractions, and how unthinkable and frightening it would be if I were obliged to leave. This was indeed the awful eventuality which in time overtook me; and I had to leave not only the garden but friends and family and all things familiar. My fears about leaving it could easily be seen as presentiments, but I do not know whether it is true or even intelligent to see it like that. Whenever I do regard it as having been presentiment, I also seem to remember that I knew (and it was true) that when I had to leave the garden, I would be alone. Adam and Eve at least had each other.

In our very early years my brother John and I were bound together by the delights of that Eden. In the beginning, though he was by four years the older and more adventurous, we were united in particular joys. For example, we were great eaters of forbidden fruit – and so were our friends, and the servants, and the children of the servants. We were forbidden to do so but (with due secrecy) we ate the apples even though they had coddling moth, and the peaches in spite of the wasps, and the passion fruit – granadillas – even though the pips, it was said, would give us appendicitis, and the grapes even though they were consecrated to the making of grape juice for my mother's tennis parties. We were, if discovered in these or other delinquencies, told off, but not told to go. There was no notion of Expulsion. We felt quite safe.

John becomes a schoolboy

Duly, even if with cruel precocity, the Expulsion occurred. My
father died, and we had to sell the house, when I was fourteen. His
death was a disaster, of course; and so was the moving. But as
many childhood disasters do, if they are weathered at all, I believe
they prepared and fortified me for some which were to come later. I
am very far indeed from being a model of the Roman ideal of 'fortitude', though always inspired by it: *fortitudo*, often with unbeliev-
able male arrogance translated as 'manliness'. It is a quality often
praised by Cicero and best defined by him as 'a steadiness of mind
when in danger, or great labour, or grief'; and also as 'the belief
that anything is bearable that can happen to a mortal' – *nihil quod
homini accidere possit intolerandum putare*. I do not, now, think
that the latter is entirely true. As one matures and as the dissemina-
tion of news about disasters and atrocities improves (if that is the
word) we are more familiar with the extremes of human suffering.
Yet it seems to me admirable if a person can at least postpone
despair. *Fortitudo* is what I sometimes think of when I fertilise my
garden soil with the long-term strength of bonemeal. This will see
them through the winter, I think, and also give them more growing
power in the spring. Or when considering how strongly, or for how

long, to let a tree or shrub have the support of a stake – if you bind it up against all the blows of winter, it will not develop its own sturdiness in its own stem. These are the facets of fortitude.

My memory of the Mornington garden has remained the matrix into which my mind flies back in times of stress; just as the ancients used to dignify and comfort themselves with the fables of Arcadia and the Golden Age where man was not vile, nor woman, and all the beasts were their friends. For example, in childbirth I have been able to extract my mind almost completely, in the early stages, from the processes which take over the body and to enter the garden at any point, and the garden then takes control. I seem to walk about it, and every plant and stone rises in my mind, and it is as though the path I am following will take me to the child who is struggling to meet me. But is that child my baby, or is it my infant self? I have, through four births, never reached a decision about that.

It was a large and complicated garden, not readily carried in the memory in all its detail of paths and trees, stones and plants, slopes and tropes, blazes and shades; but at these times it has re-presented itself to me in amazing intricacy, renewing my memory and telling me of hope and pleasure and excitement. It is as though the hundreds of thousands of times I went that or this way, in my childhood, had made an everlasting map in my memory. The strangest thing about this experience is that it seems so exactly like a passage backwards through time, to one's lost life. It never becomes dimmer, though; it has always come to me in a bright, white, morning light. I hope that it comes to me when I am dying, for it would be far better than anything unknown; certainly better than the blaze of a heavenly host waiting to greet one, a dreadful surprise party; or than a slow and fearful darkness, with which I am also familiar.

Also, the garden of Mornington is still the background of most of my dreams, especially those marvellous flights I make, when, to the amazement of all around, I rise up into the air and sail off as far as I wish, seeing spread out beneath me all the known and loved features of the garden. It is very, very dangerous, however (as

I was often told from my infancy, the first version of all the lessons about black and white), to go beyond the boundaries; in fact if, in the dream, you do, you will soon be flying over the sea, and fear will cause you immediately to develop wing failure and drop into it, like Icarus.

Because that garden has always been there, in my mind – and I have several times visited those parts of it which are still recognisable – it is surprising that it is only within the last few years that I began to think about the making of it. It has always been so real to me, a huge and given thing, like a river or a mountain, not suitable for enquiry of an amateur or personal kind. Also, there was such terrible pain in the leaving of it; and I had a new life to make. As you see, I can find excuses for delay so powerful that they prove my need to do so.

I do not think this garden had the same effect on my brother John, although he lived in it four years longer than I did, since he was that much older. He became an engineer, though always in his heart a sailor. We were exceedingly far from the sea. Odysseus, at one stage of his long journey home from Troy, was ordered by a seer to carry an oar over his shoulder and to go so far from the sea and ships (wise counsel, since he had ten years' ceaseless trouble from them) that the oar would be mistaken by the people of that country for a winnowing fan. That is how he would know when he had gone far enough. I do not know how or when my brother, growing up as he did on the Highveld, a vast province of winnowing fans, could have learned his love of the sea. He died long ago, so I cannot ask him. But I know that the sea was always as present to him as the garden was to me. I have been, variously, a broadcaster, publisher and teacher, but always in my heart (next to being a mother) a gardener, even though I have had little spare time in which to earn that name.

For my parents, certainly, that garden was an astonishing, challenging, absorbing and glorious matter. The years of it marked, sadly, the end of their time together. After my father's death my mother lived on for many years, in various flats in Johannesburg;

never a garden again until near the end of her long life John built her a cottage near the bottom of his own garden, beyond the workshop where he built his ocean-going boats. But by that time she was old, and ill, with little energy.

I used to visit her there, from England, when I could get leave from my job, sometimes taking the youngest of our children with me. I would go, if I could, whenever John phoned to say there was a health alarm or more depression than usual. When she began to recover I would sometimes try to stimulate her to a bit of planting or planning, but she responded only faintly, only to please me. I have read that in his sad and mad old age Nijinsky used sometimes, encouraged by music, to perform a halting step or two or a remnant of a dance figure with his once magical arms and legs. In such a way, with encouragement, my mother (not at all mad but certainly sad) would simulate a brief concern about whether a clump of cannas could be planted in this place or that; and what colour, or should we mix them? Or I would say, 'Wouldn't you like to put in some carrots so you can have them sweet and young for Christmas, to roast in sugar?' But it is hard to be encouraging without at the same time seeming too advisory; and both gardening and culinary advice my mother thought she had the right to reject. For her in her long widowhood, as for me until quite recently, the question of what to do in any garden after Mornington seemed an unimportant matter; whatever one did would seem wrong, ridiculously inadequate, when one thought back to what had been done at Mornington, in the Golden Age.

In the twenty years or so after my father died she achieved, in fact, many things She did not 'go under'. She was able and energetic, a great planner and galvaniser. She organised the first women's club in Johannesburg, many balls and other events in aid of the blind; during the war she raised the funds and organised the building and then the administration of a military convalescent hospital. She quarrelled with the matron over nearly everything and nearly always won. All these and many other activities were consonant with and in fact highly promotive of a very developed social life, incessant parties and high dressing. I fled from all this, a move which she considered – correctly – to be both unfilial and unpatriotic. She never turned to gardening again, or I might have rejoined her. As it is, the need I have had all my life to be elsewhere, to be sure of an alibi, was in the beginning caused by the need to escape from her and from Johannesburg, from all that (in my mind) they stood for.

3 The light of memory

~～～

Now that I have begun to invite them, recollections of my child-hood in Mornington seem to come closer, to venture further into my mind than before, to come out of the shadows into the light of memory. In the past these forms and voices have often seemed to me like those dreams which vanish with one's waking moments, often causing desperate regret and futile efforts to hear that voice again, be assured of that love, see more clearly a face and form which every moment is dissolving into the trivial realities of light coming through curtains, the foot of a bed, a familiar room. But remembering the past in order to account for one's life seems more encouraging to the shades. I suppose that is because one has to link them to conscious thought, or to the recollection of pain or dismay, of delight or distress; and therefore to whatever circumstances brought about and could explain them.

Or to surprise, present surprise. The main thing I have to account for, so it seems, is a surprisingly early determination to leave, for ever, the scene of my fortunate and comfortable child-hood. My daughter Susie, when she was a little girl of eight, asked me about this, when I brought her from England on her first visit to all the wonders of my brother's Johannesburg home: big, warm welcome; big, sunny garden and swimming pool; big dogs; big, bright flower beds; big fridge with every known kind of fizzy drink: big and lovely everything. 'Why did you want to leave Johannesburg, Mummy?' How, then, could I explain?

Deserting a childhood and a country is a move not made without effort and pain. There is the pain of separation and also the pain of guilt when, as in my case, the departure was planned over a number of years and, when the time came, somewhat desperately executed, greatly hurting the people, and especially the person, whom most I loved. In addition to the pain there is a long-term price to pay, for you lose almost all your childhood friends and acquaintances, either by losing touch with them (as I did with the black companions of my early youth) or because the desertion itself has offended some of the white.

As the foreign years pass you lose the nourishing substratum, the soil which enriches any settled life: the history of continuing friends, shared pleasures and disasters, births and deaths, the growth and changing of minds, the struggling through quarrels, the emergence of myths and funny stories. My work has brought me new black friends in South Africa – and many close white friends do remain to me, people who joined the apartheid struggle or led useful professional lives or who, like me, left, and lived and worked for long periods in other countries. There must be tens of thousands of my fellows (Whitefellows, I call them, as distinct from those who are merely white) who chose to leave their native land rather than to stay and to endure – or, for that matter, to try to help – its problems. Some of those who left have not been able to return because they are too old or too built-in where they are. They live in America, Canada, Australia, New Zealand, Holland, Israel, Spain, France; very many, like me, in Britain. The Diaspora of the Whitefellows (known to some as the Chicken Run) is very nearly worldwide.

And yet, in a certain way, by leaving my childhood so early and decisively, I find that I have preserved it from much of the decay of disillusions and dismays. I was aware, as a very small child, of some of the troubles in the land; just as sometimes in our quiet suburban garden one could feel the tremors caused by falls of rock in the deeply mined reef of gold which lay underneath and all around our city – and which was the reason for our being there, and which caused my father great anguish. But on the whole, for the first fourteen years of my life, my brother and I grazed on the sunny slopes of the great mountain of the late, late British Empire and led happy children's lives of security, interest and enterprise in our own small world of people and animals and plants.

I think that anyone who feels the intensity of my affection for my first country will share my surprise at the early appearance of my determination to abandon it. If readers found my experiences more than surprising – heroic and amazing, say, or shocking or shameful in some way – then I could expect for a short while to become famous. South Africa has been very productive of horror histories. How could it not be so, in a country so long ravaged by indigenous wars, colonial wars, massive exploitations, rivalries and oppressions: people's lives dug up and chewed and spewed out and scattered around, as the savage hounds of history have snorted through the rich earth? But about my story there is certainly nothing heroic and nothing searing or shocking. There is, indeed, great pain, but nothing as protracted as that endured for so long by countless thousands of black people; nothing harrowing like enduring repeated arrests or years of imprisonment, or tyrannical poverty, or the loneliness and bitter suffering of dissident whites; or the domestic drip-torture of whites living in a dangerous society while trying to stand against it in private ways and at the same time having to barricade homes and hearts against the violence and desperation of dispossessed blacks.

There are very many Whitefellows who would have much more than I to say about the terrible decades of apartheid, of the fight to preserve reason and compassion from behind their own daily fortifications. There is also the need to penetrate the fortification of others; I've sometimes found, even in recent months, that minds which once I trusted have become, like the forbidding garden walls of suburban homes, guarded, patrolled, dogged, electrified, spiked – almost everything but poison-rayed. There has always been, in this beautiful and boundless country, a deep mistrust and hostility not only between but *within* both black and white, arising from the coming together of different peoples from different parts and lands and consequently with differing opinions about the sharing of the power in it. Now that, after generations of deadly struggle, history has (amazingly, it still seems to me) brought about the political solution of that over-riding problem, I'm risking, with my memories, some attempts at what you might think a view from afar. At any rate, it is not a polemic, which is a nose-to-nose, growl and growl-back business.

⬅

You would be entitled to ask: how far afar? And: Are we going to get the tiny, distant view which presents itself through the wrong end of a telescope? So I have to say that a good deal of my working life has been spent in Africa. In the '50s and '60s it was part of my job at the BBC to make programmes about the new movements and forces which were sweeping through country after country south of Sahara, away from colonialism and empire and towards independence. Except of course in South Africa, where I also travelled, where the tide was on the opposing pull, towards a far more rigorous system of an internal colonialism.

When the needs of a growing family became greater than the pressures of a broadcasting life could bear, I spent a few years – before returning to broadcasting – in the African division of a great publishing company and spent much time encouraging black men and women to write or record their experiences and views; to express themselves in print, as I'd formerly caught them on the air. I enjoyed this work very much, serving as it did two intrinsically unrelated needs – my employers' commercial acumen (for the rapidly Africanising examination boards wanted to prescribe African works as set books), and my own sense of purpose.

I continue to feel that personal writing is one of the desperately necessary developments of our world, polarised as it is between what some people call 'North' and 'South'. We in the North (which before the East was westernised used to be called the West) who have the power and the means to narrow this distance are poorly motivated, on the whole, to do so. We cannot, so we think, begin to understand the widespread and enduring chaos, poverty and corruption of many African countries – or, for that matter, of certain Balkan and Asian countries. We do not know these people, we think. We have not heard them explain; we have not heard their own cries of pain and bewilderment as the pressures of the modern world distort their economies, emphasise their deprivations, force open ancient wounds along the lines of weakness, both on the land and in the mind. Most of us are not among the firms and governments that supply weapons of war to any faction which promises to pay once they have murdered their neighbours; most of us have seen all this horror only on our TV screens: people weeping, struggling, fighting, starving, dying. In the early time that I was a child there is a real sense in which I was living among black people; they tended me and taught me and amused me; and one of them loved me as her own. But I could not break the barriers between us until I had left for ever and then gone back, as though a stranger.

I did not, however, think that I myself, my white self, people like me, should embark upon anything resembling memoirs. I thought that my early life and the society which shaped it would be best entirely forgotten. That is what I thought until the day when, on the TV in my Oxford sitting room, I saw Nelson Mandela walk out of Victor Verster Prison. A few days later I scooped up my amazed little granddaughter, Sarah, who was temporarily in my care; faxed Susanna, her mother, who was working in Mozambique, to meet us when she could in Cape Town; and we rushed off. I had visited, as I've said, many times before, but not as a person who goes home. I believe that it's since that day that, little by little, a dogged sense of shame and waste has begun to fade, and the brightening light of memory has begun to bring back to me the sense of my life.

A thing I cannot do, and believe that no recollector can, is protect my memory from the overlays which time puts upon it. Each time you recall a scene, your mind invests it with something of your present self. Everything you touch, you leave upon it your fingerprints. Heraclitus put it less forensically: 'No one can enter the same stream twice.' He was speaking of time itself; I am speaking of memory. I don't believe many of the things I read in memoirs: minutely recorded conversations, adult emotions ascribed to children, even infants; total recall stapled onto events which, in later years, the writer thought significant.

Edmund Gosse in his beautiful book *Father and Son* tells of sitting in his high chair, as a baby, and seeing the family dog jump up onto the dining table and snatch in its jaws the joint of meat which the cook had left while she went to summon the rest of the family. The thieving dog then jumped out of the window, meat in mouth, and vanished. The family, arriving, saw the baby, the empty carving dish. The baby when, many years later, he came to write about it, recalled his regret and embarrassment at his lack of any speech to tell them what had happened. I can believe this incident entirely because (except that it's so funny, in a way so Chaplinesque, a silent-film sort of visual joke) there can have been nothing ulterior in the recording of it; it doesn't show a silver spoon in the mouth or betray a family connection with Lord Nelson or reveal powers of prescience. It is correctly inconsequential – though it bears out my feeling that the early scenes we recall are those invested with some emotion, even if only embarrassment.

And yet, think how boring would be a truthful account of people's earliest memories. My own, for example, is this: I saw a mouse run up a wall which was covered in ivy. After the first sight of the mouse, I could tell of its progress only by the slight disturbance it caused in the leaves of the ivy. That's all, I'm afraid. This book I've begun to write is not, emphatically not, presented as an autobiography; though for clarity's sake I feel bound to convey that there is something like a stem to the story, so that it may resemble a sprig or a spray, not just a heap of swept-up leaves.

It's clear that, like everything else in Creation, memory is subject to change (with changing experience) and decay (with castings-out and with age). But it is, in my experience, also subject to rebirth and renewal, and the factor which in my case often renews and refreshes it lies in ideas and impressions I have received through reading. 'Why were you so bookish?' asks a dear friend who has read my childhood chapters. I could only assure him that it was always so, even though there were not many books in my first home. It is something to do with isolation, with companionship, with the need for alibi in its ordinary meaning of 'another place', nothing to do with establishing criminal innocence but with the longing to see the world more widely than was permitted by the deep boundaries and shut gates of my wonderful home garden of Mornington. Whatever the reasons, I find it impossible to reflect upon my life without building in some of the writers who have meant most to me. This is especially true of Homer, who has offered me alibis and understandings which altered my days from almost the earliest (though it was after the mouse-and-ivy time) that I can remember.

4 Water, order and symmetry
～☙～

The land mass of Greece, if such a sea-eroded, wind-blasted, earth-quaked, rock-laced terrain can be said to have a mass, has always been difficult for farming. Greek literature is full of the hardships of the land and Greek history full of the attempts to escape from it, by colonisation or conquest overseas. Odysseus and his men arrived, after many delays and dangers, at the island of the Cyclops. When Odysseus begins to describe this adventure to King Alcinous, Homer shows Odysseus as a man overwhelmed, even in memory, by the luxuriance they had discovered in the place and the contrast it offered to their own longed-for home in Greece: all the crops spring up unsown; generous and unfailing rains; happy pastures for the innumerable goats; soft water meadows where the vine would never wither; plenty of land level enough for the plough; and, to crown it all, a stream of fresh water running out of a cave. It is a prospect which no seafaring Greek could possibly resist, whether a coloniser or a traveller hoping for respite and welcome.

And yet it is a very strangely disordered account of the place; and Homer was not a muddler. The listing of all the beauties and benefits is thoroughly mixed up – as in an adventurer's tale it surely would be – with censorious accounts of the 'backwardness' of the inhabitants: uncivilised people – never lift a hand – haven't got any laws – or assemblies – or even any ships! These are the reactions of a technocrat who has stumbled (in this case) upon a community of rustics. When my adventuring parents came, at length, over the sea, to their own personal act of colonising, on the veld north of Johannesburg, I can with ease imagine that same jumble of emotions and areas of ignorance leading them to similar conclusions: the prospects looked very fair (pity about the unreliable water), but what about the people, and the technologies? How shall the valleys be exalted and the rough places made plain? Who would help them to get things going in their accustomed ways, how re-create the world and the relationships which, until then, and at home, they had understood?

At Mornington they were faced, in the beginning, by three physical problems. Water above all, of course; but also there was the question of horizontal spaces: who wants to live on a vast downward slope? And then, the craving for enclosed, plantable spaces offering shelter from the sun, a longing which fights with the natural and concomitant desire for broad views and vistas. According to Douglas Swinscow, 'the source of this dichotomous strategy in the human mind' is attributable to 'the *desire to see without being seen* that must have had an important role in enabling primitive man to survive in the competition for food and territory'. And so, he remarks, 'the imperative that governed our ancestors' lives has been transformed into one of the bases of our own aesthetic pleasure.' This is worth considering as a contribution to theories of garden aesthetics; but what I think is that my mother, while needing shelter from the sun, was also anxious to revel in the space which she had never known as a child in the smoky Victorian terraces of northeast London; and I am sure she did not care if she was, while seeing, seen.

My father, in his usual firm and thorough way, must have solved the problems of water, horizontality and shelter all at the same time. I deduce this from the hydrodynamics alone. The water for this large, dry hillside garden came not by Persian wheels up the ramparts from a river, but from deep underground, pumped up through a borehole by winds which swept across the veld into the attentive blades of the iron windmill. These high, tapering structures bearing aloft their big, daisy-like wheels are stlll to be seen everywhere in dry and difficult countries; their design does not seem to have changed at all in the last hundred years or more. In most of the world's rural places they still stride about the country like giant girls, as Cecil Day Lewis observed of electricity pylons, though the frilly, bonnet-like headpieces of the windmills, with a trailing streamer at the back, make them seem far more like girls than pylons are. In fact, they rule it out that pylons should be distinguished as 'girls' at all. Hoydens, at the most.

The windmill in Mornington garden was removed long ago, supplanted by municipal plumbing, but I can hear the noise of it now – the sliding creak as the vane veers round in a gust of wind; the metallic gulping sound as the pump begins to thump down up, down up; the surge of water, just after the 'down', up to and into the pipe which leads to the tank, the short gush into the tank, the splash of the still water receiving it. If the wind is steady enough, all these singular sounds become an ordered plural, a cumulative and certain music.

The tank which stored the water was not hidden in ramparts, or lowered under the floor of a marble-fringed terrace, but stowed high up, at the top of the site, in the top of a tall, narrow, rather ugly brick structure. Very much taller than our bungalow, this tower was quite a landmark for miles around, before the trees grew tall. It had many square apertures near its roof. I don't know what the purpose was, of these apertures – perhaps to avoid giving too much resistance to the wind – but all my childhood I considered that the principal purpose of this whole structure – just because of the apertures – was to be a vast pigeon cote, which indeed it became.

My parents, both of them deeply fond of birds, often expressed alarm at the number of pigeons which accumulated inside the tank tower. My mother thought that, because of the dreadful living conditions which were supposed to prevail inside that structure, they might give us diphtheria. I don't know why this disease was chosen. I can remember thinking what a pretty word it was, and that it sounded very like a certain part of pigeon language, when they are feeling rather sleepy and companionable inside the dormitory that we could never see. It was a cooing, feathery noise: 'diphtheria, diphtheria, there there, my dear.' It is also like the high-pitched quivering sort of feather noise they make when, coming in to land and lowering the undercarriage, they curve their wings forward as air brakes. But in the end it became a word of terror because, in the name of diphtheria, John and his friends were given leave to shoot the birds, as many as they could, with their airguns.

In the beginning the pigeons often used to wait for our handouts of dried corn and other seeds, perching in the trees or in rows on the horizontal struts of the windmill. A few bolder ones would come down to one's hand, at least until the shooting period began. My father and I used to feed them together. As soon as he got out of his car after driving home from work, he would find me waiting, as a rule, at the doors of the garage, ready with a hug and the bag of food, and the pigeons waiting too. With all those eyes upon him he had no choice but to postpone for a while the rest from his labours in a comfortable chair on the *stoep*. We both used to revel in the beauty of them. I was especially attracted by the iridescence which shot through neck feathers but could only be seen in certain lights as they moved. I watched for it on necks that were pale grey, or slate-grey, or the pinko-ginger that I called 'ovaltine'. The purely white never had these magic flashes But my father favoured the white. He was a confirmed Darwinian and used to marvel at the way in which what had begun as a couple of pairs of white fantails had become an ever-increasing flock showing an ever-widening range of colours and markings.

So the licence to shoot them, which diphtheria conferred upon my brother, was for me a fearful betrayal not only of the birds but of one special bond with my father, for after the shooting began the birds would hardly come to us. I believe that I became quite ill with pain and jealousy. In sporting tradition John was allowed to shoot only, of course, during the wonderful wheeling inward and outward flights which used to give me such excitement and pleasure. A flight of birds is a very sudden miracle – the power and grace and amazing precision in the safe, small space allowed between bird and bird, as mysteriously exact as the instant obediences of a speeding, direction-changing shoal of fish. Shooting the pigeons became quite a sport for John and his friends. My distress was so intense that my memory has recorded it as the first intimation I had that my brother and I were very seriously different kinds of person.

The gravitational fall from the tank in the tower, at the top of the slope, was such that the water travelled, assisted in some cases by hand pumps, to the many places and projects in the garden where it would be needed. The layout my father devised to meet the needs for this fall as well as for areas of horizontality and for vistas must have been realised and executed well before the pipes were laid under the soil, so that they could be brought up to form standpipes for hoses, or sunken valves for pond or fountain control, or little waterfalls, or the stream in the aviary, and be exactly where they would be needed after the earth-moving had been completed. This is precisely the reason why Babur linked so closely the questions of water, order and symmetry, which accounts, perhaps, for the nature of Moghul gardens which, in the very garden that so moved me on the banks of the Yamuna, he introduced to the arid plains of Hindustan, to the garden history of the world, even – by force of logistics rather than example – to the northern suburbs of Johannesburg.

The earth moving for Mornington garden must have been a mighty task. Since I was unborn at the time, I can only speculate about how it was accomplished. I suppose earth-moving equipment as well as gang labour might have been involved. A man who had for many months driven a traction engine to make roads for the passage of an army would not be at a loss about a domestic job. But whether this was the case or not, I know that our garden was made, like the gardens and roads and buildings and mines of the whole of South Africa, by black people who had by various means been turned out of their own lives in order that their labour should be available to the immigrants and settlers who had become their masters.

The layout itself is simple to describe, in spite of the complexity which was in course of time woven into the garden by planting and various shade-giving arches and pergolas. First, the hillside was bisected by a wide path, almost a road, coursing downwards. The longest slope that was allowed, it ran from the terrace immediately around the house right down to the steps which led to the tennis court at the bottom of the garden. By the time that I remember it, this path was shaded for all its length by a pergola – we always referred to the whole path as the pergola – canopied by vines of catawba grapes and flanked by large pots of blue hydrangeas placed in between the pillars that supported the vines. It was a cool, inviting, verdant tunnel over an even, dry path (being proper-ly drained, of course) and the fact that it was so green and cool – as hydrangeas demand – although coursing down the hill, itself speaks of the quality of the water provision.

On one side of the pergola the land was divided into four ter-races, with curving boundaries. When you thought you had reached the lowest of the terraces you were confronted by yet more steps, leading to a sunken garden, serpentine, not all to be seen at once, and inviting you to delay by a stone-built pool girt with many small, flowering plants and, of course, topped with a rocky knoll out of which (if you turned it on at the stopcock) leaped a modest fountain. I myself could never turn on this fountain, anxious though I was to show it off to any visitor, because the stopcock in its little subterranean chamber in the grass nearby was usually over-laid by a heaving, throbbing mound of frogs cowering from the heat of the day.

The sides of the sunken garden were quite gentle slopes but seemed steep because they were garnished, in a random way, by huge natural boulders and, by the time that I remember, very large sentinels of cacti and aloes and other grand, succulent plants, point-

My father made a sunken rock garden, shown here newly finished, before the planting matured, and a pond. Behind is the pergola. Unfortunately, when gardening took over his attention, he seems entirely to have given up photography

ing claws at the sky. This part was, in short, the rock garden. My father took especial pride in it, for the plants here were all South African: 'They give no trouble,' he used to say, 'they are natives.' This was always registered by friends or visitors as an amusing remark, a reaction which I did not understand at all. 'Natives', to me, in those days, were black people – people, not plants! And who would suppose that they would 'give trouble', anyway? It was perfectly plain to me, and my father's words seemed to bear it out, that natives saved us trouble. He allowed my mother to dictate the planting elsewhere in the garden, and even tolerated little pockets of rather unsuitable, colourful, frilly things in the rock garden among the grand monuments to drought and desertification which are, to me as I think to him, the most appealing of the five wonderful floras of South Africa.

The sloping land on the other side of the pergola was not terraced, though it was wound around with paths. These were built dead-horizontal and properly humped at the crown – like Roman roads, my father said, with respectful approval – and drained by gulleys so that the soil should not wash away down the slope; and therefore, because of the slope, they were built up on one side slightly more than on the other. This had a faintly terracing effect, but not enough to 'spoil the view'. The place the view was had from was the sitting-room windows and the *stoep*, which is where the visitors would be.

And the view? An enormous lawn, which had been the stretch of veld my mother had described as 'all grass!!' In the course of time it was dotted about with large, shade-giving trees – I have identified from my memory jacaranda, araucaria, poplar, ilex – but never in thick enough formation to suggest a hedge or an end to the property. The interstices of the clumps of trees were planted with other, smaller trees and so far as I can recall these too were all exotic, I think because my mother wished them to be flowering. There was what we called 'pride of India' and other people called crepe myrtle, which is *Lagerstroemia indica*, unfailingly productive of reddish-purplish panicles at the ends of its branches, though very modest in comparison with the magnificent spires of *L. speciosa*, the glory of South-East Asia; and a real myrtle, callistemon, which the English (and Australians) demean as 'bottlebrush', a weirdly, brightly flowering tall shrub which does not deserve such a hideously accurate, domestic put-down of a sobriquet; and, best of all, what we called 'pride of Barbados', which is *Caesalpinia pulcherrima*, a most elegant though slightly sparse and scatty tree with a flower both gaudy and wispy, bright reds and yellows and long, trailing stamens. But these gorgeous foreigners, which I did not see in any gardens except our own, were planted some way behind the big trees, so that you glimpsed them through the spaces and thought that they were further away than was the case. I have, since those days, often come across them in the lovely gardens of Bangkok, and their proud owners – until I learned better manners – were disappointed when I greeted them as well-known friends.

My mother planted an English oak, which has grown to an enormous size, right in the middle of the big lawn. It is the only feature now left of that part of the garden. The 'parkland', the great lawn with trees planted to simulate great distances, is now entirely filled by buildings, tennis courts, a huge swimming pool and other amenities of the girls' school which, after my father's death, bought our house. I was photographing the oak tree the other day, during the school holidays, and met one of the resident staff who was exercising her dog. She told me that she believed this huge, dense tree had a calming and gentling effect on all the girls whenever they were learning or competing or idling around it. When I told her that some fifty years ago it had been planted, against all advice, by my mother, she said, 'What foresight!' Well, it was not foresight at all, at the time. It was a mistake, since by its eventual size it was bound to endanger, in later years, the landscape effect of the rest of the planting. I suppose that history has turned it into foresight.

At the bottom of the land, running right along its full width, an orchard was planted, of peaches, apricots, pears (never did very well), apples (always died, but my mother went on trying), plums and cherries, almonds and walnuts. They were among our very best friends.

The last feature of the layout, which anyone will expect me to mention who knows about the torrential falls of rain that sometimes visit the Highveld, is the drainage of the whole site. It also happens that this was a factor of great meaning for me. Quite simply, it was achieved by contriving that storm water from the hillside above us would course down two huge ditches, one on either side of the garden. When our suburb became a municipality and the roads were made up properly, these two downgoing ditches were extended to the whole neighbourhood. Under the roads they were directed and protected by culverts or, as John and I called them, 'bridges', but where they lay down each side of our garden they were open, and we often called them 'dongas', the real South African word for dried-up small watercourses. We spent a lot of time playing in them, and I spent many hours hiding in them, under the bridges.

I have dwelt on the layout of my home garden because it is, to me, rather like a map of my father's mind. I get the same kind of pleasure, I suppose, as the child of an artist does, looking at – even in memory – some of the paintings or drawings, after the artist is dead. I think that hearing the music composed by somebody who had been much loved must be almost unbearable, since there is a kind of life and movement in it. There is life and movement in a garden, too, and in the memory of a garden.

5 Boundaries

⟋⟍

The ditches at each side of our garden were not the only way in which our boundaries were marked. They ran alongside thick, tall hedges and the hedges, in the beginning, had been planted along the lines of the original barbed wire which had divided up the veld. By my time the barbed wire had become invisible, deep inside the hedges, but we certainly knew it was there and we knew its purpose – to keep strangers out, and the dogs and myself securely in. My brother John, because he was older and a boy, was not kept in. He went visiting his friends on his bike wherever they happened to live – and he sometimes took the dogs, or some of them, with him. Therefore, it seemed plain, the boundaries were kept especially for me and for the less trustworthy dogs. I accepted this classification; my lowly status and the price of being a girl seemed to be a condition of life. For a long time I too accepted the boundaries as a means of protecting me from the outside world, though I did not know what the dangers were that seemed to my mother so imminent. It appeared to be something to do with mixing with 'the natives' in the streets, but she was never specific. The dangers therefore seemed to me the more powerful, because they were mysterious: something to do with black people, and with my being a girl, but apparently too awful to be spoken about.

We had a lot of fun in the ditches, though. If it had been raining heavily and then the sun had come out, something wonderful took place; so after a storm we always tried to get there quickly so that we could influence events. The rainwater brought down to the ditches a quantity of thick, dark red mud, laterite (which, my father told me, begins at the Pyrenees. I thought that we must have some neighbours on the hill above us called Pirrany, so that this referred to their garden in the way that ours was 'the Pryces'). If you get this mud while it is sticky, you can mould it into any shape you like, place it in the sun, and in a couple of hours you will make a pot or a duck or a tortoise or (provided that you know how they go) any kind of boat. The pots cannot hold water, the boats cannot float, and none of it lasts very long but it is certainly art or craft – joy, anyway. And if you cannot get there in time after the rain, and if the sun has been fierce enough, you find an amazing sight: the mud, lying as a thick coating at the bottom of the ditch, has dried up and thinly cracked into a network of hundreds of different small, sharp shapes exactly like (and roughly for the same reasons) the crackling on a Japanese *raku* bowl. But that is not the end, for then the mud cracks more deeply along the lines of the network and the pieces begin to break free and curl up, so that in due course they resemble broken pieces of chocolate Easter egg; and then you can go with a few of these to try to persuade anyone who will listen to deceive you into thinking that you have deceived *them*, and they will take a bite into the mud … Than the bringing off of this trickery, there is no greater rapture – time after time. (I was delighted to learn, travelling in Japan decades later, that *raku* means 'enjoyment'.) Lottie, my adored black nurse, was an especially patient and rewarding victim. I cannot have supposed, even when I was young and stupid, that she would forget the trickery in the intervals between its appearances; therefore I always knew she was pretending; therefore I knew that she loved me.

Also, we had boat races in the ditches. Not with the mud boats, of course – real *raku* is also porous and cannot be put to practical use – but with what we called real boats. These races could be held only during gentle rain, or as the last torrents of bigger rain were draining away. John always won because he had some idea of how to make 'real' boats – a flat strip of wood weighted underneath (but less than coextensively) with another flat piece of wood, and in the middle of that, from stem to stern, a heavy lengthwise nail, giving greater balance because greater depth to the draught. I learned these as principles only decades later, when he came to build his really real boats, but first observed them as facts right down there, squatting in the muddy ditch. These boats had to be made very quickly, while the running of the water lasted. Sometimes John made boats for me as well as for himself but as I grew older I used to put my faith, betrayed time after time, in nature and broke off big, tough leaves from the loquat or the giant magnolia or even (I hate to put it into print) the turned-over tips of the lovely big Mexican agave leaves; brutally I cut them off; and I would put a flower on them for captain, and usually a cap or a cloak – a bud or a petal – for the captain to wear. My sad captains, though truly hand-picked and beautifully dressed, were as deficient in seamanship as their craft were unseaworthy. They had no idea of steering them to avoid the roots and stones of the shallows, of how to stop them tumbling down the muddy waters to destruction.

There was another and a dangerous game in the ditches, too: target practice. Our parents never found out, but for me the threat of telling them proved useful for a long time. A bull's-eye target would be drawn on cardboard and fixed with rubber bands onto a square piece of metal, such as the lid of a biscuit tin. John and his friends, Peter, little John, middle John, Douglas, Philip, Guy – I remember them now as little boys in khaki shorts, but at the time they seemed to me big boys with dangerous guns – would take their weapons and lie prone in the ditch, propped on their elbows, one eye shut, sighting and aiming with tremendous self-importance. The target and I took up positions some distance away, respectively in and a little to the side of the ditch. My job was to listen carefully to the sort of sound made by the impact of the pellet: if it were a metallic thud then it would have hit the target and I would run out with a pencil and mark on the target whose shot it was. If the noise were a mere muddy thud, then there was no need for me to move since it meant the pellet had lodged somewhere in the bank. I was screened by a rather low bush (in case any movement that I might make should put them off their aim). I have forgotten why I agreed to do it; perhaps to get the little spurt of power from having something to 'tell' about.

All of those boys except one were killed during or else in due course by the World War which came in their very young manhoods, even the end of their boyhoods. There was no wartime conscription in South Africa. They all joined voluntarily, two of them travelling to England to join the RAF. When I think of them now, their intense enjoyment of the pigeon-killing as well as the target practice, it sometimes seems as though, all that time, they were preparing for it. At other times it seems to me that there are wars because – well, because boys are like these boys were. It is a mistake, I know, to base broad opinions about gender differences upon early childhood experience, since change is a concomitant of growth. But my brother and most of his friends were certainly aggressive and would-be manly little boys. It is very much the white South African tradition, carried on perhaps from frontier days and of course in view of the overwhelming presence in the country of black people, who were considered, in various ways, a threat. No doubt the aggressive behaviour among black males was always nurtured by the imminence of attack by rival or schismatic clans and by the incursions of the whites.

I cannot doubt that my brother often bullied me, for I remember so many instances of it, even if they now seem comic episodes rather than the serious provocations they appeared at the time. But I do not allow myself to forget that I once most savagely attacked him. Goaded by some taunt or hurt, I picked up a china jug and smashed it onto his skull. He had been lying down on the grass, quite unprepared for a vicious assault. He ran screaming into the house. I heard a commotion inside the house and after a while Lottie came out shouting harshly about how wicked I was, and how he had had to go to the doctor for stitches, and pulled me indoors to be shut in my room. But although I cried bitterly I did not repent until my anger had subsided, which took a day or two. Whenever, now, I begin mustering some opinion about the inborn aggression of males, something inside me serves up this memory, and the opinion sidles off. This does not lighten one's view of our human future, but it avoids doing so by any fraudulent self-righteousness about 'the gentler sex'.

The 'bridges' or culverts under the roads at top and bottom of our site became, as I grew older, of great importance to me. They were my first alibis. In slow moments of fear, or sulking, or sorrow, or in rapid moments of panic, the injunction 'Under the bridge!' would flash into my mind as surely as, on such occasions, a rabbit thinks of its burrow. Under the bridges, nobody could see you unless they were themselves prepared to climb down the steep and muddy sides of the ditch. It was no good hiding there from my brother or his friends – that, whenever it became necessary, meant locking myself in the lavatory. The only other people who persecuted me, from time to time, were my well-meaning mother and Lottie, and they were both far too dignified and fastidious to attempt a climb down a ditch. They had to limit themselves to cooing shouts or to bullying shouts, but I would respond to neither.

Very often the reason for the coos and shouts was simply to get me to come and fetch my hat. John and I were supposed to wear floppy linen hats all the time that we were in the garden. My mother was obsessional about it though nobody knew about skin cancer in those days. Freckles were considered a cosmetic menace, but I believe the real reason was that my mother held a view about black and white as crude and simplistic as that of the Elder Pliny: 'It is beyond question that the Ethiopians are burnt by the heat of the heavenly body near them, and have a scorched appearance, with curly beard and hair, and that in the opposite region of the world the races have white, frosty skins, with yellow hair that hangs straight.' At any rate, the only reason I recall her giving for this tiresome insistence on the hat was that I would not understand 'until I had a daughter'. So if my hat were found lying about anywhere, empty, Lottie would be sent off to find and hat me.

The only drawback to those alibis in the ditches was the dogs, the devotion of the dogs. In the garden their company, one or some or all, was always welcome, always whistled for, except under the bridge. It is in the brisk and honest nature of most dogs that unless they are, personally, hunting, they have no idea of keeping still and silent and secret. Under the bridge our dogs wanted action of some kind, feverishly hunting for things or else slowly and solemnly smelling for things, and in either case commenting upon progress with joyous yaps or with anxious yearning whines. If anyone is searching or bellowing for you, the last thing you want around you, as you hide, are the busy, fussy noises of a small fox-terrier, let alone those of his sisters and his cousins and his aunts.

A game under the bridge which our younger and more dependent dogs found, for a while, enjoyable was if you squeezed them up close to your side, or else snuggled them on your lap and bent your trunk over them. You cannot clap a hand over a dog's mouth, unless (one supposed) it were a Pekinese or (if two hands were available) a bulldog because, in all cases except those, the grip of one's hands and the *embouchure* of one's dog are not conformable. So you had to make a ring round fox-terrier snouts with your thumb and forefinger so that their jaws could not be parted and therefore no sound uttered. The dog might enjoy the game for a few moments but before long jaws proved stronger than fingers and the victory would be yapped out to the world.

I have tried to remember why I used so often to hide under the bridge. The hat business did not cause me to hide there – it only caused Lottie to try to find me. If the onset of the danger were slow, or a matter of mood, I used to wander down to the bridge over the road at the bottom of the garden, so that any searcher would have a fairly long journey, down the four terraces or else down the long path under the pergola, round the tennis court, round the compost pit and then through the orchard. But if the alarm were a sudden one there would be time only to dive for the top bridge, much closer to the house. What were the sudden alarms? I was never beaten or even smacked, though my mother and I used quite often to exchange verbal blows which left me with a deep sense of dismay and anger.

I think that the main or most frequent cause of hiding lay in my mother's social requirements. The approach of a party of any kind – tennis, cocktails, lunch, dinner, tea or a women's committee meeting – was hidden from me for as long as possible, though Lottie or the cooks, Zwela or Albert, often blew the gaff since in the run-up times of each occasion and not merely during the crisis of it they had a great deal of extra work. Lottie, for example, had to bleach and iron a wondrous array of embroidered tablecloths, traycloths, napkins and handtowels. Each time that my mother and I sailed Home to Southampton, and back again, she bought more of these things from the merchants who used to board the ship at Madeira and for a few hours transform the decks into a bazaar, a whole *souk* of exquisitely embroidered tents, each with a predatory occupant ready to tear down the whole structure and sell it for a few pounds. My mother found their wares as irresistible as I found the small boys' dives, from the top of the ship, after silver coins thrown down into the sea. I cannot remember fearing for their safety, among the dozens of rowing boats bobbing around the great liner; I admired, only, their daring.

Lottie, too, great dressmaker and wielder of a crochet hook, loved this linen. 'Yo!' she used to exclaim, or even 'Yooooh!', on a rising note, as she spread out upon the ironing table a tablecloth which had been so extensively embroidered that while freshly damp from the ironing basket it was wrinkled and puckered, an unattractive, withered sausage of a thing. Ironing out such a cloth, with those old flatirons which needed constant reheating, was a task for many hours because the interstices of the embroidered flowers and leaves were not of plain linen, but just holes, nothing. Therefore if you passed the iron quickly over them, the pointed tip of it would be caught in a hole and, if you hurried, rip it. Each petal, sepal and shoot had to receive individual attention. It was a great pleasure to watch the sausages flattening out into exquisite blooms and sprays and arabesques; and especially as it trapped Lottie in the ironing room so that we could have games and long talks and stories. All the same, I would realise with dread that a major party day must be very close, because if these cloths were not used soon after ironing they would pucker up again, such was the intricacy and tension of their embroidery.

As for Zwela and the preparation of the meals, I was not allowed a close view of that, as the kitchen, scullery and pantry were always forbidden ground. One knew, in spite of that, from various symptoms, especially my mother's mounting nervousness or, as material things went, because of the disappearance of the table silver from the baize-lined drawers of the dining-room sideboard, and its bright and shining return – another job properly to be done only a day or two before the event, to be sure of a perfect effect.

The reason for my dread of adult visitors was, of course, that my mother wished me, also, to present a perfect effect, and her requirements were very steep. I do not know, after years of reflection, whether the mental image she made of me, beautifully dressed and couthly behaved, was primarily to do with the acclaim which she hoped might reflect upon herself or whether it were done for my sake, in the hope of training me in social graces, 'manners'. I used to think it was the former; now that, older and fussier, I am often distressed by the piglike pushiness of untrained teenagers – oh, now I can hear my mother saying something like 'I told you so!'. But I don't listen seriously. I think that a comportment which takes proper account of other people can only come from an interest in pleasing them, not from an order to do so.

All I knew at the time was that Lottie was told to bath and shampoo and brush me, put a big taffeta bow on top of my head, the latest best dress, long white socks (but these to be put on only at the last minute), black patent-leather strapover shoes and fingernails cut and cleaned, cuticles pushed down, to carry out, I suppose, impressive handshakes. I was always interested in nice new clothes, even though tortured by the hours spent at the dressmaker's, but the trouble about putting on everything together like this, for other people to see, was that it might lead them to suppose that

I must be trying to attract their attention, than which nothing could have been less true. Very often I could not utter any sound after a handshake, unless my father were there to mediate, shield and help me. For some reason my mother would usually keep silent after effecting an introduction, hoping I would produce some suitable or even creditable remark. I could, as a rule, only put on a smile and pretend that I hadn't heard their gambit. Once I was introduced to a new person by quite an old friend of my mother's, and after saying 'And this is Kitty's and Leslie's daughter Prue', she stage-whispered, 'She's very deaf, you know.' I'm afraid the alibi which this pretence affords is still among my resources.

Therefore, to return at last to ditches and boundaries (though I have been dwelling upon the most rigorous boundaries of all, which are those of the mind), I used often to hide. If there was time, I went to the faraway bottom bridge. In the early mornings, if I did not wake up until Lottie came into the bedroom with the dress over her arm, the gleaming shoes in her hand and a ferocious look upon her face, I would have to disappear *after* the dressing up, which is why the clean, white socks were never put on until (if I were found by then) the first guests were sighted. Oh, the red mud of Africa soiling the white socks of Empire! I suppose there may be more inspiring, more refulgent symbols of the extraordinary culture into which I was born.

So far from training me in social graces, these occasions engineered by my mother left me with an intense fear of large gatherings, a hindrance all my professional life; but a compensating deep pleasure in the company of a chosen one, or two or even three. This has been at the nourishing root of the profession I chose, that of producing the kind of radio broadcasting in which, in spite of its huge audiences, heart speaks to heart, *cor ad cor loquitur*. At the microphone, for a radio broadcast, the state of your socks is of no consequence; your spirit, mind, soul take the weight. On TV – well, on TV people have to worry about their suspenders, never mind socks.

6 Gardeners and engineers

By the time I remember it the garden was so developed that it needed the labour of three Zulu gardeners to tend it, and the part-time labour of two or three of their little sons – the *umfaans* – to do the fetching and carrying and minor jobs. The *umfaans* were, it was thought, being trained as gardeners. Their main work seemed to be the carrying of mowings or sweepings or prunings to the enormous compost pit by the stables, an often rotten-smelling pit screened off by a hedge from the eyes and noses of the tennis parties which caused me so often to hide.

The *umfaans* were trained not merely to toss the dumpings into the pit, but to take things further by mixing up everything that was in it, and this was best done (they thought) by jumping into it, sometimes with their wheelbarrows as well, milling around in it, pushing each other over, trying to bury each other with shouts and screams of delight, mock fear, victory, surprise, delight again. Sometimes John and his friends joined in, jumping in or even riding their bikes over the edge of it. Then the dogs, the younger ones over-excited and the older ones supposing there might be a rat hunt, would jump (or be cast) in, until the whole thing was like the Sargasso Sea with a few shipwrecks in it. What a mess!, I used to think; what sort of a game is that? I was afraid to join in – afraid of injury, not by the dogs but by the boys, bicycles and barrows, afraid of getting muddy, or green, or smelly, or buried alive. In time, of course, I learned to disguise my fear as disdain.

My mother's gift lay in the design of the planting and the mixing of forms and colours. She liked big expanses of the same blooms – not at all the cottage garden approach. She would plant not two or three agapanthus, but a bank of twenty; not a clump or even a bed of canna lilies, but a little cathedral of them. She had a wonderful sense of horticultural ensemble. It must have been latent in her until she came to live in the sunshine. Her first marriage had been to a wealthy farmer in Huntingdon, but he died a few months later, in the flu epidemic at the end of the Great War, and she had no chance to think about gardens until she met and married my father shortly afterwards. I think that the expansiveness and thoroughness of my father's transformation of the hillside, and its greening, inspired her to imaginative heights. But however grand the massing of her plants, she liked them to appear in informal and irregular clusters; and she paid especial attention to ground cover, for most tall plants need a little camouflage or softening around their stalky, soil-soiled bases; as ageing ladies do, for similar reasons, round about their necks.

She showed the same eye for the arrangement of flowers and leaves inside the house. The only physical task she performed in the garden, apart from dead-heading, was the cutting, for the house, of blooms and sprays, which happened with especial extravagance on the mornings of the parties which I dreaded so much. Yet, apart from the imminence of guests, I very much enjoyed helping my mother with the flowers – could sometimes be tempted out of the ditch to carry a wide, flat basket behind her, give opinions (advice, as such, was useless) about colour and contrast. If it were dahlias, before she arranged them in vases I would help with plunging their stems for a few minutes an inch deep into boiling water; if it were poppies, then the tips of the stems had to be burnt in a candle flame, if it were roses, stems were split and crushed – and so on, a different treatment for all the favourites. I do not know where she learned it, or developed her adventurous ideas on mixed vase arrangements. At the time, all that time, I did not think to ask. The home of her parents in Finsbury Park had no flowers, that I remember; a few laurel bushes, and all of them spoiled and sticky from the droppings of the aphids which infested a few stunted, pollarded lime trees. I have been to see the house and garden in Kimbolton where, during the First World War, she had lived briefly with her first husband; it now belongs to a famous school, but they use it as a staff house and keep the garden very tidily and caringly. I could see that this trim and elegant little house at the end of the High Street must have been the source of her sense of style and propriety.

My father's approach to gardening was entirely different. He admired my mother's assemblages, whether in the house or garden, but what fired him (once the earth-moving and hydrodynamics had been finished) was the attempt to grow perfect specimens of, in particular, roses and dahlias, to study and experiment with their needs, and by this diligent approach to please us all by the excellence of his blooms. So – well away from my mother's floral landscapes – the roses were spaced out geometrically in trim beds because systematic access to them was needed in order to spray, disbud, dead-head and cut them, and, in the summer evenings, to pick the *tokki* beetles off their leaves. I do not know exactly what these creatures were, but I would recognise one today on an identification parade with a thousand others, since the nocturnal pickings-off and poppings into a jar of paraffin often fell to me. The *umfaans* and their fathers were not expected to work after dusk, and in the daylight the beetles went into hiding.

Dahlias, too, were grown in special and separate beds and, like the roses, in strict quincunx formation to provide maximum light and space, because the object was to produce huge blooms. This also meant that a great deal of trenching, staking and feeding was arranged; and then there was the annual cutting down, lifting, splitting, disinfecting with flowers of sulphur, labelling and winter storing of the tubers. My father, as with the water, left nothing to chance. My special part in this system was, again, to exterminate the prevailing harmful insect. The enemies of the dahlias were dark grey, rather violin-shaped, long-legged and whiskered creatures, very repellent not only because of their form but because of their habit of emitting a foul-smelling liquid when threatened. Everyone called them 'stinkbugs' and my friends used to run away from them. I put gloves on for the evening cull, hating and fearing it even so, but challenged to do a thorough job by feeling an important part of so elaborate a system. I was a member of the team, I told myself; I was quite keen on the praise, too, when I showed my ugly jarful. My father used to say something playfully judicious like 'Good heavens, that must have taken you at least all night!' and Makathini, the chief gardener – for I usually kept the cull to show him the next morning – used to feign fear or disgust and exclaim, 'Too many!' (which meant 'What a lot!').

I was also proud of my special expertise with the disbudding of both roses and dahlias. Removing the side buds from the groups of three which appear in the axils, so that the centre one may develop to greater fullness, is a delicate job, much easier for a person with small fingers and no sense of the pressure of time. I was so responsive to the praise I earned from this work that sometimes I kept the culled buds, too, to show off to my father and the Chief, as Makathini humorously called himself. So there were the twin satisfactions of being a member of a team, and also of having a speciality of one's own – the ideal conditions for anyone's professional life.

In the early evenings, when not engaged on these important duties, I used to love walking round the garden with my father and the Chief, eavesdropping on their conversations. The Chief's English was uncertain, so my father, in putting things clearly for his quick and retentive mind (people who cannot read have the best memories), was at the same time putting them simply enough for me. I know that this is where I learned a feeling for plants, and for different kinds of plants, and conditions and compositions of soil, and for the seasons of things.

I also learned from my father a great, almost physical, pleasure in the structure of plants. I think it was in my case almost tactile in origin because I first remember experiencing it when I discovered

the addictive delight of snapping off the new leafbuds forming in
the axils of the hydrangeas, stationed so grandly in their pots down
the length of the pergola. I was not trying to take them down a
peg, these proud and showy plants. I must have been too young or
too stupid to realise that I was blighting their futures. Simply, I
liked the feeling of the faint, crisp snap as the damage was done. It
is not at all like the feeling of disbudding roses or dahlias, where
the tiny stems are so soft and fragile that the whole art lies in sensing exactly where to nip them. It was similar, in effect, to the noise
and the sensation of pulling the joints of one's fingers so that they
clicked, a habit I happen to have learned from the *umfaans*. I'm
afraid I can also remember introducing the *umfaans* to the clicking-
off of hydrangea buds. When the inevitable inquest on the mutilat-
ed hydrangeas came to pass, I can remember making a half-hearted
attempt to blame it all upon the *umfaans* and at the same time crying for shame at both the deed and the lie.

As I write, there is, on the table in front of me, lying in a shallow dish half full of water, the tuber of an old 'sweet potato' about
eight inches long, a sweet old yam. I noticed it sprouting in the vegetable rack and at once promoted it, for the splendour of the structure of its numerous shoots. The old tuber is lumpy, a faded purple,
bruised and blemished, shapeless except for having at opposite
ends, as ordinary potatoes do, a heel and a toe. It is as though that
family, like cowrie shells, had evolved through a million mutations
to arrive at the perfect shape to assist in the darning of our socks:
the rounded heel, the pointed toe. But its shoots have sprung up
into vigorous, tiny glory, rising straight upwards, not straining after
the light from the windows, and in their miniature way they have
many of the design features my father taught me to admire.

Their stems are strongly reinforced at the base, emerging from
the tuber through a rounded ring of purple reinforcement: a grommet, you might say, except that it is integral to the structure. As the
stems are perfectly stiff and round, their beginnings resemble the
chaste, understated bases of Greek columns – bases which remained
modest and serviceable throughout all the orders and the centuries,

even though the capitals and entablature became increasingly elaborate. They are there for the steadiness, not to rival the gracious volutes or arching acanthus of the capitals or the showpieces of the entablature which, on high, they support. The stems of the yams change, as they extend so purposefully upwards, from a purple brighter than that of the parent yam to a hectic lime green and through the gradual and improbable range of colours which lies between. On the stem below each axil even towards the tender, lighter green tips of the shoot, there is a slight swelling which is, again, purple, as though blood and muscle were being bunched up at exactly the juncture which has to support the stem of a new leaf. In the same way, just at the spot where the blade of the leaf emerges from the leaf stem, there is a purple grommet, to take the strain.

My father used to explain things in that way, from the earliest time that I remember. He derived the general approach, of course, from Darwin, though in explaining things to me he avoided the questions of origins and evolution. We concentrated on fitness for purpose of the object in question, as an engineer is bound to do. When he considered a plant he speculated upon the reasons for its features, the functions of its arrangements; he practised on these occasions what has been called 'reverse engineering'; he did not for a moment posit the mind of a Creator, or a 'creative process' which had anything to do with Intention. He enjoyed finding out what the plant had achieved for itself, so that its family had survived at all.

When I came upon natural selection, survival of the fittest and all that, I felt it sink effortlessly into my mind, a relief and a blessing. (On apprehending the force of natural selection, T.H. Huxley is said to have remarked, 'How extremely stupid not to have thought of that!') I know that my father was aware of the implications of Darwin for conventional religious belief as well as for science. I never knew him to go into a church, for example, not even, my mother said, for our baptisms, though his Quaker background may equally well have accounted for that. He knew John and I should understand what we saw, the 'what', 'why' and 'how' before the 'whence', let alone the 'whither'.

The first book I can remember him actually reading to me, not just a looking-together at the pictures, was *The Voyage of the Beagle*. I have the copy that we used, the 1890 edition, and I can be certain that as he read it to me he reduced and simplified it. We did look at the pictures too, for by this time, a generation after its first publication, it has excellent and dramatic steel engravings; these always appear, what is more, opposite the very page where they are required: a great convenience that, until recently, was ruled out by modern methods of colour reproduction, which lumped all the pictures together in the glossy colour section. I remember, from my infant listening, Darwin's incredulous delight at his first sight of the abundance of tropical scenery; and some of his 'characters' – for example the cuttlefish in the rock pool who wished (Darwin said) to get to a certain hole without being caught by him, and the many ruses it used – colour changes, propulsive squirtings, dartings and emissions of inky fluid – as it achieved the few inches of its escape from this obsessive naturalist. My father and I for some reason found this episode incredibly funny. A few years later, inspired by Homer's serio-comic account of Menelaus' struggle with the ever-changing sea-god Proteus, I wrote a story called 'The Old Man of the Sea'; and I did not mean it to be clear whether the 'old man' was the creature who in his terror put on this amazing show of defences, or the seasick naturalist who had travelled thousands of miles, under sail, in extreme discomfort, to discover it. But Darwin's account of the cuttlefish doesn't, now, appear to me amusing. It seems to me now one of the rare, magnificent moments when man and truly wild beast have met each other with deep respect, and no intent to kill, a kind of astonished understanding. I think of D.H. Lawrence's wonderful poem 'Snake', or the film of David Attenborough's inspired sitting down in the rain forest among a group of mountain gorillas.

I think, now, that in reading to me, my father must have left out Darwin's sad and terrible observations about the 'natives' of Tierra del Fuego and other places. The questions it raised – to Darwin himself, let alone to my father – about human development were painful and difficult; especially, perhaps, to us in our South African context, where mankind, as we now know, began! Darwin himself postponed for many years any explicit approach to the implications of selection for the evolution of Man – though fully conscious of it, always working on it. His reason for delaying publication of *The Descent of Man* was, as he disarmingly puts it, that 'I thought that I should thus only add to the prejudices against my views'. Neither my father nor I could have been less troubled by the religious prejudices which battered against Darwin – my father in his wisdom and I in my ignorance – but I know that in our different ways we were both troubled by the question of the nature and the potential of the black people among whom we lived, who in almost every way (as we thought in those days, having little or in my case no idea whatever of environmental or cultural conditioners) were so markedly different from us, who seemed inferior because they could not read, had no money, had lost their land, had to work for us, couldn't (even!) speak English properly; just as Homer's troglodytes had no ships.

I have to believe that my father thought they were in various ways inferior to us, since all colonialists did, if they were to avoid meeting the accusing eyes of conscience. But I can't recall ever discussing it with him and I never heard him commit himself to the view that 'the natives' were 'stupid' or 'unteachable' or that they presented any kind of threat to us. If he had a general attitude, it was probably one of thankfulness for the labour they provided in the making of the country, the mines, the agriculture, the roads, all the menial urban services, everything, including of course our own household and garden. My mother, however, had no reservations about their supposed inferiority. I shall not dwell upon or illustrate this, except to say that I know she was afraid of black people, especially black men, and that it was probably a kind of sexual fear, and that this was an important factor lying behind her obsessional over-protectiveness of her daughter.

It was my brother who learned most directly from my father. He in due course chose engineering as his profession; and, as he was older than I was, he had more time before my father died.

Sometimes I think that my pronounced antipathy to motor cars and insensitivity to their mechanical needs – a source of some anxiety to my family since I drive all the time – arise from early jealousy of my brother John. At precious weekends he and my father used to spend hours, it seemed to me, peering under the bonnet or even under the body, supine and stretched out like kippers, underneath whatever car we had at the time. I remember the names of Hudson, Talbot, Rio Flying Cloud, Hupmobile. They were before the 'modern' days of Chrysler Airflow, Pontiac, La Salle or De Soto, when the corners of the chassis became rounded and one sat less upright, in more comfortable seats, closer to the ground (harder for the kippers) and went along very much faster.

Also, there were the specimens. One of my childhood friends had a father who was a pathologist. The story goes that she once, at the Zoo, watched a giraffe urinating, and (whether from the time it took, I do not know) remarked, 'Oh crumbs, what a long specimen!' The specimens which my father brought home were those of, you might say, a pathologist in metals. They were fragments of a very heavy metal, usually short, tubular sections, often damaged in some way. They did not interest me for a moment, except for the fact that they appeared to both my father and my brother to be of great importance, and would be the reason for their going off together for a long time to the microscope in one or other of the laboratories, either my father's specially built one leading from the garage, or John's, made out of an old stable at the bottom of the garden and where, for reasons which will appear later, I was not allowed to go.

It was not until after my father's death that I came to know the nature and purpose of those specimens. They were fragments of the bits, that is to say the biting parts, of rock drills, such as were used down the mines for exposing the reef, making holes for the correct positioning of explosives and, when the right rock had been exposed, for the more sensitive extraction of the gold. The great problem, in those days, was that the hardness of the rock and the heat engendered by its abrasion of the drill would often cause breakages in the steel of the bits, which would severely delay the progress of the work. Untold money, working hours, profit, was lost.

It was my father, by this time consultant engineer to a large consortium, who solved the problem, and I have been told that since that time, over sixty years ago, his invention has been used in all such drills throughout the world – including dentists' drills. The solution lay in keeping the steel as cool as possible by means of water coursing down a hollow centre in the bit. To protect the steel against corrosion by the water, the central canal or tube was lined with stainless steel. That is what all the samples of steel were about; and mysterious publications in Swedish about steel that was *rostfri*, and a delightful Swedish engineer who several times came to stay with us and who, much later in my life, saved me from despair. I believe that after my father's death his employers refused to extend the payment of royalties on this invention, even for a limited time, to my mother, on the ground that the development was simply part of my father's duties in his research laboratory at 'the office'. My mother, of course – my father dying so early – had little other source of income. Each time I have a tooth drilled, this reflection increases the tension I feel: the heat of the embers, I suppose, of my mother's anger and disappointment.

〜

My father's interest in the structure of plants and in their habits of growth were closely related, since a plant of any size will grow suitably to fill the space of light and air allowed to it, and if that is insufficient or irregular, the plant will modify its development in conformity with its chances. He often tried to illustrate this point by showing me how my mother's crowded plantings 'worried' some of their growth, even though he would admire the general effect and never interfered with her decisions. I could feel, though, that he was better pleased when he inspected the sturdy platoons of his dahlias and roses: no weakness in the stems, an even distribution of the laterals, no misplaced extrusions, no faintings or boltings, no etiolation, and the base of each plant perfectly surrounded by its own saucer of earth, to retain whatever moisture god or man might provide.

Some things, of a rather different order, I learned for myself. If you squeezed, very, very gently, the closed and pendulous buds, their futures folded tightly inside them, of the white datura (which we called moonflower) it felt exactly like my mother's evening gloves of finest, softest, white kid: the special ones with dozens of tiny round pearl buttons and opposing cream silk loops right up to the elbow. The gloves were kept – as I keep them still, never to be worn – in a fine oblong boxwood glove box, together with their wooden tongs or finger-stretchers. The gloves were kept well out of my reach, on top of a chest of drawers; so I must have been a very small girl at the times that they were worn. I was allowed to squeeze them, before trying to help with the glove buttonhook, on the special occasions of their wearing, occasions made even more exquisite by how beautiful my mother looked, and smelled, and how happy she was on those evenings. What is more, about the datura, is that if in addition to squeezing the buds you also gently stroked them with a moist finger, they very softly squeaked, as fine leather does. The flowers and the buds hung there, from the huge shrub under the far end of the pergola, in great numbers all the summer long and were never put away in boxes. I was told not to touch the datura, since it is in all its parts extremely poisonous, so I squeezed and stroked it secretly, not even showing the *umfaans*, or my dearest friends, and certainly not my brother.

It seems to me that in the whole history of human domestic settlement, there can have been few garden-makers as fortunate as my parents and all that generation who went out to South Africa in the years following the Great War. They went to virgin land, with a cheap and plentiful 'labour supply', and found themselves to be living in the midst of what many botanists say is the richest flora, or combination of floras, in the world. They were able to create all the spaces and places and conventions and inventions that they wished, and – if they could beat the water problem – to plant them with trees, shrubs and flowers of a variety and splendour they can hardly have dreamed of.

Before they went to South Africa, my parents can have known nothing, for example, of the great array of daisy-like flowers, with the violent colours of little sunbursts, that are today so common in the gardens and greenhouses of Europe – arctotis, gazania, ursinia, gerbera, venidium, mesembryanthemum, osteospermum. Can my mother have dreamed of all the tall lily-like ones – agapanthus, clivia, schizostylus, true amaryllis, zantedeschia, kniphofia, ixia, galtonia, sparaxis, nerine, crocosmia, strelitzia? I remember all these in her plantings; and great banks of *Plumbago auriculata* (the favourite of Cecil Rhodes, and to my mind showing the clearest, palest, liveliest blue in all nature) around the *stoep*, and roundels of streptocarpus (crudely called the Cape primrose) on the edge of beds of phygelius (crudely called Cape figwort) or pelargonium (perhaps South Africa's most popular contribution to the world's gardens), and bands of chlorophytum running through colonies of the delightful felicia. I did not then know the names of most of these plants but I have sought them out, over the years, and have tried to make some of them grow, often in hostile soils and unsuitable climates. I cannot end this litany, drastically shortened as it is, without recalling that lobelia, all the small, humble, blue lobelias, are my co-natives. Bluefellows. They grew everywhere in our garden, year after year, as did the wild *Freesia refracta*, ancestor of all the freesias.

My parents would have known, before they arrived in South Africa, not one of these plants. Mornington was not the bright morning of their lives, as it was of mine; but it was in every sense their flowering time, blessed and fortified into life by the strong, clear light of the Highveld.

It was well understood by everybody that I was never to go out of the garden by myself. Even the dogs knew. If John got his bike out of the shed, the dogs would press and prance round to see if it was going to be an outing or just dirt-track stuff round the drive or pelting down the pergola – fun, but of the second class, not a patch on getting out of the gates. But if I went to get my little cycle – hardly a whisker of interest. So I had no knowledge whatever of the outside world (as I thought of our town or even our suburb) beyond the little that was revealed during occasional bus rides with my mother to dentist or dressmaker. It is true that several times she took me to England to visit her family; and once a year my father would drive us all down to the sea, Durban or Cape Town, to stay in hotels. But these adventures were so exotic that they didn't seem to relate to ordinary life. It was more like going to the bioscope, which I was allowed to do, if suitably accompanied, when I was older.

But I had a look-out point which nobody knew about, not my father, not even Lottie, my dear Xhosa nurse – as I continued to refer to her long after nursing had turned to what you could call general management, spiritual nourishment and divine reassurance. At the far corner of the bottom of the garden were the stables and the carriage house which had been built, in horse-drawn days, by the previous owner. The stables and tackrooms and storerooms were disposed around a courtyard, in the usual manner, and there

were wide double gates onto the road for the carriage to pass
through. I was not allowed into this courtyard, because the stables
and storerooms, in our day, had been converted to use as the rooms
of the male servants and their little sons. My brother had one of
the rooms as his 'laboratory'. I once made a strong move to have
another as my 'museum', but this could not be. It was a men's compound.

I pointed out, to no effect, that my mother sometimes went
there, men's compound or not, because the adjacent carriage house
was used as a vast storeroom. 'I am going to the stables' meant she
was going to search for and fish out some item of furniture or
decoration or clothing from the English past, or to freshen up the
mothballs for the furs and the Epsom salts for the linens, in the
trunks and crates. A hoard of her treasures from her brief but
elegant life in Kimbolton remained in boxes down there: lace for
collars and cuffs, large feathers for hats, fichus, jabots and other
frills of one kind or another (I have many of them still, stowed
away as, on her death, she left them, wrapped in blue or black tis-
sue paper) and an assortment of furs – tippets and stoles and capes
and muffs and long, full coats, some of which she sometimes
exhumed to take on winter trips to England. The furs I have certainly not kept, though I am bound to say that like most women of
my generation I became conscious of the wickedness of them only
in my thirties. I have always loved animals of all kinds, and yet I
was so slow in waking up to the wickedness of furs, of killing for
vanity. I awoke only when I saw a huge poster in the London
Underground, showing a painting of a woman in a long fur coat
which, behind her, was dripping blood. The caption said, 'It takes
300 dumb animals to make a coat like this; but only one to wear
it.' (Perhaps the reason why our royal family has not yet got the
message is that they have never travelled by Underground.)

Of course, fashions had changed drastically after the Great
War, so that most of these treasures were no longer wearable; and
then my mother had moved to live in the sunshine of colonial life
so that many were unsuitable to the climate as well as out of fash-

ion. Whenever she went down to the stables she took the dogs with her, in case there were rats. Once, a dog got hold of one of the furs, a whole, flat, gutted fox – and other dogs disputed it, and it was torn in two. Its horrible dried head with glass eyes, a tortoiseshell clip substituted for its lower jaw (for it was supposed to beautify a woman if this thing curled round her bosom while biting its own tail), was all that remained intact. It went into my museum though, this dead, dried head of a once beautiful beast.

Because of the embargo on my visiting the stables, the men's quarters, I was obliged to set up my museum in one of the three summerhouses higher up the garden. These mud-walled, thatched, cool, dark little houses bore a remarkable resemblance to Zulu huts. They were used for countless purposes in addition to hiding, sheltering from sun or rain, or sulking. (It was only I who sulked; if John were hurt or angry, he didn't go to earth but struck out in some way.) One of them housed, at the end of each day, all the garden tools, which would have been scraped and washed off under a sluice close by – another manifestation of the waterworks. One of the huts was almost filled by the paraphernalia for the dahlias: shelves and pigeonholes for storing the tubers, each according to its labelled kind. Its floor was covered with sacks and bags of corn and seeds – big and coarse for the chickens, finer for the pigeons, small and delicate for cagebirds – ants' eggs for the goldfish, grit for the chickens, and charcoal biscuits and lumps of sulphur for the dogs. These little huts did not have much ventilation, so the smell of this hut filled one's head and lungs with what I thought was a sort of glory, the smell of love and care and fruitfulness.

The hut I chose for my museum had the racks for drying the seeds from our flowers, most of them hanging down in their various pods, next to pendent horsetails of different types of twine; and there were stout shelves for the bags of rather odoriferous fertiliser, *muti*. It also had a rough old kitchen table, and upon the table was the big attraction: the elaborate machine which John had invented for unwinding the silk from the cocoons of our silkworms. It began with a series of cigarette tins with holes punched in the lids, in which the cocoons were stored, and ended with the thread winding round a cotton reel jammed onto the spindle in the centre of the turntable of an old gramophone. There were a few intervening mechanisms which caused the threads to pass through water. (In Thailand, a lifetime later, I learned that this is unnecessary if you have first boiled the cocoons; but they were our pets.)

The reason why this wonder was not kept in John's laboratory was that I had been flattered into the minding of it, the endless repairs to the thread: women's work, naturally. It gave me control of the gramophone, though, and since the revolutions of the turntable did not interfere with the sericulture until the reel in the centre was full, which sometimes, due to breakages, took rather a long time, I was allowed to borrow some records from the house. I think it is those long sessions which gave me a lifelong affection not only for silk but also for Gilbert and Sullivan, Albert Ketelby, Adelina Patti, Richard Tauber and a lump in my throat all the millions of times I have heard or overheard 'Land of Hope and Glory' – especially when, so incongruously, it is played at commencements in the United States. I cannot possibly see in these early musical tastes the foundation of my love for classical music; that is something which began a long time afterwards and in spite of these beginnings.

My father had helped John to make a crystal receiving set, with a 'cat's whisker' and two sets of headphones, which had originally to my great dismay been kept in John's laboratory in the stable-yard, where I could not go to listen in to its dreadful whines and howls. But at about the time that I set up my museum this treasure, also, was lent to me. It was difficult to tune in – difficult for anyone, let alone an infant novice. I clearly recall sitting there wearing a pair of the headphones and making the atmospheric noises for myself, squeaks and groans and windy howls, with the same kind of satisfaction as little boys derive from roaring out '*vroom vroom*' while seated at the wheel of a car, safe on their fathers' laps. Hearing the real atmospherics used to frighten me.

The summerhouses, though cool and full of interesting smells, were rather too dark for museum display, as I always apologetically explained to anyone I could persuade to come inside. Sometimes I had a torch, but usually they had to take on trust my account of the wondrous specimens on the shelves which my father had put up for me: the dead butterflies and centipedes, oak bolls, a jar of knocked-out *tokkis*, and so on, and the fox's head, of course; so it was a great boost to have those two machines, even though they reflected upon me no personal credit, only the half-pride of co-ownership, a junior partnership. But they attracted people to come inside.

To revert to my look-out point at the bottom of the garden, in the stables: the carriage house had a corrugated-iron roof sloping gently down from the front to the back, so that rainwater would not collect in the stableyard; and if you got up there – taking a newspaper with you as the roof was usually too hot from the sun to sit on, and if you sat on the brick parapet you would be seen from the road – if you got up there you had a view not only of the lower road and the front garden of our 'back' neighbours but also, of course, of everything that went on in the courtyard of the stables, the forbidden territory. I used to get up there quite simply – not, naturally, from the courtyard, but by climbing a peach tree which had been espaliered along the back wall of the carriage house. Its branches were slim and fragile, and I would not have risked harming them; but the Chief had fixed training wires and wedges which were as strong and regular as a climbing frame, and that is how I used them, to ascend to my look-out.

The thrill was to be there at all as well as to be there secretly. I cannot say that I ever witnessed anything remarkable, though patience was sometimes rewarded by a shout from the street or a rap on the carriage gates. One of the servants would go to open them and admit a visitor, always a man, sometimes two or three, and there would be great hospitality, sitting round on logs where the men, unless it was raining, took their meals, and endless conversation in Zulu, of which I knew only a few words. None of these seemed to occur during the talk, so my spying produced little in the way of information or understanding.

All the same, I was happily interested whenever observing the Chief and Zwela and Albert or Thulani and Samuel, or their sons – Moses 1 and Moses 2 (they were both rather small, but we called them, for clarity, Big Moses and Little Moses) – Aaron, Bolly, Beko, Makhaya, Joseph: so many names, it seems, over the years, yet they were all alternating long-stayers. I was disappointed if they kept to their rooms for any length of time, accessible only to hearing or not at all. Often John was in the courtyard too, sometimes with some of his friends, and I felt uneasy about spying on them: frightened, for one thing – if they were to discover me there would be, at the least, terrible teasing; at the worst, disclosure to my parents. I calculated that the most likely result of being found out would be John's use of it as a counter-threat to my disclosing of the airgun range, which would deprive me of most of my little power. Yet in spite of my fear, there were certain rewards to listening in to John and his friends when they were there by themselves. For example, I learned quite a few of the facts of life, some of which struck me (as they still do) as absurd and badly thought out, in particular the awful proximity, confusion even, of the organs of generation and excretion. I could hardly believe my ears.

What I dreaded, though, while patiently hiding up there, was the starting-up of an old Hupmobile engine which my father had bolted to a stand in the courtyard so that John could learn about internal combustion and how to fix things in a car and so on. At least this engine had a decent separation of functions, since the spots for the ignition and for the exhaust (the only processes I could identify) were at opposite ends. But its noise and smell were dire; and the boys – the three Johns and Peter and Guy and Philip – would spend so long gathered around it, talking about it, cleaning and polishing it. Sometimes when the roaring and chugging began I would begin a descent down the peach tree wall; but without cover from the racket, it was not safe to move. Once I began my descent as the Hup began its emissions, but after a moment or two it coughed and choked into silence; and I was caught on the espalier wires, and the Chief was close by working at the compost. I was terrified of discovery and had to remain on the wires a long, long time, like a trapped bird.

Sometimes, if the men were there at the same time as John and his friends, there would be playful mock-fights between black and white – though I quite often saw this in other parts of the garden too, for there was nothing secret about it. The initial stances of it often could be seen as a sort of ritual greeting at the day's first meeting of black and white, men and boys only. If it developed, the Chief, a huge and powerful man, would pretend to be holding a Zulu assegai in his right hand, aloft, over his head, and in his left hand a shield in front of his body, and he would raise one leg, knee bent, as high as he could, pause with it there, and then stamp it violently down to earth again with a fearful utterance, something between a grunt and a yell, at the same time bringing the assegai down with a huge thump upon the imaginary shield. Then he would raise the other leg and at each step slowly advance towards

John and the Chief, Makathini, 1936

the 'enemy', jabbing in the air with the assegai, thrusting his head forward and back in a most threatening manner. Had he been the Zulu warrior he was enacting (or possibly remembering, from his father and father's fathers), John and his little friends would have died of fright. As it was, they scuffled about doing the quick little fist movements, and feints, and dancing up and down on toes, that they had learned in boxing lessons at Mr Hadland's preparatory school. How, I wondered, could these two kinds of fighting ever meet? I never saw, of course, a blow landed or harm done. Nor did I ever see one 'side' trying to teach the other how their mode was done. Makathini did once bring John a small shield and spear, from one of his visits home to Zululand. It ended up in my museum, stapled by my father to the mud wall so that it could not be used! It was only about a tenth of the size of real ones, a toy.

Makathini's stance as Zulu warrior, and the power and precision of his war-prance and the menacing syncopated rhythm of his approaching steps and the frightening battle grunt, were so convincing that the incongruity of his khaki shirt and trousers hitched up at the knee and blue apron was not observed. Also invisible on these occasions was Makathini my patient friend and teacher in the garden, who taught me many useful habits which remind me of him almost daily as I work in my garden.

For example, don't waste time by going to work without string and a knife in your pocket; and if you have a knife, lay it horizontally in the pocket or it will eviscerate you when you bend over; don't throw away strong twigs, however small, for they will do to prop up something or other; don't hesitate for a moment to crush a snail effectively at the first sight, or it will drop into the leafage and escape. This is the Makathini that I remember now: the Chief. All the fear has gone. I heard many years later from his eldest son Moses that after my father died, he went back to Taylor's Halt in Zululand and became a shoemaker. I could never trace him. I feel sure that, like all our servants, he died a poor if not a destitute man, in some remote and unproductive part of the country called, in all the years of apartheid, a 'homeland'.

Most of the time on the carriage-house roof I watched the comings and goings down the dirt road and its wide unpaved pavements, with a few wild bushes and grasses of the veld still sprouting. Sometimes there were gatherings of the neighbours' servants, men and women laughing and joking together, who could rarely have much contact in the conditions of their captivity – if their regimes were anything like that in our house. There were young black men on delivery bicycles with huge, high front baskets, delivering orders which the white mistresses had phoned through to the chemist, grocer, butcher, baker; there were horse-drawn carts with men selling fresh vegetables from a nearby farm. And there were many, many tired and ragged men trudging from front gate to front gate asking for work. I did not know, then, about the Natives Land Act of 1913, which, long before apartheid, effectively delivered tens of thousands of black peasants into servitude, since it divided the land into 'white' and 'black' areas, making hopelessly limited provision for the latter, so that working for the white man in the towns seemed safer than looking for another 'master' in the country. The men and boys walked through the suburbs of the towns and cities, looking for work. Naturally, I knew nothing about the Land Act or, indeed, about Trekkers and Settlers and Frontier Wars and Boer Wars.

I have tried to think back to what it was that I thought. Somehow, while all blacks seemed to be poor, the roads and pavements – at least those not in the centre of town, not macadamised – belonged to them. There was almost never a white person on the road, unless driving along in a big, upright, sharp-cornered motor car like ours. Nearer to the mark than I can have realised, I wondered whether the blacks' 'possession' of the streets was why I was not allowed to go out of the gate. How, then, was I ever going to get out? I had no prospect of becoming black. Or perhaps, if you were white, you had to be a boy, before you could? Or quite old – my parents often said 'older', but never how old. All that was clear was that even if the streets were mostly for black people, the houses and the gardens and the motor cars, and the money to buy them, belonged to white people. I cannot remember ever feeling proud about this, though I did when very young feel proud to be British as distinct from merely 'white'; but I do remember from earliest times feeling, in spite of the longing to be free, a measure of simple, rather puzzled thankfulness about my whiteness as I spied upon the poverty in the street.

The girls and women servants, as distinct from the men and boys, could never have visitors because their rooms were on the top of the slope, right at the other end of the site, spaced around the yard directly outside our kitchen door and so in full view of the side of the house; and anyway, because our boundaries were so strongly reinforced, visitors would have had to come in through the front gates and would surely have been seen by us, even if they were willing to brave the excited throng of fox-terriers.

There were several rooms around our kitchen yard. The largest was the laundry, with a huge copper bowl, called the copper, set in whitewashed bricks over a fireplace in the corner of the room. The copper was for boiling the white uniforms of Lottie and Zwela and Albert (uncle and nephew, who alternated as our cook, arranging their home leaves to suit) and the white uniforms that were punctiliously worn by the gardeners whenever they were transformed into dinner-party waiters or tennis-party handers-round (even the *umfaans* had white suits for posing as cloakroom attendants) and my parents' tennis clothes and, of course, John's school cricket and other white things. 'That will have to go in the copper, Lottie,' my mother would say, looking at some garment of John's which dogs or the compost pit or cricket had made disgusting. I once heard her trying to persuade John not, when preparing to bowl, to rub the seam of the ball up and down in his groin. She probably thought it was some kind of sexual twitch, undesirable in itself as well as the cause of ugly red scars on the white flannels. When he explained the necessity of it for a good spin, she asked if he could not take a little cloth in his pocket, such as a face flannel, to do the polishing!

Round the sides of this room were several big washtubs with slop-ing corrugations for scrubbing and drubbing built into their nearer sides; nearby were big lumps of white, blue-veined soap, looking like slabs of Gorgonzola.

There were three kinds of laundry day. One was for the ser-vants' clothes, one was for ours, and one was for the white things of all; racial segregation did not seem to apply to the last because the prime object was that the white clothes should be truly dazzl-ing, and the white laundry was a very great labour. In the first place the fire in a rather poky little furnace under the copper had to be brought to a stabilised roar, and then the water in the huge cop-per up to boiling point, and then there was the stirring of the clothes, which was done with an old cricket bat.

There was a great row with John about this cricket bat. Probably it had been his; probably he resented the loss of it, even if he had been given, as I suppose, a replacement. He had annoyed me very much by asking whether Lottie was a right- or a left-handed batsman. Sensing the antagonism of the question, I replied, 'Neither. She only goes up and down.' This occasioned a fearful ridicule, in front of his friends; my loyalty to Lottie caused me acute pain and storm and I took the matter to my father. I showed him how Lottie had to wield the bat, up and down like the pump of the windmill; up and down, as I learned in later years, as women all over Africa pound the grain with mortar and pestle: the slow rise into the air, the heavy, guided fall down into the mortar, the slight rounding movement around the crushed grain as the pestle is lifted again. It is back-taxing, arm-testing work. Tearfully I pulled my father into the laundry, though no boiling was in progress at the time, and made Lottie show him how she used the bat. She was unwilling, cross with me and frightened, as though she had been doing something wrong.

My father observed that the copper was too high, or else Lottie too short, for the operation to be fully effective. He went off to his workshop to make her a step 'so that she would have greater pur-chase'. We did not know, Lottie and I, what that meant, neither of us being mechanical engineers. When the step came, made out of a stout soda-siphon box, Lottie saw at once the help it would be and I suppose we both gained an inkling of this meaning of 'purchase', one of the most elusive and interesting words, bequeathed to engineering by, of all things, the science of hunting. All the same, in spite of the greatly improved purchase, this work was very hot and tiring, such was the great capacity of the copper; and then there was the subsequent close examination of the garments, still boiling hot, for any remaining blemish, and then the repeated rinsings. The whole long process was Lottie's great pride. She always had one or two young girls to help her, but the drive and the planning and the standards were hers.

After the immersions the yard would be strung across several times with thick wire (to form another vital feature – the line) and I would often help her by handing up the pegs (handing up is what I remember, though Lottie was a short woman) as she hung upon the line the billowing aprons, overalls, petticoats, upside-down shirts fat with the breeze, dangling trousers, and always pair after pair of white cotton gloves, some big, from the waiting and handing-round, some small, from the taking of coats and hats. There was a short, low-down line on which Lottie allowed me to hang up the gloves by myself, and any white socks there might be including my own hated long ones, the white socks of Empire. On this low line, too, Albert used to hang his chef's caps, which he always starched himself to make sure they would stand up proudly enough. These smaller items were a humble side-attraction to the great white laundry show which transformed our yard on the sunshine days, the days of the show, of the ballooning white sails of Lottie's pride.

When I look back, now, on the pleasure and interest which Lottie's white washing days afforded me, it seems a grotesque part of my experience. I must have known it was part of her servitude; a very hard part. I must have known that her high standards were in one way or another a response to my mother's requirements. I am not now and was not then at all interested in domestic processes as such. All I can do is record that the way Lottie did the laundry gave me my first experience of a proper professionalism and – I have to come out with it – a sense of beauty and dignity, at least whenever I see anything resembling, even remotely, the shining, billowing whites on our long-ago backyard washing line. White sails, for example, which, even as I am writing this, I can see swaying and filling as their craft gather in the roadstead outside Simon's Town harbour; or at home when a family of swans processes up the Oxford Canal to the bottom of my garden, their cautious grace, calmness, confidence in my most willing hospitality – their whiteness untouched by the muddy greens and browns of the water – it is, to me, as inspiring as Lottie's laundry used to be.

Perhaps our sense of beauty is always to be accounted for by a memory of someone whom we loved; perhaps a sense of pride and order always comes from a memory of helping with a given, small, important task, and receiving thanks and praise for it; as I did, also, for the stinkbugs. It is not at all clear, as Darwin knew, how we may account for a sense of beauty since it is not to be connected to the idea of a beneficent Creator who made the universe to please, specifically, us. Darwin resorted to theories of sexual attraction and selection. But I do not know, though in university days I tried very hard, of any satisfactory type of aesthetic theory. As the decades have passed, accompanied perhaps by a softening of the brain, I am more-or-less content with my Lottie's Laundry theory.

Next to the laundry proper was the ironing room where there was also a fireplace, in this case under a stove with large square plates, for heating the flatirons; and filling almost all the rest of the room, a table – very large, for upon it rested a huge basket for the rolled-up iron-ready clothes, stands for the flatirons, space for the ironing itself and, fixed against the wall above it, a big rack for the ironed garments. Underneath this rack there was a place for me to sit, to amuse Lottie while she ironed or me while Lottie ironed. As the rack filled with the pressed clothes we gradually became invisible to each other, which did not seem in the least to matter.

To the side of the ironing room, but a few yards away, was our family privy, before sewerage came. On the other side of the laundry was a servants' shower with a privy for women (I was told) on one side and for men on the other and next to that 'the girls'' rooms. Our Lottie was a mature woman, but she was, in the way of those times, always referred to as a 'girl', just as the grown men were referred to as 'boys'; which is probably why, saving confusion, the real little boys were usually called *umfaans*.

As far back as I can remember there were two, sometimes three, young girls – teenagers, *izintombi*, or *ntombi* as we called them – who not only helped Lottie with the laundry but also cleaned the house, under her eye. Some of them were the children of one or another of her relatives. She used to go in the car with my father to fetch them at the station when they came up from the country. None of them stayed very long; only long enough for Lottie to teach them a few things to prepare them for schooling at her church mission. She taught them not only their household duties but how to make their clothes, in a European style, how to walk in shoes (they used to giggle a lot, finding this an absurd thing to do), and basic English. One day I went running to Lottie to tell her that the oldest girl, Lena, had had a terrible accident – blood was running down her legs and there were bloody footprints in the yard. She must have cut herself on something, I thought. Lena was crying pitifully and crouching down by the wall. I went and crouched down with her but Lottie just sighed, went to her room to get something and, with what seemed to me a reprehensible calmness, went out to cope, leading Lena to the shower room; and that is how both Lena and I learned about menstruation and how to put up with it.

I did not get to know any of the *ntombi* very well since we had hardly any common language, and they were very shy. Lottie was very strict with them. I suppose she had a sort of auntly pull. She would not allow them to play with us and the *umfaans*, probably because, except for me, all were boys. Knowing my careful, foresightful father, I should think that their presence was part of the same policy as accounted for the *umfaans*: an attempt to ensure that our family should have, till kingdom come, a continuous supply of trained and loyal servants and no need to have recourse to the dispossessed who roamed our suburban streets. This colonialist employment policy was not inconsistent with trying to give the children of our servants the best start in life that seemed, in their circumstances, to be possible.

And then, next to the ironing room, there was Lottie's room; and always, and all the time, for she never went on leave, there was Lottie.

8 Lottie

She had, when I was young, no children of her own. I can tell now, and am sure I could then, that she gave me the care and love, though perhaps not the iron discipline, that she would have given a daughter of her own. The care was total except, I believe, for breast-feeding, which my mother for some reason, in later days, often assured me that she had performed herself. In almost every other way Lottie was my carer and keeper, bather, dresser, feeder and watcher and singer-to-sleep.

I have very early memories of the feeding, in particular. She had to sit with me at table – until we were about ten or eleven John and I ate with our parents only for Sunday lunch; otherwise always in the day nursery. John used to bolt his food and then be allowed to 'get down', but I was a reluctant eater, it seems, and so was given my food on a special plate kept hot by having a sort of pewter chamber underneath for refilling with hot water, as the meal dragged on. Lottie was patient and resourceful. I would complain that the food tasted like soap, or dirt, or *kak* or any horrible thing I could think of. '*Aikona!*' Lottie would exclaim. 'Oh no! It can't be! Let me smell it!' – and in this satisfactory way, once Lottie had seen that in spite of many encouragements there was no future between that meal and me, the lump on the plate would piece by piece disappear into some bag or cloth on Lottie's lap, with many ecstatically funny faces pulled by both of us at the strange flavours which I

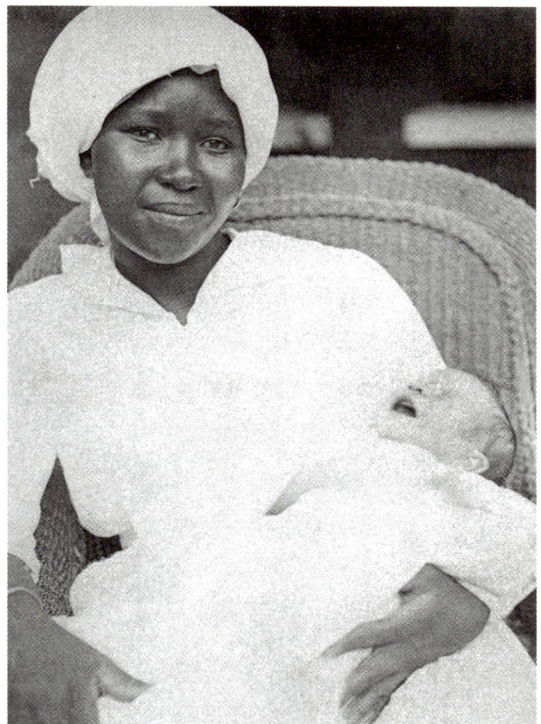

*This is the only picture I have of Lottie. We were both very young
at the time and do not seem yet to have established the closeness
which meant so much to me*

was inventing. Unless memory will one day take me back to the
cradle itself, this may be my earliest intimation of Lottie's skill and
wisdom in managing her tricky position of surrogate mother, on the
far side of an enormous cultural divide, without either criticising or
(noticeably) deceiving her employer.

As I grew up, and my mother had no younger children, Lottie
became more my companion and confidante, while in the household her duties changed to the charge of the everlasting laundry
(which in very early days a turbanned *dhobi* used to do, carrying
huge bundles of it over his shoulder, on his back – never a bike,
never a cart – kicking out, poor man, at the dogs), and to the

training and supervising of the *ntombi*.

We did not have a high turnover of staff in our family, though some of our neighbours were always hiring and firing. My father was a kind and just employer, very paternalistic. Like many English in those days, he wanted only Zulu servants – there are signs of a British–Zulu *entente* even today. It is rather surprising, seeing that the Zulu are the only nation in southern Africa to have inflicted defeat on a British army. Nevertheless, the defeat (or victory) of Isandhlwana forgotten (if it was known about), Zulu is what our servants had to be and, for the most part, they came from one village too – Taylor's Halt, to the west of the Valley of a Thousand Hills, in Natal, KwaZulu-Natal. When the season came for one of the men to go home for ploughing and sowing or harvest, a relative would be sent in his place. But this applied only to the men.

Lottie was not part of that system and moreover she was a Xhosa, from the Eastern Cape. She had a husband, called Meshak, who was a delivery-cart driver for Solly Kramer's bottlestore in town and lived in Alexandra Township. That is all I know about him, and I did not once see him, in fourteen years. He was not allowed to come to our house. That is how it was.

On Sunday mornings and every other Thursday Lottie would put aside the blue overall and starched white apron with its top that covered her great bosom and travelled over her wide shoulders to descend down her back in broad bands to a crisp bow at her waist; put aside, too, the starched white cap which concealed her many tight little pigtails. On Sundays she would put on a dark, smart, sober, high-necked and long-sleeved dress, whatever the heat of the day, and on her head either a *doek*, a scarf tied at the back, or a dark cap of crochet-work coming over her brow and almost concealing her ears. It was Church, of course. I do not know whether Meshak joined her at the church – if he did, I suppose that he would have had to conceal his connection with the bottlestore – or whether they had any home life beyond every other Thursday.

On those Thursdays, she dressed quite differently. In the first place, she wore quite a different sort of cap. All the caps, which were rather like acorn cups, she made herself. I watched her, so many times, with a stout crochet needle and thick thread, black for Sundays, white cotton for everyday, but for Thursdays coloured silk – pink, yellow, green, bright. She made them by beginning at the middle with a round disc which ends up, when the cap has been completed, on the crown of the head; this disc is then progressed round and around, and outwards, getting larger as the hook is poked in and out of the circle just completed, Lottie's quick brown hands, with the pink palms, twitching the thread around. But it doesn't end up as a flat circle, as a doily, although there were many of these on the surfaces around her bedroom, and indeed around mine, which she made for me, and in a lighter thread with beads round the edge hanging (against the flies) over our jugs of milk or home-made lemonade. She taught me, in time, to make stunning doilies; but caps are a different matter. They have to conform to the shape of a head, so once the crown is big enough, they have to start to go roundly downwards and this is an aspect of the art which I could never learn. If I, no matter how closely supervised, took two or three stitches together into the hook, to begin to reduce and redirect the circumference, things got very lumpy, out of hand and off the hook.

On Thursdays Lottie wore no makeup or jewellery except modest earrings. Her going-out dresses were always plain and matronly, but on Thursdays they were much brighter than on Sundays; and Thursday caps were no less than joyful, with little arabesques or points around the ears. Her Thursday demeanour when we said goodbye was also bright and joyful; loving, but smiling and eager to go. I was always asleep by the time she came home, and she never told me anything about life in Alexandra Township, and was never willing to answer any questions about it.

I didn't often visit the laundry. If Lottie was in it, poking the boiling copper with the old cricket bat, or drubbing with the Gorgonzola, she would be too busy to talk. It was in the ironing room that nearly all our reading took place – that is, my reading to her – but the greatest pleasure of all was if she asked me into her bedroom, in her free time.

Lottie's bedroom had a black iron bedstead with a white coverlet she had crotcheted herself, and her pillow lay in a white pillowcover with the word 'Home' worked on it and shown up by a pink backing. A tin trunk covered by a large, white embroidered cloth served as bedside table. Upon it was an alarm clock, a candle in a blue-and-white enamel candle-holder (we had electricity but not in the servants' rooms) and a beer bottle full of sea water which I brought her, by special request, every year from Durban or Cape Town. All these objects sat upon doilies of their own, and a china cake-stand which was also on the 'table' supported, on a very big and fine doily, a battered Bible. There was a chest of drawers and a washstand with enamel jug and bowl A wooden fruitbox, covered with a pretty cloth, supported a hand-operated Singer sewing-machine which she sometimes took away to Alexandra on a Thursday, balancing it, of course, on her head.

9 Reading and writing

None of our servants was literate. They were numerate, but only in their heads; they could not write or read either the words or the symbols for the numbers. It is important to distinguish these skills, not to use 'illiterate' or 'anumerate' as synonyms for the altogether foolish. In my youth it was the custom to do so; all too often even now. But no one could do so who has worked with non-literates in any way which – as in the building and tending of a garden, for example – demands an accurate understanding of 'when' and 'how many' or 'how much' or 'how often' or 'how deep' and so forth. The Chief did not need to take notes of my father's copious daily instructions about the garden; nor Zwela or Albert my mother's verbal sketches of how to make a plum duff or cheese mousse; nor Lottie the elaborate details of my complicated routines. They just remembered what had been said. They supplied the lack in their formal education, as all intelligent pre-literate people do, by mental discipline and by what often seem to us amazing feats of memory.

When I look back on the little I know of my father as a mining engineer, and Olive's carefully kept photo albums, I seem to think that my father learned this fact about non-literate people very early in his career. I do not think that a person would go down the world's deepest mines, almost wholly dependent upon the manual skills, attention, alertness and memory of non-literate black people, had he not reached certainties on this head and a trust in their

abilities. There are a couple of pictures of him on the Simmer and
Jack Mine: a group of several tired men in shirtsleeves, with dirty
clothes and faces, sitting chummily even if wearily together on the
steps of my father's bungalow. Two of the men are white, my father
and Mr Wetherall (from the traction engine of Boer War days); and
the rest are black. Olive in the caption describes the latter as 'black
colleagues !!!'. The exclamation marks are patronising, of course. I
cannot tell whether they were supplied by his sister Olive or copied
by her from the letter in which he had sent the picture; but the
group, because so informal, is indeed an unusual one for the time. I
have concluded that my father and Mr Wetherall were undergoing
– perhaps had just come off shift – their training to get their
'underground ticket', which is a statutory requirement of the industry for miners and engineers alike; and that this was the team
which gave him the training, a small group used to working together and trusting each other in dirty, difficult, dangerous circumstances.

I can't remember ever discussing the question of black abilities
with him, but I remember very many illustrative incidents. For
example, the only time I saw him lose his temper: some people had
come to 'sundowners', drinks on the *stoep*. It was usually the
women who got together to talk about 'the servant problem', but
on this occasion it was a man who raised the question. He was one
of the few bachelors we knew, an untidy and unhappy man always
making loud and silly jokes. At 'sundowners' even I could see that
he drank too much. The 'joke' he told that evening was about his
new 'boy'. Ordered, apparently, to bring his master drinks in the
garden, the servant had put a bottle of water and the bathroom
mug on a large tray and presented it to him. 'Ha ha ha, the damned
fool! I ask you!' The teller nearly died of derisive mirth; the company giggled; my father got up and went over to the man. I thought
at first that he was going to refill his glass, or something, but he
stood in front of him and asked him to leave the house. My mother
was fearfully embarrassed; I suppose everyone else was too, and it
was only in response to their defence of the joker that my father, in

the end, really exploded. I don't remember what he said, but the man left in a huff and a hurry and was never seen again, and nor were some of the other guests who left shortly after, and it was a cause of grievance between my parents for a long time. Clearly, my father, normally the gravest and calmest of men, had been incensed beyond endurance, not merely by the man's crass insensitivity but by the general attitude which had been revealed among the guests. Sometimes I think that the main thing may have been because the man was drunk; but perhaps that was only part of my father's excuses to my mother in the many rows they had after this event.

My mother, because she was the domestic and the socialising one, and took a great pride in both these roles, naturally had far more to do with the servants than my father did. Yet she did not have nearly so sure a touch with them. Naturally, she was at first inexperienced, but it was also a matter of temperament and imagination. She had a quick intelligence, but it operated in fits and starts; she didn't think things out, or through, or over, so that when it came to training or giving instructions to servants (or us children, for that matter) her edicts were often incomplete or even self-contradictory. The servants' attempts to reach clarity about her wishes must often have seemed to her to be evidence of their failure in understanding or of language slowness, so that she sometimes fell into the common absurdity of simply repeating the faulty instruction more slowly and more loudly.

However, lest it be thought I am claiming that literacy is an unimportant matter (or unimportant for servants!), which is a million miles from the case, I should explain how we all got by. If there was anything calling for reading and writing that was either important – such as weevils in the bag of meal that had been dispatched to a wife in Zululand – or dangerous – such as anything to do with the police – then it was a matter for my father. The men would come up from their quarters at the end of the day, after my father had returned from work, and ask to see him in the kitchen. The matter would be talked out, sometimes at great length, everybody standing, and my father would listen, ask questions, read any

papers that were produced, and at the end he would often write
something to give to them, or say that he would write or telephone
about the matter, and that was that. I was allowed to attend these
meetings (though I cannot remember my mother or even Lottie ever
being there; perhaps I was too young to be considered a female)
provided that I neither spoke nor fidgeted.

I sometimes understood little or nothing of the case. One I
remember clearly was when the Chief had had news that one of his
sons had run away from home to 'join the mines'. He was deeply
upset, and the *indaba* was called to ask if my father could retrieve
the boy. I remember how puzzled and worried my father looked –
it was probably in those days a thing impossible to achieve, even
for a consultant engineer, even if one knew which mine the boy had
gone to. But the whole atmosphere cleared when my father asked
when the boy was born; the Chief, Makathini, told him the precise
date and it turned out that he was – ten, I think, maybe as much as
twelve. So my father assured everyone that he would not be accepted at the mines. That was the first problem over; but what about
the next: where was the boy? Would he become one of the many
thousands of 'lost ones', those who never made it back to their
homes? Nobody could answer that, but a few days later little
Moses, for it was he, turned up at our front gate and joined our
ménage. Big Moses, the son of the Chief's senior wife, wasn't too
pleased, but was due to leave soon anyway. Lottie told me she
thought that little Moses had never intended to join the mines; only
to ensure that it was he and not some other son, or son of some
other servant, who took the place of big Moses.

The *indabas* were a vital part of my parents' (my father's, at any
rate) relation to black people who could not read, write, telephone
or otherwise protect themselves in their world at the bottom of the
order which the white men had imposed. But everyday reading and
writing – that was my job. They would not ask my mother, or
John, who was most of the time at boarding school anyway. So it
was that I read their letters from home, which had always been
written in English, on behalf of the sender, usually by the post-

master, sometimes by the storekeeper, at Taylor's Halt. Their news
was always sad and bad. After the long customary greetings and
thanks for any money or food that had been sent, there would be
news of illness, hunger, the death or birth of infants, drought
(sometimes floods), failure of pumpkins, mealies, millet ('kaffir-
corn', as all races called it). Then a few days later, I would be asked
to write the responses – 'Dear My Wife ...' – for the postmaster or
the storekeeper at Taylor's Halt to read and convey in Zulu for the
wives. English had to be the written medium because I knew only
English, and I was a vital link in the chain. The letters were one of
the few ways in which I learned about the world outside my
boundaries.

Apart from that, I read for them all kinds of other things: labels,
instructions on medicine bottles, newspaper headlines, recipes
('Take a quarter of an ounce of ... Well, Zwela, it says here that
you put in *nearly nothing* of ...'), pamphlets from the street,
prayers on 'holy cards' from the missionaries, invoices from
traders, dispatch dockets from the railways, seed packets, warnings
on bags of fertiliser (always called *muti*, medicine, as I do now). I
also wrote various things for them.

One recurrent thing in particular, a very uncongenial job, was
for the police, a Pass. 'Please pass boy "Maka," or "Albert," or
"Zwela" until 11 p.m. tonight.' Then one would have to put the
address and the date, and fake a scrawly, grown-up type of signa-
ture. I can remember doing this even before I could do joined-up
writing. The Pass Laws were strictly enforced – though they applied
then only to men – so I suppose that, for them, necessity overrode
the humiliation of virtually having to seek permission to come and
go from a white, a child – and a female, at that. As for me, even
while I faked these documents I wondered what sort of fools were
in the police force.

From the time I was about ten, a very serious and almost obsessional kind of reading developed. My taste has matured a little
since those times but I feel sure that the obsession with it, which
remains, has its origin in the days when reading was the source of

the only knowledge I had of the world outside my garden, or of intimacy with people I felt to be, sometimes rather remotely, like myself. Reading was not therefore an 'escape' for me, as people so often suppose; it was a reality, a mode of experience which informed and enriched my real and conscious life.

The reading of those days concerned Lottie and me only. The men and boys could not come into the women's compound, and the *ntombi*, whose English was marginal, were very quickly bored. It began when Lottie brought home from church some battered and well-thumbed little books of pious and tragic little tales. They always ended happily – in Heaven. Although we knew everybody would get to Heaven, Lottie used to savour the trials on the way, and if there were sadnesses of any kind, like undeserved punishments or lingering illnesses, she would ask me to read those passages over and over. It was as though she could never have enough sadness. In time we had read all the church booklets, and they had to be returned anyway, so a terrible vacuum occurred.

Lottie's Bible had been given by her church, though unlike most of the missionary churches they apparently made no attempt to teach her to read it. It was a precious object to her, placed on its special doily on the cake-stand, her lectern, her bold, brass Gospel lectern. I don't, for some reason, remember reading to her from the New Testament, but we tore through the Old, which often frightened us in its cruel savagery but provided me with at least a cursory knowledge of great works which I was never, in later years, obliged to read. I had a hard time with much of Genesis, all the 'begats' so faithfully chronicled from the beginning of Creation, which Lottie would not allow me to skip. But we both deeply enjoyed all the adventures of Abraham and his amazing family. Lottie refused to explain to me how Lot got both of his daughters pregnant, and it is still (for different reasons) unclear to me, considering that he was at the material time unconscious with wine. Predictably, Lottie's favourite was the Book of Job. I recall that it was very hard to read aloud unless one shouted and thundered all the time, whether the speaker was Job, or Satan, or the Comforters, or God himself, for they all uttered words that were so wild and dreadful, awesome, resounding. You couldn't just say them; you had to utter or, at the least, intone; and you felt more equal to it if you stood up and walked about. I tried to ignore the giggling of the *ntombi* in the next room.

My parents did not have very many books. Darwin, of course, at least the *Origin* and the *Beagle*, *Pears Cyclopaedia*, Lord Tennyson in crinkly red calf, Bowdler's Shakespeare in ten small volumes ('omitting all such words and expressions as may not, with propriety, be read aloud in a family'), Edgar Wallace, Sapper's *Bulldog Drummond*, Ruby M. Ayres (who was my godmother and sent us copies of the three or four novels which she produced annually), many stacks of *The National Geographic Magazine* which, together with some engineering journals, came regularly, All these, in their widely differing ways, were unsuitable for reading to Lottie. They were not very suitable for me, either, though the pictures in the *National Geographic* excited and sometimes deliciously frightened me – beyond all reason, as my mother said: volcanoes and earthquakes or the deep sea creatures, the huge ones, or the ones that lived in such utter, deep darkness that they had their own electric lighting systems (so I thought), as miners had Davy lamps.

In the later years of my childhood I had a few books of my own, a strange assortment: Homer, who changed my life; the Canadian nature-novelist Gene Stratton Porter, a great favourite (*Freckles* and *A Girl of the Limberlost* – if only I could find them again in some compost heap of a bookshop, where the good old things moulder along with the bad, to our general great enrichment). I had beautiful editions of *Alice* and the Grimms' grim stories and Andersen's soppy ones, and a semi-religious aunt sent me *Pilgrim's Progress* and *The Holy War* and a few such others that I tried to conceal from Lottie so that we would not have to wade through them. And I enjoyed John's adventure novels, Jack London and R.M. Ballantyne especially. But Lottie reacted in horror when I tried to read her the latter – *Black Ivory*, I had chosen. I had thought that, substituting elephants for huskies and tusks for

teeth, it might be a sort of counterpart to the thrilling *White Fang*.
Unfortunately it turned out to be about the slave trade, with harrowing pictures. We abandoned it in something like hysteria.

So my mother wrote to her father in London, who believed that
only one writer was worth reading, and kindly sent us his own
leather-bound copies of *The Old Curiosity Shop* and *A Christmas
Carol*. They provided us with marvellous interest, and sorrow, for a
very long time, in view of all the repeats for sadness. I think my
grandfather must have considered, rightly no doubt, that the rest of
Dickens would be over our heads, so he sent other books of which
I remember only the titles: *The Wide, Wide World*, *The Lamp-
lighter* and *A Peep Behind the Scenes*, which was an amazingly
tragic tale of circus life. I have never come across these novels since
that time, though I read recently in the journal of Elizabeth Lees
Moffat (whose sister married David Livingstone) that upon her
return to the Moffats' remote mission in the northern Cape after
completing her education in England, she brought back with her
the first two of them. The date of that entry is 1854! I feel sure,
from that date, that it was my grandmother's contribution of books
she had loved as a child. Then one day *Sense and Sensibility* and,
unfortunately, *Wuthering Heights* arrived. My grandfather was a
man largely self-educated yet of strong and cultivated tastes. But –
if only the latter had been any other book, by any Brontë other
than the fierce, passionate, marvellous Emily!

This wonderful novel was, during one of my years with Lottie, a
source of great trial and worry to me. I found it very frightening
and I could not understand why all the characters, male and female
(except Lockwood, who was not a part of that world and Nellie
Dean, whose amiability serves to show up the rest), were so vile-
tempered and mannerless, rude to each other when they were not
downright cruel, weak when not overbearing, sly when they could
not prevail by force, and often murderous.

The main trouble was, in Lottie's day, that I could not understand any of the characters emotionally and one of them, the hate-
fully religious manservant Joseph (in whom Lottie pinned great

faith because of his biblical quotations), not even verbally, since Emily's rendering of the West Riding of Yorkshire dialect is impenetrable. As I recollect reading to Lottie in her little room, she working away at the crochet, me lying on her bed – there was only one chair – I am full of self-admiration for the time and care I must have spent in these unlikely circumstances, stumbling through sentences such as 'Aw wod hev ye tuh look aht, Miss – yah muh be t'next. Thank Hivven for all warks togither for gooid tuh them as is chozzen, and piked aht froo' th'rubbidge! Yah knaw whet t'Scripture ses …' I used to pick Joseph out, all right, if I saw him coming, because of *his* rubbidge, and stifle him, for if you started him Lottie would make you go on, for the expected bit of Scripture.

We struggled with this book for months. Sometimes I felt I couldn't face another instalment and would take something else along to Lottie's. On such days she would become sad and silent; at best monosyllabic. Her broad, round, brown face, usually so bright and loving, would close up and her mind would go inward. Even if she spoke a word, she would not show her wonderful, white, even teeth, but her lips would bunch up around them, hardly moving (why do people pout, when sulking?), her voice very low. Many sighs, even if I were reading hilarious stuff out of the Sunday comics to which we descended once a week. This reaction is unbearable and unbeatable. It's a kind of sulking which might well be called 'wuthering', a sort of sub-withering, resorted to by servants or underlings or oppressed children who do not risk speaking out. Whenever Lottie began to wuther consistently *Wuthering Heights* had to come back. What can have attracted her to such a sombre, mysterious and – to us – foreign tale?

I had not, of course, read Charlotte's Preface to her sister's work, and would not have understood its rather veiled import if I had – veiled because many of the themes were based upon local family stories which had been imparted to the Brontës in confidence. Mrs Gaskell records that, walking on the moors with Charlotte, she heard stories about the local people which made the people of *Wuthering Heights* seem virtuous! Now that I have the benefit of Charlotte's introduction and of several learned articles by Christopher Heywood, I can see what held Lottie's attention.

Heathcliff is a black man! The abandoned son of a slave! I have thought, all this time, that he was just gypsy-like or dark and glowering, like Laurence Olivier. Near the end of the work, Heathcliff far gone in his demented longing for Cathy, there is a reference to 'his black father'. But it is not dwelt upon and I for one (before I read Heywood) took it as a reference to the devil. The book as a whole is a covert indictment of a slave-owning society, or rather of the lives, in Yorkshire, of the sugar plantation entrepreneurs who grew rich on the miseries of the slave trade, drew their profits back to England, expanded their estates – and brought with them their racial attitudes and, indeed, some of their slaves. They were especial objects of loathing to Wilberforceans, Quakers, many churchmen and, it appears, the Brontë family.

I think one of the most telling incidents revealing this slavery connection is that when the hateful Linton is discovered 'sucking like an innocent' (though a grown man) at a stick of sugar candy. Throughout the decades of abolition and emancipation there are many accounts of sugar boycotts by Wilberforceans, sugar being regarded as the evil source of the plantation slave economy in the West Indies and hence of the moral corruption of those who conducted or condoned it. One is reminded of the boycott of South African products, which were such a feature in England during the forty-odd years of the apartheid regime. And I have supposed, all these years, that the novel was about the bleaker regions of a cold, long-dead and 'foreign' society!

It seems clear to me now that Lottie must, somehow, have picked up the essentials of Heathcliff's position from the start. I certainly did not. Old Mr Earnshaw, Cathy's father, had found the small child, 'as dark almost as though it came from the devil', he told his wife, 'starving and houseless and as good as dumb', abandoned in the streets of Liverpool, and brought the boy home in his arms, sixty miles on foot, to share his home with his hostile family

and the bewildered Nellie Dean. The child was referred to by the
rest of the family, even by Nellie, as 'it', given no welcome, not
even a bed; slept on the stairs, was turned into an outdoors servant.
The fact that Cathy takes a strong liking to him is the source of
much of the family feuding thereafter: is Heathcliff a servant, or a –
person? Because he is treated so badly, his nature deteriorates. He
hates and is hated by everyone except Cathy, but even she, later on,
will not marry him. I think now that in Lottie's view all this
stemmed from his being black, or being a servant, or both. Lottie's
place in life and her remarkable non-reader's memory caused her to
pick up and to store all the clues which escaped me – and which
Emily had taken great pains to hide.

10 'The servants and the dogs'

'Really, Prudence! All you care about is the servants and the dogs!'
I quarrelled with my mother quite often, even when small. I think I
was a strangely wilful child, considering my shyness. Whereas she
often seemed to me impatient and unreliable, though I know that
mothers, as a rule, have less time for questions and discussions than
fathers do when they come home to rest from work. What irked me
in particular was that she had very fixed ideas about 'appearances'
and how to keep them up, and this seemed to me to cover everything in the world and to be her main interest in life – my life,
unfortunately, as well as hers. When we quarrelled she would often,
at the end, boil it all down, in exasperation, to the servants-and-
dogs accusation. I would think, on these occasions, though not of
course admit, that (making an exception of my father) she was
right. 'You are dead right,' I would think, the 'dead' expressing the
anger I felt rather than affirming a correct judgement; not at all like
the praise and encouragement of 'Dead on!' that I would shout out
if some boy's air pellet had, a foot or two from my face, hit a bull's
eye.

Perhaps this servants-and-dogs world is true of many childhoods, in certain societies and ages of mankind. Consider the great
Odysseus – my earliest hero, though (before my manic persistence
won her round) he bored Lottie to death. After ten years' fighting
in Troy, and nearly ten years after that trying to get home to Greece

in the face of almost every kind of maritime and erotic disaster, finally he gets home to Ithaca. But he cannot declare himself, because his wife, Penelope, is besieged by more than a hundred suitors who must first be killed off. So he invents an immensely long story about being a blameless refugee and makes for the hut of his old swineherd. 'The noisy dogs suddenly caught sight of Odysseus and flew at him, barking loudly.' Well of course, Lottie and I agreed, after an initial shock: those dogs did; those were dogs that didn't know him – they were born after he had gone to the war. The swineherd doesn't recognise him, nor does his own son, Telemachus, who turns up. They go to spy out the palace:

'Stretched on the ground where they stood talking, there lay a dog, who now pricked up his ears and raised his head. Argus was his name. Odysseus himself had owned and trained him, though he had sailed for Troy before he could reap the reward of his patience. Now ... he lay abandoned on the heaps of dung from the mules and cattle ... There, full of vermin, lay Argus the hound. But directly he became aware of Odysseus' presence, he wagged his tail and dropped his ears, though he lacked the strength now to come any nearer to his master.'

Odysseus, fearful of betraying his identity, makes no move towards the dog. This always seemed to me to be one of the greatest of his trials and tests of his strength of purpose – quite as stiff as the murderous seas thrown at him by an angry god, his capture by the cannibal Cyclops or the disastrous songs of the Sirens. The swineherd talks about the dog for a while: his former speed, power, beauty and devotion to his master – of course, to rub in the agony of this moment – and then the men move off. 'As for Argus, he had no sooner set eyes on Odysseus after those nineteen years than he succumbed to the black hand of Death.'

As for humans, the person who first recognises Odysseus is not his loving wife, Penelope, and not his son, nor his father. It is his old nurse, Eurycleia, now nearly blind, whom Penelope details off to wash the stranger's travel-worn feet. That does it! The feet! The scar from the boar tusk wound! 'As the old woman passed her hands over his scar, she recognised the feel of it and abruptly let go her master's foot, which ... dropped against the basin, upsetting it and spilling all the water on the floor. Delight and anguish swept through her heart together; her eyes were filled with tears; her voice was strangled with emotion. She lifted her hand to Odysseus' chin [What a marvellous brushstroke: exactly the way in which an old woman would touch a child] and said, "Of course, you are Odysseus, my dear child. And to think I didn't know you until I'd handled my master's limbs!" '

We had many dogs, in those years. They were nothing special, as breeding goes; they were for the most part the mongrel puppies of our smooth-haired, loving and most loved fox-terrier bitch, called,

Beloved Puppy and the shaggiest of her sons. Puppy always looked you in the face, like this, intelligent and loving

into her extreme old age, Puppy. She lived with us, but in spite of the barbed-wire fences and the hedges and the ditches she visited widely. There were holes in the hedges, sometimes combined with tunnels, which were called 'Puppy's holes', through which she escaped to her escapades. The *umfaans* were supposed to keep them blocked up, but Puppy could scratch away anything. She was our chief ratter – indeed, the chief of every dog affair – and sometimes with her excavation techniques she most usefully turned over almost the whole contents of the compost pit, four legs flailing, searching for rats, her tiny stump of tail feverishly oscillating, yelping occasionally as though reporting progress.

Puppy's puppies were shared among neighbours, but we kept most of them, until my parents put a secret surgical stop to the supply. The neighbours knew about the qualities of Puppy and always hoped for the inheritance, but on the whole they went in for big, strong guard dogs. Two or three of Puppy's puppies – if all were indeed her offspring and not hangers-on – were shaggy and weird, but on the whole what predominated was Puppy's foxy little black face with a white parting and brown patches at the base of the whiskers, her sweet and loving intelligence and her sense of fun. Puppy and nearly all her children could *smile*. She would raise her upper lip (not at all the prelude to a 'guttural gnarl') and wag the whole of her hindquarters – not just the little docked tail, but her whole behind so that, in turn, first one back foot and then the other left the ground. Then would come the sneeze – an essential part of the smile – with a violent shake of the head proceeding horizontally as a quick convulsion of the whole frame; then the upper lip reverted to normal and she would resume prancing around, waiting for the next amusement. She was particularly likely to smile and sneeze in this way if she had been made to feel foolish. It was like a light-hearted confession that she had been mistaken or inept, an acknowledgement which humans find such a challenge.

Puppy was an attentive and faithful mother, but when not in brood she seemed to be wholly and entirely at *our* service. The great Roman, Lucretius, has a touching passage about the dreams of horses and of dogs, and he divides dogs into the hunting and the domestic types and accordingly interprets the movements and noises which they make in their sleep. I find it, as I find most of Lucretius, entirely convincing. 'Hunting dogs' – he means big and serious ones – 'will when asleep sniff and quiver and jerk their legs, and chase the empty images of stags, as though they saw them in flight, until they dissipate their delusions and come to themselves.' But, he says, 'if the friendly breed of dogs which live in the house catch sight [he means in their sleep] of an unknown face and form, they hasten to shake themselves and to leap up from the ground.' Puppy, exactly. She was always on duty, always thinking (so I believe) of us.

Puppy and her children, who were collectively called Puppies (or perhaps, I don't know, Puppy's), came to perform feats of understanding of our childish games. They helped us to develop them. They were always very actively helpful, fetching and finding and appreciating and urging us on. 'Hide and seek' was easy, of course. If when you stood counting with your eyes closed you had a Puppy with you, then when you let it go it would streak off to the nearest hiding child, then on to the next, and the next. Puppies sat, not very happily, but faithfully, in 'dog carts', as we wrongly called them – wooden whisky boxes mounted on a plank with wheels, pulled by John, as a rule, behind his bike; or else I would be put in the cart, usually sharing with a dog, and pushed down the slope of the pergola, though mostly rescued at the last minute from crashing down the steps to the tennis court. Puppy always stayed in with me to the end, but her children jumped overboard long before.

The dogs were closer to us than the birds; more responsive, more playful, more 'normal'; but for as long as I lived at Mornington I know that I was obsessional about birds. Sometimes when people asked me what I would like to be when I grew up, I used to reply 'a bird', and it would not have occurred to me to say 'a dog'. Perhaps it was because birds are free and mysterious, whereas I was trapped, and overseen by everyone. Or perhaps I was trading on my father's interest in them, in order that we could have long discussions about their peculiarities.

For quite a time I was especially impressed not by their flying but by the ways in which they got about the ground, which seemed to me amazing. I can remember trying to wrest from him an explanation of why all small birds, wild or free, have the habit not of walking but of going pop-pop-pop along the ground. 'They do not go, as people say, "hop hop hop," ' I insisted, demonstrating the nature (in case he did not know, for he surely, never in all his life, had hopped?) of a bona fide, one-legged hop. 'They go popping along, both legs together like fixed pins, never putting one foot before another. They bounce along in little spurts, like a dropped ping-pong ball, pop-pop-pop.' I bounced around him, demonstrating. In his usual grave and thorough way he asked me what muscles I was using, to do that popping. My thighs, I supposed. And what else? My ankles? Yes. And could I point to where on, say, a sparrow the thighs were? No; upon reflection, I could not. Somewhere under the feathers, I supposed; but if there are any, they must be negligible, no thicker than their little sticks of shins. As for ankles: who could say what was ankle and what was knee? Or even elbow? My father, philosopher and engineer, pointed out the conclusion: creatures equipped so differently from us had to get about by means of what, exactly, they had; which in this case meant popping: and terms borrowed from other creatures were useless deceivers.

I was not satisfied. Some birds, in my opinion, walked more properly: bigger birds, though even some of those had silly walks. Take pigeons: a pigeon as it walks, may put one foot forward at a time alternately, but it thrusts its head forward and back to accompany each step, so that its head moves at exactly twice the speed of its feet. What an expenditure! And what does the bird gain from it? My father referred me with confidence to *The Origin of Species*. We tended to use Darwin in our house as an encyclopaedia, for 'the truth' about everything. I did not realise until years later that it embodied a great new theory, and so have always regarded its main contentions as a matter of common sense as well as common knowledge. My father said that Darwin would be sure to know about this head-nodding as he was particularly a pigeon man – and so indeed he was. He wrote with amusing mock-modesty in the first chapter of this earth-shaking work, 'I have taken up domestic pigeons. I have kept every breed which I could purchase or obtain ... I have associated with several eminent fanciers, and have been permitted to join two of the London Pigeon Clubs.'

My father helped me check every pigeon entry in the book. I would not be surprised if it was after this intensive research that a new respect was acquired for the breed and that a stop was put to my brother's licence to kill. We learned about every pigeon fact imaginable. No wonder that, according to Richard Leakey, 'when Darwin's publishers submitted the manuscript of the book to a referee for an opinion, the referee wrote back regretting that Darwin had not simply written a book on pigeon breeding: "Everybody is interested in pigeons," he insisted. "The book would be reviewed in every journal in the kingdom, and would soon be on every library table."' My father and I combed through all the inexhaustible pigeon matters of domestic variation, transitional forms, fertility (though we knew all about that), linkage, reversion, bone structure and so forth. We read about everything down to the type of skin between their toes; but about locomotion, we found nothing.

Both my parents loved birds, wild and captive. For the captives my father built a large aviary, which had – of course – a stream running through it, and a fountain and paddling or dipping pool, which gave all the birds, and us, great pleasure. I am certain that these birds were happy, though you will know by now that a theme of these memoirs is the direness of captivity. These birds had been hatched in captivity by Mr Lopis, a famous local dealer. My father used to come home from work sometimes, after a visit to Mr Lopis, with a little brown paper packet, or usually two, since he bought in pairs; the packets were tightly sealed, with holes punched in the sides, and little scrabbling sounds coming from within. I cannot ever have felt such delight, both at the gift and at the knowledge that I, personally, could set them free – into our big aviary, that is. I have sometimes lived in a Buddhist country, and sometimes still do, and try to repeat the thrill whenever I see in markets or at street corners birds in little bamboo cages for sale, to set free and make merit (as the Buddhists say) for the purchaser. As the little birds dart off and upwards in a panic of liberty, I feel a burst of pleasurable sadness. I always hope the birds, rather than I, will get the merit, to give them a better chance next time round.

The aviary my father made had a large orange tree growing in the middle of it; indeed the cage had been built around the tree – as Odysseus had built his bedroom 'round the the long-leaved olive-tree, which had grown to full height with a stem as thick as a pillar'. The resemblance (I thought) did not end there, because what Odysseus did with the olive tree after that was to fashion it into a living bed, for his love-nest with the young Penelope. Our orange tree lacked inlays of gold, silver and ivory, but our birds too used it for roosting at night, pairs or even whole necklaces of them (so tiny were some) huddling together. This had certain consequences for the tree. Whenever I asked Makathini if there was a garden job I might do, he would hopefully suggest the cleaning of the leaves of 'the birds' orange'. The *umfaans* were often landed with this task too, but it was fairly considered down to me, because for quite a while, before her own place was built, the orange tree was the domain of my Abigail.

She was a fat and usually green chameleon, large, about eight inches from her nose to the end of her wonderful, tapering tail; but she could not be measured in that way because, except when she was stalking, the end of her tail was curled around, like those fireworks called 'Catherine wheels'; more exactly, like the whorls which were the beginnings of Lottie's crocheted caps. Cleverer than chickens, Abigail could look at you with one bulging eye while swivelling the other to check any approaches from behind. Both eyes rotated nearly all the time, as the lamps of lighthouses do, scouring her little horizons for flies or bugs. If you were communing with Abigail on the lawn or on a table, trying to tempt her with captured insects, she often seemed awkward or primitive; moved much more slowly than even the tortoises, her Y-shaped feet scrabbling uselessly on a flat surface; her whole semblance like a minute dinosaur, out of time, out of space.

But on the orange tree, or in her later enclosure which she did not have to share with alien avians, Abigail, especially when hunting, was a miracle of precision engineering. Approaching her prey, each Y-shaped foot clasping a twig would stealthily be detached from it and then moved slowly forward, one at a time, millimetres at a time. Sometimes with one or even two feet free (one at the back and one at the front), she would gently rock to and fro, rather like javelin throwers before they run up to the line. Was she testing her balance; or pretending to the prey that her whole body was a swaying leaf; or steadying her nerve, or her muscles; or adjusting herself to slight changes in the attitude of the prey? All those things, I suppose. 'She is arranging her purchase,' I liked to explain to watchers or passers-by, remembering Lottie at the copper with the cricket bat. Abigail's movements were so slow that watchers rather soon turned into passers-by.

The attack itself was over in a moment. I knew the mechanism of it, from a book, but I could never clearly see the immensely long tongue (how do they stow it all? – folded up like a fire hydrant?) whipping out, trapping and returning to base. It was like a whiplash; the whole show, apart from the purchase arrangements, over in a blink – a great disappointment, because even to be present at the critical moment one had had to wait there, still and silent, for a long time.

Chameleons should not be kept as pets; their requirements are too particular and their temperaments too exacting for children, at any rate, to cope with. I took a lot of trouble with Abigail and she gave no evidence of being unhappy; but then, she gave no evidence of happiness either, or ever altered her behaviour in any way in response to mine. How unlike the instant responses she made to the vegetable world in which she lived, changing colour and tone and pattern according to the exact mini-milieu into which she moved. I found her dead one day, still fat, her complexion still beautifully verdant. My father kindly said it was sudden old age. After a decent interval her leafy cage was used for dozens, later hundreds, of stick insects which John brought home from boarding school. I often thought how wonderful it would have been, if the day were considered long enough, to watch an engagement between a stick insect simulating a twig and Abigail simulating a leaf.

But the canaries which my mother kept in cages next to her bedroom, in a 'sleeping porch' of the house, which we used only in hot weather, did not seem to me to be happy. They sang very prettily, which gave my mother great pleasure, but they fought too – love affairs I supposed – and were often foul to their hatchlings, attacking them, or turning them out of the nesting boxes to die. My mother took endless pains with these ugly, pathetic little rejects, though I could hardly bear to look at their tiny, featherless, yellow bodies and closed, swollen, purple eyes. First she wrapped them in surgical cotton wool, then she dripped brandy down their beaks, then she put them in the top of the kitchen range where plates were heated, and an hour or two later she removed the little corpses and sadly put them through the front doors of the stove, for decent cremation among the coals.

But none of the many birds we kept could possibly have qualified as companions; they could not even have come as close to it as poor Abigail. We did not play with the birds. It would be gruesome to think that John and his friends were playing with them when they shot them. And I did not, exactly, love the pigeons; I admired them and I loved to be with my father, feeding them. I spent very many hours looking at birds. I still do – looking at and spying on and tending them. This year the steadiness of my 'fancy' was rewarded when a pair of wild, mute swans from the Thames, a couple I have known and fed for several years, chose to build their huge nest in my garden, which borders on the Oxford Canal. I felt very chosen and honoured, willingly put up with their depredations of stems and leaves, even the flowers of my best rhododendron which the male artistically scattered about when the work was done. We raised, the birds and I, five beautiful cygnets.

But the dogs, the dogs! I cannot think of my childhood, cannot recall even a vague impression of the wonderful years at Mornington, not the roughest sketch or ground-plan of it, without a sense of the loving and companionable, attentive busyness of Puppy and her puppies. Even more surely than this, I cannot think of my life as a whole, all the decades and the whole me of it, without the root nourishment so freely passed to me by the forbearance, warmth, care and patience of those whom we called our servants.

This chapter may appear, in the climate of the newly enfranchised South Africa, patronising and altogether unacceptable to all black people and to those of the whites whose opinion I respect. There is not much I can do, though, except tell the truth as I feel it and have lived it. All this talk about servants ... well: until the day after I left school I joined (tried to join; in the event just went to meetings) the Communist Party of South Africa, I had never spoken to a black person who was not a manual worker or a servant or, like the tired men trudging our suburban roads, hoping very fervently to become one. That is what history did to the land, and to me. If I write with love and praise about the servants that I knew, it is certainly not because I consider that they 'made good servants'.

History is a given thing; its complexities are not so mighty as those of Evolution, yet no one person can find a way out of it. To make the best of it we need on the one hand good intent and on the other forbearance and, if we are big enough, forgivingness; and neither will come easily unless we can learn something about how the thorny problems of history germinated, and in what soil.

—⌒—

I loved my home, and home garden, that my parents had made out
of the bare veld, and so far as the pleasures and amenities went, it
was very much as I expect to find Paradise. But it was haunted by
the existence of another home or, rather, Home, which my parents,
especially my mother and some of her friends, used to talk about.
Whenever I heard 'Home' with a capital *h*, there would be a small
flare-up of objection in my mind, a brief danger signal, like a flick-
er on the dashboard meaning 'no oil'.

My parents were English, conscious of it, proud of it. My father
always played down a certain Welshness, though his oldest friends
called him 'Taffy'. I didn't like that, because

> Taffy was a Welshman, Taffy was a thief,
> Taffy came to my house and stole a leg of beef.
> I went to Taffy's house, Taffy wasn't there,
> So I took him by the left leg and threw him down the stair.

That was very funny, of course; one became hilarious, time after
time; but – disloyal. My mother didn't like the 'Taffy' either, since it
was not dignified, so it gradually dropped out of use.

'Home' referred, of course, to England. In those days we did not
use the word 'Britain' – though I know a Scottish family who did –
or 'British' of a person; only of British-made imported goods, or of

the British Empire, where I am sure it was thought that the adjective gave an even greater glory to the noun. Nor did I hear 'United Kingdom', let alone the degenerate 'UK'. 'Home', capital *h*, meant England and any adult who chose to say 'England' rather than seize the opportunity of saying 'Home' was thereby shown up, at least in my mother's eyes, as a mere South African or some other sort of foreigner.

She went on a visit Home every two years or so, to visit her extensive family in London. When I was very young I was taken with her, though never my brother. The glorious days at sea afforded by the Union-Castle Line almost erased my grief at leaving my father and Lottie and Puppy; and when they were over, there were the glorious days of the return journey to look forward to. I think the voyages were so delightful to me for three reasons: first of all, and strangely enough, freedom. There was no 'outside' that I pined to get to. There were, for children, secure and clear boundaries but we did not aspire to cross them, not even I. They were on a par with the deck railings which prevented immediate access to the ocean, closed doors to the bar and the smoking and billiard rooms, staircases to the forecastle and crew's quarters and, most rigorously forbidden, to the Second Class. To feel secure as well as free is a rather rare form of happiness and my little friends – there were always several near enough to my age – indulged it to the full. And our freedom was very busy, and could not easily be supervised by an anxious parent.

The Deck Quartermaster always introduced us to the many deck games and helped us, if we needed it. I remember with great affection one whom we called 'Old Bill', who sent me postcards for several years afterwards. He showed us how he plaited oily ropes into little rings suitable for competitive throwing into little buckets or for use as 'tenniquoits'; he taught us all kinds of sailors' knots; and he tried to teach us his sailor's knitting or macramé work. We teased him about that, thinking it a feminine pastime, being so ignorant or uncaring about the lonely male lives of sailors.

Two of the greatest possible excitements of a voyage, in those days, were 'the crossing of the line', when selected sailors and sometimes passengers were given a ceremonial 'shave' by a sailor dressed up as Neptune. The novice, supposed to be someone who had not crossed the equator before, was amid much pantomime covered in foam and then ducked into a canvas swimming pool erected on the deck. And then the arrival at Madeira, or sometimes Tenerife, the coming on board of the merchants selling the fine embroidered linens made by their wives and by nuns and novices in the convents. The deck was transformed into a magical *souk*. My mother loved it as much as I and bought a copious supply of all kinds and sets of heavily embroidered cloths, to give to her family and also to take back to Johannesburg, where they added to Lottie's problems in the ironing room.

There were many other pleasures. As the voyage progressed the climate changed so that suddenly one day all the crew appeared in whites, white everything, even shoes; to us children this was also a sign that we were approaching the equator and – just as important as the imminence of Neptune and all that – the appearance at eleven o'clocks, instead of beef tea in blue cups (though that was delicious enough), of icecream in little silver (we thought) goblets, pink or white or stripy icecream, sometimes even second helpings.

Apart from the freedom and the games and icecream and all other things to do with the voyage, I did not as a rule much enjoy the visits Home. There was my grandfather, a dear man for years overwhelmed by his wife and clamant family of daughters, and my cousin Beryl, my age. The three of us clung together and escaped when we could from all the relatives, often just going round the corner into Finsbury Park.

And yet an even stronger reason for disliking Home emerged if I was not taken there with my mother, for then I would be sent to stay with Madame L. in a tiny house in a new suburb of Johannesburg, with a high wall around it, almost no garden, only one dog, fierce and mouldy, and two or three other unhappy little girls. We were all so insecure and miserable that we were often as spiteful to each other as only little girls can be, unforgiving and aggressive. I suppose that, like me, the other girls were children of first-generation immigrants, so that there was no kin in South Africa to mind them or take them in if the parents had to go away for a while. Madame L. was herself an immigrant, from Belgium; perhaps she too felt the need of a family.

Yet my father did not go away, to England or anywhere else. It must have been considered that it would be in some way improper, or careless, for my mother simply to have left me at home in Mornington with my father and my beloved Lottie. He would have to be at work all day of course, so could not 'keep an eye on things'. What things? He came to fetch me at the weekends, but they were poisoned by the thought of the approaching Monday. I used not to understand why these awful periods of detention were inflicted on me. But of course, I do now: my mother's great fear of – the dark. 'Fear of the dark' is what I learned, long ago, to call my mother's lifetime inability to trust or love anyone whose skin was dark.

On one occasion I had been delivered to Madame's and had put myself straight to bed, though it was before supper. I remember the terrible pain of that time, the thought of all the days and nights that lay ahead, the longing for Mornington and for parents, and my brother, and Lottie. I could not even cry. Madame noted my dumb despair when she came to my bedside to see whether I was ill. She said, in a kindly way – or I thought she said – 'Do you want to go Home?' 'Oh no, oh no, not Home. I want to go home!' I assume that she telephoned my father to report my confusion, for he came and took me home again and left me in Lottie's care for that week.

In later years Home was not such a threat to me, but I grew to dislike the attitudes that it spoke of. I seemed never to understand or even to see the pathos or nostalgia of it. The voice is always my mother's:

'At Home you would never get rudeness like that from shop-girls.'

'At Home, of course, servants can be trusted.'

'At Home you can get to the seaside in a few hours.' (Even this was a feather in the cap of Home!)

'Be sure you send me Home-made jam. What? No, of course not your own.'

'I would like John to go to boarding school at Home.'

'When Leslie retires, I expect we shall go Home.'

But in my very young days, because of all that sort of talk, I suppose, it is possible that I had a tendency to confuse Home with Heaven; because for a while God appeared to my infant imagination in a very strange guise, that of King George V. This semblance was at any rate much more reasonable than the picture I had seen somewhere of God as a white pigeon sending forth rays. Our white pigeons, in spite of their glory, were noisy and greedy and sent forth no rays. I found a suitable picture once, of an old man with a long white beard, but was disappointed to be told it was Moses, not God himself.

There was a strongly implied, but unseen, God who dwelt behind the little silk curtains on the main altar of the Convent, the infants' school of which I briefly attended until my father won his battle for my real school to get me a Latin teacher, not usually thought necessary in the infants' classes. (The Convent taught me some Latin prayers which my father, though Quakerish, must have thought better than nothing.) But – if God was behind those dolly curtains ... I had hoped he woud be bigger than that.

King George was much more like it. We had his picture on a biscuit tin, very dignified, next to Queen Mary choking with high-neck diamonds. Then, one amazing day, I heard his voice! We had acquired a big and proper 'wireless', a most mysterious object to which were attached numerous wires. It was about three feet high and in addition to dials and knobs its wooden front was adorned – architected, you could say – by a series of interlocking, pointed Gothic arches. The arches were filled by a shiny, brown-gold cloth stretched across them – not as shiny as the little chapel curtains, but tending that way; a tincture of holiness.

This wireless, the first time I saw it, had been placed on the

dining-room table and everyone, including the servants, was summoned to hear the King's first broadcast to the Empire. To my
father's distress, reception was so poor, so cacophonous – a series
of wild howls and croaks, surging and receding – that I, at any
rate, heard only one word, 'abundance'. A good, substantial word,
but who knew what it meant? It could have been the voice, and the
vocabulary, of God? This supposition was soon corrected and
Home disentangled from Heaven. I think it had meant almost nothing to the servants either. I discussed it with Makathini and Moses
shortly afterwards, as we were squatting around digging out weeds
from the top lawn (they had old, broken kitchen knives but I was
permitted nothing so dangerous, only an old teaspoon). They
thought it hadn't even been the real king. The real king, they
assured me, was King Solomon Dinuzulu, in whose name – as they
had taught John and me to do – all solemn oaths were taken. I
didn't know that Dinuzulu had died in exile, a defeated king and a
broken man, ten years before my birth. The Chief knew, of course
– and every Zulu in the land.

I once caused great amusement to my father, and annoyance to
my mother, just after returning from one of the visits to Home on
which she had taken me. The two of us had gone there for
Christmas that year. I had greatly enjoyed 'the boat'; there had even
been an extraordinary episode of flying fish, flapping around the
deck and the awnings! I had high tea out on that many a time. In
London my grandparents and aunts and cousins had showered
attention and Christmas presents upon me. Because I can remember
some of the presents, I can tell how young I must have been – a
wind-up rabbit whose ears cocked up and down? A small girl-teddy
with a flowery bonnet? I was five, or six, or seven.

At bedtime on the very day of our return, my father asked me
what I had enjoyed most about the visit Home. I knew that he
wished me to describe the lovely Christmas and all that. I delayed
for a while, and then told him that the best thing was when our
train up from Cape Town had stopped, during the previous night,
at a siding, so that our sleeping compartment was right alongside

an open wagon of tightly packed sheep. I could hear them *baa*-ing
right in my ear, as I lay on my bunk, and when I raised the blind
and looked through the window I could see silver moonlight on
their crisp and woolly backs. So much for H.

12 Lottie at the gate

The servants' letters from Taylor's Halt, and their replies, and the
people I watched in the road from the roof of the carriage house –
these, among other signs, all told me something about the world
outside, but all the news seemed bad and frightening. One fearful
and recurrent message, which only came at night, was glimpsed
only by peering under my drawn curtains. This was the 'donkey
cart'.

My bedroom was in the front of the house, its windows about
midway round the crescent of the drive, so that anything stationed
there, even in the unlighted dark, was plainly to be seen. 'The donkey cart', which was in fact drawn by mules, but mules are not in
the nursery pantheon so I misnamed or misidentified them, was a
long, low-slung tubular wagon, a tank in effect, drawn by five or
six span of animals, and there were rows of quite attractive red
lights, hanging storm lanterns, swinging along its sides. Neither the
cart nor the animals made much sound, and the men who came
with it made none at all. So it came to my view only by chance,
interrupting sleep, and I did not know, nor know now, how often it
came. Some of the men used to disappear in the direction of the
backyard and return each carrying a large bucket.

It was, of course, the sanitary cart. It must have come very late
at night, so as not to embarrass grown-ups returning from wherever it was that they went. Before I understood its purpose, I was

anxious to see it again, and to discuss it, but nobody would talk about it, not even Lottie – especially not Lottie. Sometimes when I asked Lottie awkward questions she would laugh and tease me with ridiculous answers before referring me to someone else; but questions about the donkey cart were received in gloomy and sulky silence, not unlike 'wuthering' behaviour, with, at most, 'I don't know'. I slowly began to understand that the entire city and its suburbs was served by black men in this way; and that to them it was a source of very great shame. Not only shame, but anger. I did not know, until my political education, that the 'bucket boys' were a significant element in the black labour force of a city which, founded solely for its proximity to the gold-bearing rock, had no natural channel for its effluent; and I did not know that following a successful strike by white power workers, the 'bucket boys' went on strike, also for higher wages, but, being black, were put down and penalised with great severity. That was not long before my birth.

Another terrible message: my father, as I have said, was a consultant mining engineer. From time to time in Johannesburg, we would experience earth tremors, and they used to electrify my father. Wherever he was, sitting on the *stoep*, talking to the gardeners, playing with me on the little putting green, in his workshop or anywhere else, he used to break off, hold up his hand for silence, the better to gauge, by sound, the severity of the rock fall in the mineshaft. Sometimes he would say something under his breath and without any explanation hurry into the house to telephone.

Then, there were the visitors at the front gate. I have described the arrangement at the back or bottom gate, the carriage gate leading to the men's compound. Out of sight or earshot of the house, it was possible and perhaps even allowed for men (only) to visit there. I never found out the rules because I could not, by questioning, reveal that I was a spy. But the front gates, at the top of the site, one at each terminal of the crescent drive, were quite a different matter. The gates were always shut – though in contrast to what largely obtains today in all white or wealthier South African suburbs, not locked or barbed or electrified or computerised. All the same, no black men or women could enter through those gates without permission, and I can't remember any permissions except to the regular 'delivery boys'. Our dogs, unlike those of some of our neighbours, were not encouraged, let alone trained, to bark at strangers, yet one was often alerted to a stranger waiting at the gate by unrest among the dogs, or experimental yelps from one of the pups. If I were near the gate the man (always a man or boy) would shout out, and the message was always the same: '*Nkosazana, ndicela umsebenzi* – I am looking for work.' (There seems no acceptable or even accurate translation of *Nkosazana*. Lottie always told me it meant 'Princess'; ordinary words like 'miss' are not respectful enough.) There were very, very many of these callers throughout my time in Mornington. They almost always came singly to the gate, though sometimes you would see them paired up on the road. They were of all ages, raggedly dressed, and they never wore shoes; nor, when the little *umfaans* came to us from the coun-try to be 'apprenticed' to their fathers, did they possess shoes – nor, for some time, could tolerate them. Their fathers used to make them sandals, at first, out of old motor tyres, and so slowly break in their feet (like everything else) to captivity.

If we were near the gate when the men came to ask for work, we – John and I – would simply say, '*Uxolo, asinawo umsebenzi* – Sorry, we have no work', for we didn't get our servants this way. But quite often we asked them to wait, and we would send one of the servants out to talk to them; or at the gate the callers would ask for water, which came to the same thing, because the servant who came out with the water would always be ready to talk. I used to go and fetch Lottie, as a rule. I thought she gave them a better time: she was more generous with her offerings of food and drink than the cooks, Zwela or Albert. She would cut a couple of thick slices of what was known as 'boys' bread', and smear them with 'boys' jam' and sometimes serve out a small bag of 'boys' meal' or mealie porridge and put them, I suppose, onto a 'boys' plate', with some milk, and march up to the gate. She never tried to hide it. It must have been either sanctioned or nodded through by my mother.

Lottie sometimes allowed me to carry a beer bottle full of water or a huge enamel mug of sweet, strong tea; and she always allowed me to hang around for the long conversation which followed.

I did not understand the contents of those talks, but I have never forgotten the form of them, the slow and thorough reciprocities, not properly begun until the stranger's eating and drinking were done, the two of them sitting there on the edge of the dirt road, myself a few paces behind them, hopping up and down the rungs of the five-barred gate, leaning over it, swinging on it, not allowed out of it.

I have never forgotten those particular slow and thorough reciprocities, so integral to the mutual understanding between human beings, but in normal, modern, European converse so attenuated, as though, even if we are not in a hurry, we dreaded the onset of any particularities. I once, as a brisk young classics student, added up the thousands of lines which Homer devotes to lies. I'm not referring to the amazing transformations and all that – I believe, on the whole, in the gods of Greece and their machinations and I know that if there is anything in it for them, they will, like politicians in power (unless defeated by dissenting colleagues), bring about any kind of deception. I refer to the lies which goddesses, in particular – also Odysseus when forced to conceal his identity – actually tell to mortal interlocutors, because people expected in ancient times to go through the same intricate social forms which used to take hold of Lottie and the suppliant visitors at those sessions at the Mornington gate.

The deities have to conceal their identities from mortals when they visit them. The mortals usually know after the conversation that there had been a divine visit, but at the beginning they have to be fooled or they would pass out with reverence and terror; and so the deity has to take part in the long, country reciprocities, and invent a most elaborate disguise and pseudonymous identity, purporting to explain most minutely who they are, where they have come from, what they are doing. Not to do so, when conversing with a stranger, would excite immediate suspicion and resentment.

Pallas Athene, for example, who always did her best for Odysseus, when she visits his son to galvanise him into something more positive than moaning at what his mother's suitors cost in food and drink, presents herself in a long account, pages and pages, as 'Mentes, chieftain of the sea-faring Taphians'. (After she has done the galvanising, however, she doesn't bother to spend any time on withdrawal. She turns into a little bird and pops off through a hole in the roof.)

Country people everywhere give, and expect, care over introductions. The gods and heroes of Greece may have had on occasion to invent their histories and personae according to immediate needs, but in most real places where strangers come from far away the pattern is exactly as Homer perceived it to be: a sizing-up, an attempt to place, a mutual appraisal, a soliciting of interest and belief, perhaps of help. Lottie and the stranger would network at great length. It did not seem to be one-sided but a real and leisurely exchange, though in the nature of the encounter it was he who was seeking help and advice; and between them there was almost always an air of reflective sadness.

In my later life, as a teacher-trainer for radio education, I have often had to encourage African men and women to record interviews, in villages or in the bush, with peasant farmers or their wives, who would be hoeing, or pounding meal, or harvesting or even doing nothing but sitting on the ground. And you can forget all your own training about how it's done in Europe, with smart, sharp questions expecting factual replies or sly evasions, forget the advice to make, yourself, no exclamations of surprise or sympathy or long laughter or throat noises-of-encouragement, all of which might interrupt the replies. For in Africa these are the expected signs of attention and sympathy. Also, in rural Africa you sit right there on the ground with them, no awkward standing around. An interview that in terms of rural African society is worth anything, and especially if it is to be used in a programme aiming to show the heart of a matter, must warm and reassure the interrogated heart, treasure and encourage all that it may unfold.

I have all through my life thought of Lottie so often, not least Lottie on the roadside behaving like a goddess, but with more compassion, more dignity; and certainly telling no lies.

13 Comities and amities

It has perhaps been an exaggeration to present myself as a captive in my home, though I often felt like that at the time. But I went to school, of course, a marvellous school, Queensfield, where all my schooldays I was very happy. Queensfield, however, was just over the road (in the course of time it covered all the roads round our house) so that often, if pressed for time, I got to school through one of Puppy's holes. The fact that I had to make no journey to or from school probably accounts for the delay of my entry into the big world. But I used to go on the bus with my mother to the dentist, and dreadfully often to the dressmaker, and sometimes to the houses of her friends who had children; and sometimes Lottie took me to other houses to play with my special friends. There were the several long voyages Home, with my mother; and once a year, as I have said, my father took us in his motor car to the seaside – Durban or Cape Town – where we stayed in hotels which we thought were amazingly posh. They look very humble today, squatting modestly between the towering apartment blocks which line the sweeping curves of the modern sea front.

My first experience of a real somewhere else, outside, came about when Lottie was 'lent' to my brother's preparatory school in Johannesburg. She took charge of the black women staff there during some crisis, while a new – white – matron or housekeeper was looked for. The headmaster and his wife, Mr and Mrs Hadland,

were close friends of my parents, and Mrs Hadland was one of the
few adults whom I felt to be a friend to me. She was a masterful
sort of person, though kind and quite jokey in her manner, and she
always, when visiting my parents, came to find me and have a talk,
knowing that at the first sign of visitors I used to rush off to the
safety of the ironing room or to hide 'under the bridge', in the big
culverts that took the stormwater under the roads into our big
ditches. Sometimes Mrs Hadland brought me things for my museum. I remember a deformed double tomato which gave immense
pleasure, before it rotted, because it resembled a bright red human
bottom; and a sort of glass phial in which there were layers of differently coloured sand, or ash, from Vesuvius. When Mrs Hadland
realised the heartbreak which the lending-out of Lottie was causing
to me, she had a long conference with my parents, and then with
Lottie, and it was decided that I could go and stay with Lottie at
the school!

A little bungalow, the school sanatorium, at the far end of the
grounds, beyond the playing fields, well out of sight of the pupils
but near the servants' quarters, was thought to be a suitable temporary home for Lottie and me. It was understood that it was to be a
rather secret arrangement, and that if any little boy came down
with an infectious disease, or needed any nursing care, I would
have to return home. Lottie slept in the bed next to mine. This was
in itself a great treat, for both of us: at home, if my parents went
out at night, Lottie used to come and sleep in my room, but not in
the spare bed; she brought her own bedclothes and had to sleep on
the floor. She did not complain but I can remember myself crying
and fussing about it. And at the Sannie we had our meals together
in the kitchen, and Lottie cooked only the things I would eat without persuasion, and our reading was done either lying down on our
beds or grandly in a tiny sitting room. The whole thing was a
wonder. For the first and only time, Lottie and I were together as
mother and daughter.

In the daytime when Lottie was busy I would sometimes go to
read in the school library; or when the boys were playing another

school at cricket I was allowed to join the throng at the edge of the pitch, among the rest of the boys who shouted out at every opportunity 'Come on, the School!' – though I was too shy to do more than whisper it. I rather liked, too, to watch them doing PE on the cricket pitch, especially a weird exercise called, I think, *rectus abdomini*; for the effort needed to constrict the muscles of the abdomen often caused the trousers to fall down of the hipless, hapless little boys. When Lottie was busy I liked, most of all, to go and be with Mrs Hadland in her house.

The Hadlands were Oxford people, which was even grander than just coming from Home. Mrs Hadland was a grand woman in all respects – very tall and broad with a kind, large face and an authoritative, rather masculine but, I thought, very mellifluous and 'English' voice. She had lovely, pure white hair with a yellow streak in it from chain-smoking in a long holder drooping out of her mouth, since her hands were always busy mending little boys' socks or knitting or typing. It was she who introduced me to Homer, first telling me some of the stories and, seeing my interest, she then gave me her own copies: they were the *Iliad* in the translation of Lang, Leaf and Myers and the *Odyssey* in that by T.E. Lawrence, whom she said she had slightly known in Oxford. Imagine, I wondered to myself, imagine (for I had never heard of Lawrence of Arabia or *The Seven Pillars*), imagine knowing someone who understood the real language that Homer spoke!

It was a bad day for Lottie when these books were given to me and I brought them, in pride and delight, to the Sannie. Lottie could not take to Homer even during our sitting- or lying-down sessions, our lovely reads, and especially not when I followed her round the house or the yard reading out bits for her especial attention. She thought the *Iliad* a totally boring work, obscure and dull, even though I tried to leave out all the lies, and battle scenes, and genealogies; and she pointed out, a final damnation, that it did not even seem to be Christian ... She would not allow me after that, at the Sannie, even to open the *Iliad* in our reading sessions, laughing at the very mention of it. There was no 'wuthering' behaviour in the Sannie. I think that she felt (and indeed was) the mistress of that little house, and so I was her child *only*, and not, as at home, her mistress as well as her child. So instead of wuthering we had protests and laughter and mock threats. I gave up with Lottie and the *Iliad*, of course, though in later months I inveigled her into the *Odyssey*; but Mrs Hadland's gift changed the course of *my* life.

For me the Sannie was a life adventure, not just a holiday. I was very happy there. If any small boy from the school was brought by the staff to the Sannie, I'm sure I looked upon him with such focused anxiety, even hatred, that his germs must have been destroyed and all wounds cauterised, as with a laser; so that nothing occurred to alter the arrangement that, until a white housekeeper had been appointed, Lottie and I should remain together, so closely, in such amity.

✦

'Mind you don't suck the railings!' Whenever Lottie and I set off for the Zoo, this bizarre piece of advice was issued by my mother, in the attentively automatic way that she would also put a handkerchief into my pocket or adjust the ribbon in my hair. In those days the Johannesburg Zoo was one of the very few public places, in fact I can think of no other, where blacks and whites were allowed to be together on an equal footing. There were separate 'conveniences', but for the main actions – even the elephant rides, even the swings – there was mingling. Commercial considerations, I suppose. So what was in my mother's mind about the railings? It was the uneasy thought that I would be climbing onto, or looking through or otherwise getting intimate with, railings which were being used by black children, or adults, in the same way. 'Mind you don't suck the railings!' is something I still say, an arcane family joke, to my own grown-up children as I see them off to foreign parts.

The Zoo was always an enormous treat, for Lottie as well as for me. It had been quite difficult to arrange, at first; or we thought it was going to be, since the Zoo was the other side of town, my mother did not drive in those days, and public transport was segregated. The solution was found by my father. Sometimes it was permitted for the conductors of 'white' buses and trams to allow blacks to occupy the two rear seats upstairs. Knowing they had discretionary powers, therefore, my father gave Lottie some cards to show to conductors, with his name and address and a polite request 'to whom it may concern' (as on the men's Passes) to allow 'nurse-girl Lottie' to accompany his daughter on the public transport. He had such firm, regular and authoritative handwriting that I had complete confidence in these cards. Rightly so. There was never any trouble. I was always allowed to sit in the tram next to Lottie at the back, upstairs, though I am sure my parents supposed that by the force of my father's card we would be allowed into the 'whites only/alleen vir blankes' seats in the front.

The trams in those days were very high and narrow, shaped in general like a box of dates, rounded at the ends. Since they ran on rails they were not able to turn around, only to reverse; so for the return journeys the backs of the seats, which were made of wooden slats fixed to iron frames and hinges, could be flapped over, at each terminus to enable the passengers for the return journey to face the direction of travel. At the termini the conductors did this at great speed, passing down the aisle and stroking the seat backs so that they would all go in sequence '*skwee*-CLAP! *skwee*-CLAP!' After the first rather nervous trip to the Zoo, we gained confidence and would ourselves flap over (gently and secretly, no *skwee*-CLAP) the seat in front of Lottie's, so that we had our own little compartment to ourselves; we could face each other, or put our feet up, or use it as a parcel rack. It was an enormous privacy and somehow a sock in the eye for – whoever it was. It was an important part of the thrill of going to the Zoo.

The Zoo itself was exciting for me, because it was outside my garden and therefore in the real world. It was also (I thought then!) a visit to the real animal kingdom, or as near as I was going to get. Since those days I have taken my family to visit many of the great game reserves of East Africa and I know how pathetically limited

was my childish view. All the same, I felt then, very strongly, that
the Zoo put me into touch with the great families behind the animals we kept at home. I liked, and like, to watch any kind of small
animal, if they are happy; and as for big animals, just to gaze at
them, hear them, smell them, be near to them. I have the feeling,
which I could not at that time have expressed, that at such
moments one is at the interface of all the species. Somewhere, in
spite of immense physical differences, one is very close to, in communion with, an animal who for all the millions of years of life on
earth, of its evolution and of mine, was born during my minuscule
lifetime, is with me now, has many gifts and abilities far exceeding
mine, is hearing and smelling me and accepts me as a presence at
the same time as it asserts its own presence. There is a certainly a
comity between us.

I have felt it with Leviathan himself. A few years ago I went on
a small two-masted schooner from Vancouver Island down the
Californian coast, accompanying the annual migration of the
Pacific Grey Whale from the Arctic to its breeding grounds in the
Gulf of California. It is something that only a sailing vessel can do,
for the sound and vibration of an engine would drive away the
animals, interrupt their singing, each to each. I would like to know
what the whales thought we were doing. They seemed not to pay
us any attention, but of course they were all the time, just by avoiding collision with us. The sea was turbulent with their activities,
heaving and boiling with their numbers, but there were no nosings
or bumpings; and not any games with us as I have seen dolphins in
the Aegean sportingly pretend to be guiding our ship by crisscross-
ing before the prow in a daredevil manner. (Perhaps they just hitch
a lift on the bow wave, as geese do following their leader when
they fly in strict V-formation.) The Grey Whales rose mightily from
the sea from time to time and crashed down, splashing us a little if
there was a cross wind.

I had intended to film them, as I have filmed the Southern Right
Whale from headlands at the Cape; but on the deck of a small ship,
in a wind, you have to hold onto the rigging and then the vibration

of the ropes thrums through your body, turning any kind of photograph into a hopeless blur. I have no idea how real photographers, or real sailors, do it. So I gave it up and just watched the whales, was with them, hour after hour, encircled by the hundreds of them, their dark backs arching as they leaped; admiring the slow, marvellous, huge and precise going-down of their great, fluked tails.

There were many other things to watch, for most of that coastline is a marine biological reserve. Between our ship and the bruise of pollution along the California skyline there was not only the endless wheeling and dealing of the gulls but also promontories of yelping seals, flotillas of brown pelican, strings of fishing cormorants and sometimes, if you watched closely, you could make out little bobbing families of sea otter. They float on their backs a great deal and use their bellies as tables on which to sort out the findings for their picnics; and sometimes, on their chests, bash open shellfish using stones as hammers! All the time, between these delights, there was the efficient and to me mysterious activity of the four or five young men and women who were sailing the ship; but the overwhelming need was to be with the whales. The whales accepted us as part of their enterprise. I felt very deeply the comity between us all, a bond which makes of no account the endless passage of the ages and the tropes of evolution.

In his answer to Job, God tries to terrify and humble him by speaking (shouting out, in my squeaky young voice in Lottie's room) about the wondrous, mighty animals that he, God, made and Job had had nothing to do with – was not even there at the time, when the morning stars were singing together. Hast thou given the horse his might? 'Hast thou clothed his neck with strength, he who swalloweth the ground with fierceness and rage and saith among the trumpets Ha, ha ...' Let alone Behemoth the crocodile, who moveth his tail like a cedar and drinketh up Jordan; or Leviathan who maketh the deep to boil like a pot, treateth the sea like a pot of ointment ... Quite, quite contrary to the assertion of that God, I felt a miraculous closeness to very large beasts, and I feel it even more keenly now, many decades later, when I have learned that we can and do, all the time, perform the very things which God told Job were impossible – 'draw out Leviathan with an hook, fill his skin with barbed irons, open the doors of his face and fill his head with spears ...' Amity is what we may feel for other humans, if it turns out, after circumspection, to be possible. Comity we can feel with animals as we may feel it, all our lives, with our cherished dead: a being together across fixed and immeasurable distance.

This experience is not as simple, nor I as simple-minded, as may from my account appear. It was important, after all, that I was having my comity with the whales from the stance of a sailor, or sailer, one with their own mode of treading the ocean. I would not say 'from the safety of a ship' – that is a different point, though valid. We on the ship were not competing with the whales and not even disporting, which are the two modes in which humans, as a rule, consort. We were certainly together, but each on our own paths, own ways. I have disported with a dolphin, in the sea, off Cape Verde, the very westernmost cape of Africa, in Senegal, where I had been interviewing Léopold Sédar Senghor. I don't know which encounter was the more frightening, that with the first President of Senegal and Africa's greatest poet or with the lone dolphin which for some reason sought human company around a certain bay. I put myself in the way of being found by him, and how I regretted it! He looked forward to the sort of games he loved to play with the young fishermen of the shore, weaving and jumping around, doing all the dolphin tricks (except the miraculous walking backwards on the water) and doing them with such power – and such screaming. Dolphins do not merely flap fins or wiggle tails to get around. Much lither than sharks, they bend strongly from the waist, propelling themselves up, down or sideways by the might of their muscles. As everyone knows, they can do this even in the air! So I was knocked sideways, most of the time – not by this one's body, which never touched me, as flamenco dancers never touch, but by the power of the water which it moved around. I was not nearly quick and strong enough for that – or any – flamenco disporting; and he surely had no interest in the companionable, calm comity which had been in my mind.

At the Zoo, Lottie sometimes grew a bit restless during my comities, and anxious to pass on to fresh wonders, especially amities; though she was very patient considering that the main part of the outing for her was to join the crowd of other women who gathered on the pleasant green slopes around the Zoo Lake. Some of the nurses used to leave their charges swinging in the playground, or even wandering around the Zoo, while they went to join the throng around the lake; but Lottie would never have done that. She took me along with her.

On Sundays and Thursdays, the gatherings could be very large indeed, for there would be not only nursemaids in their uniforms but a crowd of other women, all kinds of workers and servants, who were having their day off, if they were employed at all. They wore many different types and styles of clothes, they were of all ages, and they spoke in several different languages. These women – there were men there too, but on the whole they kept to a different bank of the lake – had come together from the villages, slums, townships, and 'girls' rooms' of a vast country, driven there by poverty and need and the disruption and dispersal of their homes, societies and nations. They were witnesses, no less than the vast slave populations of Greece and Rome, to the might, arrogance and greed of their masters. But they came to the Zoo Lake as to a festival. At gatherings like this they could try to reconstitute their lives and ways, or make new ones and try to forget the past. Captives' networks are made of the minds and the pasts of other captives. There were few, if any, institutions of the state to make good the damage which the state had caused. The women congregated in different groups, of course, and there was quite a lot of high-spirited calling out from group to group. There were some quiet ones, some very young, sad and lost ones, but by far the most of them, certainly Lottie, had almost non-stop (I thought) excited or emphatic conversations. I didn't know the words, but I saw the modes and the moods, and I, too, enjoyed it. Sometimes they spoke to me, usually in the indefinable ways which are called 'motherese'. I never spoke if not spoken to; just leaned against Lottie or lay on the grass with my head on her lap.

An essential feature of Greek and Roman slavery was that there were no races or even nationalities specifically targeted to be slaves. They were enslaved by the victors after warfare wherever there were wars, or they were bought from traders, and their kinds and conditions were many and various. And many of them, though the lot of most was one of servitude and often misery, were people of more education than their masters and became privileged teachers to the household; and many were manumitted, or even bought their freedom, and so passed easily into the population. These paths were not open to the blacks of the Southern States, and it was not open to the great servile black population of South Africa.

The possibilty of such paths, on any appreciable scale, has had to wait for the miracle of our own times, a much greater social and political revolution than ever shook the pillars of an ancient state. The women whom I watched at the Zoo Lake, and the people who served us at home, were made into captives for all their lives, and their children after them and, so far as they could possibly have foreseen, their children's children, for ever.

From the women at the Zoo Lake I never felt anything but kindness, playfulness and care. I was quite scared, all the same, of some of them: some were very demonstrative, some were very bright and large, some very talkative, and I could understand little of what they were saying. Perhaps you would think it comity rather than amity; yet they were embraced by the love and trust of my amity for Lottie. I felt as though I were surrounded by a flock of large and wonderful birds, and everyone knows that birds have this hidden cleft in the feathers of their breasts, the brood patch, so that their eggs and their hatchlings may be kept near their bare skin and nursed by the warmth of their pumping hearts.

There was never between Lottie and me any conspiracy to deceive my parents, but we must both have known that these gatherings of the women would not have been thought suitable or desirable for either of us, any more than my sitting in the black, back seats of the tram. And the hard-won Zoo outings had to be protected at all costs. I remember very well, because the essence of it was absorbed into our family web of funny stories, a conversation with my mother on these lines:

'Was the tram alright today, darling?'

'Quite OK, thank you.'

'And what did you see at the Zoo?'

'The lions. The poor old polar bear. Parrots and things. Prezzawoofski's horses.'

'*What?*'

'Something like that.'

'What are this person's horses doing in our Zoo?'

'They're not personal horses. They're a special kind. The end of the line, or something.'

'What else did you do?'

'Lottie had an icecream, and I had an Eskimo pie. I was going to choose an iced lolly but Lottie said you can't trust the water. We bought nuts for the monkeys but I ate them all. I went to the toilet and waited outside Lottie's while she went ...'

My mother, as intended, would get bored by the minutiae and ask no further questions. If my father questioned me, after he came home from work, I would certainly have deflected him onto the mystery of Przewalski's horse.

14 The view from below

⌒

John and I, and the *umfaans* and our friends, always ate freely even
if secretly of the fruit in the garden, but one thing which was forbidden beyond all others was the fruit of the granadilla or passion
fruit vine. This plant has the most wonderful flower, exotic beyond
dreams. Lewis Carroll wanted to use it as a persona in the garden
of *Through the Looking Glass*, but on learning that its amazing
arrangement of sepals, petals, stamens and stigma was held to symbolise various aspects of the Passion of Christ, he changed to the
imperious tiger lily.

My parents' objection to the eating of the fruit of granadillas
was not, however, on religious but on dietary grounds. They
believed that its mass of small, black, hard seeds would lodge in the
appendix, leading to grave danger, surgery or death. The embargo
on eating this fruit, imposed as it was not only by my anxious
mother but also by my mighty and reverenced father, had all the
weight of God's interdiction of the fruit of the tree of the knowledge of good and evil. In exactly the same way, as time passed, the
fruit became irresistable. Out of sight of the house we used to eat
dozens of granadillas, searching eagerly through the mass of leaves
for the ripe ones, which, wrinkled and shrivelled, always look like
the dead ones.

One night I was disturbed in my sleep by stomach pains so
severe that the doctor was called, and shortly afterwards I was

wrapped into a blanket and my father carried me in his arms out to the car, and to the hospital. It was, indeed, appendicitis, but the pain, and the fear of my first experience of surgery, were as nothing to the thought that all my cheating over the granadillas would be discovered. My appendix would be found stuffed to bursting with little black seeds. The doctors would tell my parents. I would never be trusted again, for obedience, for not stealing or for not lying. We were told later that pips of any kind had nothing whatever to do with appendicitis but before that release I was in a state of acute moral sensitivity as well as beset by the fear of imminent suffering or death. So I was, I suppose, exceptionally responsive to the endless and boundless firmament of stars which wheeled around my head as I was carried to the car. I had never imagined such immensity of space, such throngs of what I thought were other worlds like ours; such overwhelming and unbelievably vast spaces filled with beauty and brightness and yet, by their huge darkness, oppressive and threatening. My father delayed for a little at my exclamations, then hurried on. In the car, trying to comfort me, he said that he would ask the doctors to put my appendix in a little bottle, for my museum. I was so vehemently against this idea, though normally a very greedy curator, that he must have thought my glimpse of the infinite had unhinged me.

And in an abiding sense, it had. I felt overcome by humiliation and fear, discovering so suddenly, merely by accident, that all that I (or anyone else) could hope to achieve in world, life and time was – nothing. The view from below revealed the pitiful size of the world we knew, and its vulnerability. It did not much alleviate the distress and the fear when I later discovered that there was no human or other 'life' upon the stars that we could see. In a sense it is harder to bear that all we can hope to know and love of our life may be blasted away by some brute event in the universe, gases or rocks or solar winds or planetary wanderings or unimaginable temperatures. Annihilations of nearly all living things have happened before: some say many times before, some say five times before and that we are awaiting the dreadful sixth, which we will bring upon ourselves. The fear of it relates closely to our unwillingness to die at all, *timor mortis*, which drives us into churches of various kinds to listen in reverence to anyone who seems confident about 'salvation', 'afterlife', 'immortality'.

I have not, knowingly (one doesn't go around asking), met anyone else who can remember their first glimpse of the night sky or, therefore, anyone for whom the fear and wonder of it had so many lasting consequences in terms of their beliefs and interests. I don't care! I know I am on safe ground just as the great Lucretius knew that he had a firm and distinguished guarantor of the same experience – whom with simple reverence he calls 'a man of Greece'. Epicurus, Lucretius and I share the experience and the certainty that it is our view from below which may darken all our lives; and what to do about it.

> Humana ante oculos foede cum vita iaceret
> in terris oppressa gravi sub religione ...

'When man's life lay for all to see foully grovelling upon the ground, crushed beneath the weight of superstition which displayed her head from the regions of heaven, lowering over mortals with horrible aspect, a man of Greece was the first who dared to uplift mortal eyes against her ... For fables of the gods could not deter him, nor thunderbolts nor heaven with menacing roar, but all the more they gave courage to his eager soul, so that he desired, first of all men, to burst through the gates of Nature ... He traversed the immeasurable Universe with his intellect and in triumph brought back the knowledge of what can come into being and what can not; of how everything has its own function and its own, deep-set, boundary stone.'

Roughly, perhaps, this is our ultimate reason for keeping gardens, or animals, or both, or keeping near to them. I can't answer for the great (or any) scientist who goes so far as the great Epicurus, to set out to search for knowledge; but it seems to me plain that keeping a garden of almost any size or kind, even a few dwarfed plants in a little dish, is a hedge against unsightly fears of the natural world; our comfort and certainty in face of the dangers revealed by the view from below; a consolation for our own negligibility and transience.

It takes some boldness to generalise about gardens; but I believe that there are only two kinds of them, even if there are many gradations. There are gardens organised on a formal basis, for the display of attractive plants and the cultivation of edible ones; and there are gardens which (usually with infinite contrivance) simulate and pretend to tame wild nature. They cannot be characterised as, respectively, 'town' and 'country' gardens. The monstrous regimentation of Versailles was marshalled in the country, and many thousands of portentous estates after it. As to 'country' gardens in towns, we tend mistakenly to think that they need a lot of space; that they are either very private, like Buckingham Palace, or very public, like Battersea Park, and most people don't relate very keenly to either.

It is much easier to illustrate the urban country garden from Chinese or Japanese examples, such as the small (but still mighty) part that the public is allowed to see of the Emperor's Palace garden in Tokyo, where lakes and hills and vales and groves, all man-made, magnificently symbolise the wild nature that most Japanese never see. But to observe the devotion to 'country' gardens of the modest and even poor Chinese or Japanese town-dweller, you have only to look at almost any odd space that occurs outside the house, or shop, or hotel: there may be a frilly purple cabbage or two in pots, or a shelf of *bonsai*, and there will almost certainly be, somewhere, a miniature garden of rocks, trees and sand, even if it is in a little dish. In the West we tend to regard these gardens as toys of a kind, and we trick them out with little figures, temples and bridges. But in the East, without these playthings, they are part of the long 'country' garden tradition, concerned with ancient verities and Man's place in Nature and the struggle of the soul towards the infinite. They are different only in scale, or in artistry, from the most sacred gardens that I have seen, the great temple gardens of

Kyoto; and some of these are surprisingly small.

Needless to say, I knew nothing of all this as a child. I thought a garden was a garden and that if one were very lucky it would be like our garden. All the same, I felt almost knocked out with wonder and delight when one day my mother (I think she had been to a charity bazaar) brought me home a little 'wild' garden made in a roasting tin which had been painted green. There was a tiny tree, jagged stones for rocks, some 'bushes', and glistening, clean sand had been sprinkled on top of the soil. They were mostly succulent plants, needing hardly any root room and little water. I kept it on the window sill of the *stoep* where it would get only moderate sun; and each day it was the first thing I rushed home from school to see, before the dogs, before Abigail, before any of my feeding duties in pen or pool or cage. There was little one could do in the gardening way with it, cultivation or improvement, but I have never forgotten the wonder of it . I think it is in the memory of it that I have kept succulents all my life, inside the house, in unsuitable climates and conditions as a rule, in pots and pans and little dishes. Perhaps it spoke to me, as it does to people in China and Japan, of the Outside; a glimpse, merely, yet a fearless glimpse, a powerful little symbol of wild nature which by this image of it we could, after all, control, see the whole of, see the beauty of, and so use for our comfort. At a desperate time later in my childhood, when my world had changed almost beyond bearing, I began to make dozens of little wild gardens. It was considered a bizarre symptom, as indeed it was, of approaching breakdown.

Two or three years after the granadilla scare and my first inkling of the unbearable Infinite, I had an experience which, although not frightening, was in a way more confounding, since it was unconnected with any mood or preoccupation of mine. I went one day to play with my dear friend Elizabeth in her garden, in a neighbouring suburb. Lottie took me there on the tram, then left me in the charge of, I suppose, Elizabeth's nurse. But we were not seen as, greatly daring, we wandered out of the back gate. We passed through some dry fields, nervously as there were a few cows in it, animals which I, at any rate, had encountered only in pictures. We ran downhill to get away from them. The grass grew greener and soon we found ourselves released from the world we knew onto the broad, flat stones on the bed of a small river.

It was, perhaps, the most purely joyful moment of my life. Elizabeth felt it too. We could hardly believe that those lovely, smooth, flat stones were 'wild'; they were so much better than the broken crags that had made our 'rockeries'; so were the big round boulders on the banks or clustering in the middle of the stream, some of them with convoluted thorn trees wriggling their way out of clefts within the rocks. And the river rippled so waywardly, rolling over stones or dropping into pools, dashing and fanning out and splitting against fallen boughs and boulders. Even my dear father could not have arranged things so well.

It was, to me, like my first sight of the stars, a cosmic revelation – before I ever heard of the cosmos. But so far from the fear which I had felt upon first sight of the night sky, in this new experience in a wild place of the earth, in the bright sunshine, there was only joy and wonder. And also surprise: it seemed to me the most unheard-of and unthought-of chance that there should be, in a place untouched by mankind, such detailed perfection, and that I should feel such joy in it. And the joy was in *me*, a *person*, not a tadpole or a bug or anything which belonged to and had grown up in that habitat! One would expect a garden to be designed and tended and made beautiful according to the ideas of its maker; but who, or what, made this? And what did they know of me, that they could so deeply please me?

I know better, now, than to ask questions in such a form – or to ask questions at all (as distinct from raising problems or examining one's own mental processes) when it cannot be clear to whom or what they are addressed. But I am still, in wild places or when observing plants or animals wild or tame, often blessed by the bewildered thankfulness which led me, so long ago, to ask those questions, on the banks of the Jukskei River, on the Highveld, north of Johannesburg.

15 Dissolution

‿∽‿

My father died, suddenly and unexpectedly, in his early fifties. I had just turned fourteen. It was during the Christmas holidays and on the day that his death was discovered (for he died alone), meaning well, I suppose, my mother sent me to stay with a schoolfriend some distance outside Johannesburg. My friend and her family, also meaning well, I suppose, did not mention my father during the fortnight or so that I was there. I can remember asking my friend, after a few days, if she knew about my father. She said 'Oh yes' in a hurried and frightened way and plunged the conversation into dogs, or horses, or clothes. By the time I returned home the funeral was over, no more friends were calling at the house, my mother was distraught with business affairs, negotiating to sell the house to the school, acknowledging wreaths and flowers and letters.

Whatever course world and time, chance, likelihood or supposition had marked out for my life was blown to fragments by his death; not fragments even, not so solid: blown into vaporous gases so that the universe was blasted free from whatever before had tethered it to sense and solidity. I feel, after all this time, the terrible pain and pity of it. Whenever there have been other deaths, especially that of my husband, at every blow near to me, and many that are far – disaster and sorrow, cruelty, genocides, wars, famines – the pain and the pity move in predatory circles around my heart. The death of my father was the fundament of all other sorrows; it was the bedrock on which have been laid, over the years, the sediments of all other griefs. Grief, like loneliness, courses down the riverbed of memory, laying down its detritus, in flow after flow stirring up and augmenting its gravels.

For some years after Michael, my husband, died I could barely cope with the pain and the loss. My balance and endurance, I believe, were saved by the love of our four children; and also, since they were still young and dependent, I had to work very hard. For the pain, my closest friend persuaded me, greatly against my will, which was binding me to the stake of Effort or Determination, to go to a psychotherapist. In many of the opening sessions, I was unable to talk to her at all, but could only weep. Slowly, with encouragement and reluctantly increasing faith in the therapist, I began to speak in words and even sentences. After a while – I remember so clearly my own shock as well as hers – she exclaimed, 'You are speaking of your *father*!' She said I should try to complete – after more than thirty years – the mourning for my father, for there could be no healing without it.

I believe (it may have become apparent) almost everything that Lucretius says about the universe; and he, on the whole, was adapting, and in his verse fixing into our civilisation, doctrines which he had in essence inherited from Epicurus, who lived some two hundred years before him; that is to say, about 2300 years before me. I believe, in particular, that thought and feeling form a continuum and that the mind or intelligence (as Lucretius puts it) 'has its abiding place in the middle region of the breast. For in this place throbs terror and fear, hereabouts is melting joy: here, therefore, is the intelligence and the mind.' Any reasonable person, however modern or lately born, will agree that 'around the heart' is at least the archive where emotions are stored. However much they may be stirred up or activated by messages from elsewhere, that is where we feel them, where they seem to come to rest or residence. In some people, the emotions do not come to rest. Heavy or repeated blows of fortune may keep them in a constant state of development. The Greeks called this condition *lupe* and the Romans, who thought it a form of illness, *aegritudo*. Jane Austen refers to it as Sensibility. These days it is often confused with Sensitivity, but it is separate and should remain so.

Sensibility is not at all a desirable condition or quality. The Stoics mocked it. Seneca writes scornfully of one Fidus Cornelius who burst into tears because somebody in the Senate called him *strouthocamelum depilatum*, a plucked ostrich. Neither is it a desirable quality in any close associate, even if one doesn't go so far as to call it an illness. In *Sense and Sensibility*, a tale of two sisters, Jane Austen bestows the Sensibility upon Marianne, the sister who is so unguarded as to fall in love with a confused and deceitful young man whose scrupulous and unceasing devotion to self-interest (as Jane would have put it) inflicted immeasurable pain upon her and in the end, most satisfactorily, upon himself. (Lottie put far more succinctly the scorn we felt for Marianne: 'Yooh!' she said, 'True as God, she is mad!' Exactly what Seneca would have thought.)

By far the greater part of the novel is about the burden which Marianne's unbridled Sensibility, expressed so copiously in grief, illness and despair, inflicted upon her sister Elinor, who is, of course, the one of Sense, but who has nevertheless a difficult and sometimes desperate love affair of her own to cope with, which she has to bear in secret and in silence, tending only to the emotional needs of her sister, until almost the last chapter.

✌

I understand very well why the sorrows of other people may be burdensome, and the motives questioned of those who choose to display, or even to mention, their suffering. But as I have said, it is not essentially, even if primarily, my own life that I write about even though I cannot forsake my eyes, my ears. And I cannot write about my country, even though I will not dwell upon my father's death, without an account of how terrible, after that event, 'outside' became. It is as though, by his death, I emerged from

childhood and saw, for the first time unprotected from it, the pain
and sickness of the whole country.

An early consequence of my mother's decision to sell the house
was that old Puppy, it appeared, had to go. The other dogs were
variously adopted by neighbours; but Puppy, our matriarch, was by
this time old, rather solid and stiff-legged, slightly uncertain of temper if taken by surprise but to me at any rate still her old, sweet
and sporty self, loving and funny and anxious to help. I thought
she would surely move with us into the flat which was projected.
Later it appeared that dogs were not allowed. I thought that one of
the neighbours would surely take her in, with one or other of her
children; she was so *known* to everyone, visited them so often
through her holes, was so (I thought) loved. Friends and neighbours
did take the young dogs; but old Puppy was sent off, out of the
front gate, in a bag, a canvas postman's bag, strings drawn tightly
at the top.

I had heard a commotion coming from the kitchen, Puppy
snarling and screaming! I ran down the passage to get to her, but
she was already in the bag, slung over a man's back, and he was
running out through the yard, down the drive to the gate. The bag
was wriggling, Puppy's stiff old legs crumpled up, poking at it, her
cries choking and muffled, calling for me. She was vanishing into
the unknown and terrible outside. I assume that I was held back,
that my mother assured me – what else could she say? – that Puppy
was going to a 'good new home', in the way she had assured me
that the servants were all being found 'good new jobs'. But she was
able to tell me the addresses of the good new jobs; not that for
Puppy. In any case I knew that no other home could be any good
for Puppy. Many months later I was surprised to find myself hoping that it was indeed death that she had been taken to; but I never
heard the truth about it – or, after that, believed everything I was
told.

We had to make plans about the disposal or dispersal of our
other animals. The chickens gradually diminished in number. I suppose they were killed off and eaten. The pigeons were left alone,

the problem being insoluble. It was thought that the school would wish to preserve the aviary, though we heard later that the headmistress had simply opened the door and driven all the little birds out, to *their* terrible outside. It was assumed that the school would wish to preserve the sunken garden with its fishpond and the tortoises; and so they did, until decades later the need for more buildings and the pressure upon space grew too intense.

I left South Africa for good as soon as I could after my father's death, although I was trapped there for several years by the imminence and then the outbreak of the War. After that, I visited sometimes from my home in England, for broadcasting or teaching work or to see my mother, but in those years up to my mother's death, I never once visited Mornington. I did so only, to be exact, forty-six years after we had sold the garden. I was spending a weekend with one of John's sons. 'Why don't we go and try to see your old garden?' Richard said, and kindly drove me there. It was during the holidays; the watchman at the gate let us in, after hearing our explanation. Buildings were going up everywhere, tennis courts, a huge swimming pool. The sunken garden had just been filled in and levelled off, and the labourers had left a large crane on the site and, hanging from its chained jaws, the very last of the big rocks from my father's rock garden. It had waited for me up to its very last day.

I am afraid that the worst part of the dissolution, apart from my father's death, I have yet to tell; though I have no wish to vie with the tearful Marianne or to choke with *lupe*. It is worse for me to write about than for you to hear.

A little while before my father's death I had been told that Lottie had to go home on a visit to her village in the Eastern Cape. I realised at the time that this was unusual; normally it was only the men who went home at certain times of the year, to help with harvest and planting. So I was surprised as well as dismayed when Lottie went; but she seemed to want to go, and my mother said she would soon be back.

But my father's death and the dissolution intervened, soon after.

No more servants, no more dogs; only nothing, nothing. We stayed on a while in the house, and the new term at school began. At break-time one day, at the school, one of the cleaning maids came up to me and said there was a visitor for me – 'at the gate, *nkosazana*'. She said you would know.'

I rushed to the storm drain so as not to be seen going out of the school gate, crept down it under the road, under the bridge, and came to the gate where I had so often admired Lottie welcoming and instructing the strangers. She was sitting on the pavement, dark dress, dark cap, bowing over a baby which she was breast-feeding. I recall only confusion and distress and a conflict in my mind about which to deal with first – my father's death, or her return and her baby. It was sorted out, with many hugs and tears. She had heard about my father; she wanted me to tell her, to the smallest detail, what I knew, which was not very much. I told her all I could, both of us sobbing. I felt as though I had not been able to shed, or share, any of my shock and grief until that day. She had not gone home to her village, but to Alexandra Township, to Meshak. She had come to see me because of the death, though she also wanted to show me her little new daughter. As we sat on the pavement's edge, she found a way of hugging me with one arm and supporting the child with the other, so that I could watch the little brown face, solemnly sucking, close to mine. For some of the time Lottie was keening as well as crying, swaying from her hips, to and fro. I know now that this is a natural movement of grief.

I learned the truth about her 'going home' – sent away, of course, for pregnancy. 'But that didn't mean she had to sit here, on the pavement, out in the road? Her room was still there, the bed, the chair; there would be food in the kitchen … she could show the baby to my mother …' She would not; she would not come, she would not show, she would not eat, she would not let me go and fetch. She had been sacked. In the end she won this battle, as most others. I forsook school and walked with her to the queue for the Alexandra bus. She unwrapped the baby from her back and let me hold her in my arms as we queued, until the very door. I watched her driven off in a shaky and overcrowded old vehicle, driven off, out of my life, her new child in her arms.

In a strange way I have come to think, after all these years, that my opportunity to spend that little time with Lottie grieving for my father, sharing it with her, set me free to live at least adequately without him, without the reliance upon him which had shaped my life; and I seem to see in these memories of impressions and emotions a correspondence between that meeting and the way in which the setting free of Mandela and all that has followed have enabled me at last to write about my childhood that I had thought was lost. I cannot explain it; but I know that there are many Whitefellows who, whether living abroad or not, have felt themselves set free and in deep ways re-created by the freedom of Mandela – in spite of the rages and resentments which that freedom of itself has in some, both black and white, set free.

I sat on the crowded pavement of the Alexandra bus stop a long time after her bus left. I remember the black legs and dusty feet or worn shoes gathering round me, discussing me, and wondering, I suppose, what to do about me that would not land them in some kind of trouble. I knew from the shifting crowd of legs that there must be quite a large gathering of people. A group of women led by one who spoke English tried to question and to help me. Each time that I tried to explain to them, my sobs made my words unintelligible. In any case, what help or what solution could there possibly be? One of them said the others should go away and she would wait with me; which she did, just quietly sitting down beside me and waving others away, exactly as one would need. When I had calmed myself and when I thought school would be safely over for the day so that I would have no re-entry problem, I thanked this woman so fervently that she was embarrassed; and I went home to tea.

My mother was sitting on the *stoep*, with the flowery china and silver teapot and lace tablecloth. She was worried, distracted, as usual. I told her, with difficulty, about Lottie and the baby; but she could not deal with my problems as well as her own. She must have known, too, that I wanted to hurt her with the news, not only because of the sending away but because I had been deceived about it and now had the truth. She did not let herself seem troubled or hurt at all; if she was; only politely interested. I tried again with what I thought must be a deadlier thrust – 'And she has called her little girl ... Prudence.' My mother briefly laughed, as though this were some kind of joke, or a rather flattering piece of impertinence.

16 Nepenthe

A few weeks after my father died my mother took me to England with her. Again, Home. Again, John was left at his school in Natal, since interfering with a boy's education might damage his career. I do not think the visit comforted her, and it upset me a good deal as I was sent to a nearby London school which turned out to be unsuitable to my needs and unpleasing in every way. It had no garden; and the classrooms were small, cold and smelly – and the same was true, I considered, of my fellow pupils. To try to make up for my acute deficiency in mathematics I had to go to classes two years down from my age, so of course any friendships were out of the question. In our early life even one year is a whole generation.

When we returned to South Africa my mother had to face the dismembering and sale of our home and removal to a flat hopelessly too small for our possessions; and also the impending removal of my brother – to England, where he had been entered, by my father, as an apprentice to a large engineering works in the Midlands, for a year's practical experience before starting a university degree in London. The professional wisdoms about engineering training were a source of great anxiety to her, since she knew nothing whatever about any of it. It had all, naturally, been my father's province. In their plans she had been in charge of questions of winter underwear and fixing up somewhere for him to lodge.

What to do with me was also a problem. There were a lot of

miserable arguments, between three miserable people. In the end, the solutions had to be drastic. The surplus possessions were sold, the flat was let for a year, my mother took John to England and I was entered at Queensfield as a boarder; and for the holidays and for general care was passed into the kindly and reliable hands of old friends of my parents, Mr and Mrs McKenzie. They were appointed as my legal guardians, a precaution which made me feel especially insecure. Why, I wanted to know, was it necessary to involve the law? It infected me with fear rather as those little way-side shrines do, little plaster Virgins in glass boxes placed on poles which distract you at the worst points of the hairpin bends over the mountains of Italy. Was my mother intending not to come back from England? Was she going to stay in England for the five years it would take John to become an engineer? *Was* there going to be a war, which would prevent her return? Or even kill her?

In this period of painful insecurity began a lifelong habit of keeping almost every personal letter. As I re-read those which my mother wrote to me from Cape Town, from the ship, from Southampton, from London, I can see her deep anxiety for my welfare and above all my 'security'. But I didn't feel it then. I thought it was the usual fussing and bossing. I felt only loss and a kind of betrayal. Now, I can see how little reason there was in this feeling; how unfair to my mother; now, indeed, I can see that so far from being an unfeeling person, in her racial attitudes and in her ideas about the feeding and clothing and general 'good behaviour' of children she was entirely a product of her time, doing her best in the unusual and alien and often difficult circumstances of what was, to her, a foreign, inchoate and rather dangerous country. She learned the garden lessons of soil and growth and care quickly and very successfully; the management of my growth, at least of my mind and nature and their needs, she never understood and never achieved.

Sometimes I wonder if the fixed and scarred no man's land between us, which lasted (though often camouflaged as the mere distance between continents) all her long life, was due to the entirety with which my early years had been handed over to Lottie. It is possibly the most important factor in it. I can feel no regret, though, to smear the thankfulness and love I feel for Lottie. The hostility towards my mother may be the price I have to pay for that source of comfort, that lifelong certainty of the love that is possible between black and white even in a context of servitude and selfishness; and Lottie, after all, was one of my mother's arrangements.

It was interesting, at first, getting to know the McKenzies' house and garden, so different from our own. It was an attractive, long and somehow low-lying bungalow, with white-painted walls and a red-tiled roof, and doors and windows painted bright blue – all much more modern and colourful than our modest brick and corrugated iron. I think their house seemed low-lying because the land around it was completely flat, not sloping and terraced as ours was, so that its surrounding trees seemed very much taller. In all these important matters of siting and aspect, relationship to the sun and the surface of the earth and to surrounding growth and nature – the considerations which make the Chinese science of Feng Shui so endlessly interesting – the McKenzies' house was entirely different from my home. Perhaps it was the stimulus of these radical differences which disguised, for a while, the pain and depression which quite soon came almost to destroy me.

It is apparent that my mother was right to entrust me to such a well-set-up, dependable and worthy couple. Also, there was the swimming pool! Something John and I had often begged for at Mornington, but the nearest we got was John's invention of a brick-and-canvas arrangement in which the water barely covered one's feet. The McKenzies had a proper one, built for their son Jamie and his friends, but since he went away it had fallen into serious disuse. My mother had said she would ask if it could be cleaned and filled again, and perhaps some of my schoolfriends would come and disport with me.

So it was a disagreeable surprise for everyone, including myself, that for the first several weeks – months and months, so it seemed to me – in spite of the novel and stimulating Feng Shui, in spite of the 'independence' and the swimming pool, I sickened and pined and sulked and hid in my luxurious apartments, attended by every physical care. Nobody ever came to disport, for (Mrs McKenzie said) I was not well enough, and the pool was never cleaned out, though it was emptied. Only a tranche of dark, evil water remained in the deep end, full of frogs.

I will not allow Sensibility to lead me on to describe those awful weeks. Also, to be truthful, I have forgotten the quality of the suffering. I know that the essence of it was the isolation, and that – as in grief for the dead, with which of course I was still often overwhelmed – there was a very strong strand of fear. I know that, as in all grief, when I woke in the mornings it was to the knowledge that something appalling was wrong, even before consciousness presented the facts.

Mercifully, intense suffering, if we can weather it at all, seems to carry the makings of a delayed-action forgetfulness; as the pains of childbirth do, or who would try it again? *Nepenthe!* This is the drug which, in the years after Troy, Helen (reunited with Menelaus) used to mix in the wine of any visitors likely to rake up embarrassing reminiscences about the war and its causes. One would think they would be already far gone in drunkenness before raising that subject in the presence of that hostess; perhaps she had to increase the proportion of Nepenthe as the evening progressed. Nepenthe, Homer says, 'had the power of robbing grief and anger of their sting and banishing all painful memories'. I do not think kind old Mrs McKenzie put Nepenthe into my evening Ovaltines; I think that perhaps my Other, with whom I was shortly to get acquainted, slipped it into the secret ducts and channels of my metabolic network, the first of many good things she has done for me.

All the same, it is generous of me to praise the Other, seeing that what at the moment I am attempting is the reconstruction of that misery. I have to do it by symptoms, merely, since I cannot recapture the essential nature of the sadness. First, the terrible headaches. I did not learn the word 'migraine' until I was very much older – still suffering from it, as I do today. It must have been thought, then, that it was not a condition appropriate to childhood, or perhaps not even possible in the young. The headaches were ascribed, first, to recurrent sinus infection, so the sinuses were scraped and then opened up for drainage, so that they have been especially liable to infection ever since. When the pains persisted, impacted wisdom teeth were suspected, so they were dug out of their safe and, I am sure, blameless sockets; after that, it was felt that my eyes, or sight, must be to blame. Poor Mrs McKenzie took me off to an optician, who in due course supplied what can only have been clear glass in some very impressive (I thought) tortoiseshell frames. She did try, poor Mrs McKenzie; she tried everything, including nightly advice, as she tucked me up, to cheer up and get a hold of myself and make the best of things and think of my mother, and not let her down, and so on. She even counselled me on one occasion, to 'think of' my father!

It was after the useless spectacles that I began to make little 'wild' gardens, in any dish or tray I could find about the potting shed or even the rubbish dump, using cuttings and leaves from succulents and stones and bits of wood. I am not sure if this was a symptom of my illness or of my fighting it. The making of each garden was a sort of ritual act. I feel sure it was something to do with my mother, who had given me the prototype: perhaps to show her, when she came back, that I had forgiven her about Lottie and everything else; or perhaps it was an apotropaic act for her safe return. What is clear to me now is that whatever the immediate causes it was in essence to get the better of a hostile universe by reducing it to a minuscule size, making a sort of effigy of it. There must have been a therapy in the making of them, or why would one, one only, one apotrope, oblation, apology or sacrament, not have been enough? When Mrs McKenzie asked anxiously why I had to make so many of them, I'm afraid I asked her why she went to church every single Sunday. What thought-free, thorough wisdom, from a suckling! I didn't mean it rudely even though I was anxious to preserve the right to make even more gardens. But she took offence, especially as I had always declined to go to church with her. I overheard her complaining to Mr McKenzie that she was sick and tired of trying to make me out. Poor Mrs McKenzie! Worse, much worse, was to follow.

Although my Nepenthe prevents me from re-experiencing the suffering of that particular time, I recall very clearly, in addition to the bizarre symptoms I have described, the journey to the bottom of the world; for that is a journey I have made on several occasions since then and it is where, usually, I have met my Other. It is as though she waited for me there.

✒

On this first occasion, looking for the bottom of the world, I chose the steps of the empty swimming pool, partly because the bottom of the empty pool was indeed like the bottom of the world. It was a disgusting place, consonant with my mood on that day of many days. It stank of putrid water and there were tidemarks of thick green slime in horizontal stripes around its cracked and peeling sides, and on the surface of the dark water that was left there were floating rafts of suppurating yellow stuff, I suppose dead algae.

I remember very clearly that I thought that my world had shrunk to the four dirty walls of that pool. There was only me, in that space, and a frog or two. Anything else, for good or bad, had to come out of me. Anything I said would echo back at me. It stood, too, for the whole of the McKenzies' house and garden. The apartment where I was quartered was virtually closed off from the house, 'independent'; and the garden had no vistas, no resonances, no secrets. I could expect no visitors, partly because Mrs McKenzie told everybody I was ill, partly because my close friends had all gone, as I used to do, on summer holidays to the coast. In the house and the garden there were no reminders, no promises, no prospects; not even any jobs I could do, for the servants would not allow it. I had been saying to myself, for some days, without under-standing it, 'There is only what you can see.' And at the

McKenzies' I was walled about, not only when I was in the dirty, empty swimming pool; and could see very little, and none of it gave pleasure. Sitting on its steps, at a very low point on that bright, sunny morning, I first met the Other.

There is nothing in the least mystical about it. It is explained quite simply and factually by, of all people, that most baffling and grandiosely mysterious of atheist philosophers, Nietzsche – whom I did not read until at least ten years later: 'my heart shies away from believing that love is dead. It cannot bear the icy shivers of loneliest solitude. It compels me to speak as though I were Two.'

I did not say that I heard a voice; I said I 'met' ... Words came into my head, cogent messages, though brief. But I had sat on those steps many times, going over the worries and sadnesses that seemed to distress me on so many sides. If you are lucky enough to have the kinds of problem which do have a solution (as grief by itself does not) it is likely that in thrashing around, the solutions have in fact presented themselves to you before they occur in the form of a command by an interior voice. That is why the 'voice' can speak briefly; there is no need to go over the old stuff. The understanding and the will to obey are instant. It is rather like La Fontaine's (or was it Aesop's?) fortunate frog in the pail of milk who, unlike his despairing fellow who drowned in his panic, struggled round the pail so often, looking for a foothold, that the milk turned into butter; so he could, and did, hop out. I remember, too, my dear Thai friend, Noot. We were sitting on a sunny beach of the Gulf of Thailand, sunbathing. I was telling her, for some reason, about the importance in classical times of divination by eagles in the sky – good omen if they were seen to your right, bad if to the left. She was puzzled: 'Khun Prue,' she said, ' if you see them to your left, you can just turn your feet around 45 degrees and they will be to your right ...' We laughed immoderately at the thought of this victory of the mind.

There are people who 'hear voices' in ways different from this, of course, and there are others who not only hear voices but see visions of creatures of various kinds who or which are speaking the

words. The Old Testament, after all, is full of them. Isaiah and
Ezekiel are special examples, who saw the most thunderstriking
companies of creatures, which they describe in the greatest particularity as to numbers of eyes and wings and heads sprouting under
wings and, in Ezekiel, the precise day of the month of the year, and
in whose reign, what year of it, and who or even what large company of people was present at the time who were seeing him seeing
these things (he never says whether they too saw them.) I remember
Lottie's fear and distress when I read this sort of thing to her,
though I did not clearly know whether it was feigned or not, since
a lot of amazed laughter was mixed up with her peals of protest.

William Blake, in his divine, visionary and and expansive cheer-
fulness, Blake who painted the companies of angels and prophets,
virgins and martyrs, all with the rather stunted bodies and penuri-
ous robes of the British working classes, and who even as an old
man wrote poetry of the bright simplicity of happy childhoods,
Blake of the many meetings with God, tells us that he invited both
Isaiah and Ezekiel to dinner: 'and I asked them how they dared so
roundly to assert that God spoke to them … Isaiah answer'd "I saw
no God, nor heard any, in a finite organical perception; but my
senses discover'd the infinite in everything, and … I was then persuaded, and remain confirmed, that the voice of honest indignation
is the voice of God."'

17 The Hadland Settlement

⌐∽⌐

It is surprising how briefly the Other speaks, as a rule. I have never known mine to discuss, or argue, or even appear doubtful. Nor does she, or (in the case of others' Others) he, ever apologise if proven by events to have been wrong. Think, for example, of Abraham's Other – a disgraceful case. In the course of time the converse between Abraham and his Other developed somewhat, even to the extent of including a few quite cheeky questions from Abraham (such as 'How do I know you are speaking the truth?' Gen. 15.8) or – falling on his face and laughing! – 'How do you suppose an old man like me could fertilise an old woman like her?' (Gen. 17.17). But in the decades before they had achieved such bonhomie together, Abraham's Other, whom he called Yahweh and whom a modern theologian has called 'the single most stupendous and widely-influential literary personality ever created', extended the converse only by adding to his instructions and offering – as for dessert – grandiose promises, sweeteners, about the Promised Land; never explanations, never apologies, never any question time. This is how strong men get on: Yahweh is a pattern for them all or, as we ought to say, that is how they made him.

Well, my Other was like Abraham's, in the very beginning – non-bending, very terse, not at all loquacious. Abraham, after all, on the first occasion, was just told to move his tribe: 'Get thee out of thy country, and from thy kindred, and from thy father's house.'

(Well, in my case, I often reflected, it is my father's house that has left me.) So Abraham and his following, with their goods and animals, left the fertile crescent and moved into the desert, where the famine was so acute that they had to move on to Egypt. No apologies, even then. I wonder what Abraham said to the tribe; or was he too, modelled as he was on Yahweh, stronger than the need to explain? My instructions from the Other were not as clear as that, and they did not let me down, though they certainly, in the end, involved leaving my country.

'You cannot see anything,' she remarked on that day on the steps, 'because you do not know anything. Get out of here.'

I believe that at the time I thought that 'Get out of here' meant something fairly metaphorical: Leave this dirty pool, slough of despond, snap out of it. It certainly did not, then, seem the instruction which later developed into a 'Get thee out of thy country' and became an obsession and which (after nearly wrecking it) entirely altered my life.

I had begun work on the 'see', because it had been so much in my mind, during my depression at the McKenzies, that there was nothing there to see. And yet, only a year before, and all my life up to that time, I had been so absorbed by things that I could see: to see exactly how things were, or what they resembled, how they moved, colours, shapes and similitudes. But at the McKenzies, I seemed to need sight only to find my way about – not that it was difficult, but using my eyes only because I was not blind.

Looking back, though to a time well beyond the McKenzies, I can feel that this is what befell my mother, too, towards the end of her life, in the few years she had in the little house that John built for her at the bottom of his garden, where she was never happy, did not feel free, had no wish to improve or change anything, or even to work on the garden. She withdrew from old friends, ceased to bother about the dressmaker, found fault with most intended kindnesses; would not have bothered to eat if black Mary had not persuaded tasty food into her thin, old body. In her little house she lived in three or four beautifully furnished rooms which were full of the treasures she had, in the beginning, brought from Home, many of which during my childhood had been stored in trunks and crates in the stables. But at the end of her life they had all dwindled into Things. As it was for me in the McKenzies' house and garden, there were no vistas, purposes, secrets, promises or resonances. The little house of her old age must have been to her as the empty pool, or all the McKenzies' domain, had been to me.

It comes down to solitude, of course, and in my mother's case, as in that of most old people, nearness to death. After her death, when I went to clear up her possessions and her house, for I was executor, I found that she had gone around her things and onto many of them had stuck or pinned notices addressed to me: 'I think that Richard would like to have these horse brasses and they go well with the fender and tongs' or 'You could offer these fish servers to Anne unless you think Dorothy would make more use of them' or 'My mother's workbox – I especially want you to have this, Prudence.' I wondered about how she had felt in the many days she must have spent in this mournful exercise. Or perhaps it all came to her and was done in a rush, under pressure from the advance of her final illness; but even if it did, I am sure the decisions were the result of many hours of reflection in solitude.

Her possessions had always meant so much to her. It moved me inexpressibly; not only to see how thoughtful she had been about which of our family would be a suitable recipient, or her evident wish to help me in such decisions; but also to think that she had come to a time when all that she saw in her things was – what other person should have them. They, and the little house and garden, had finally failed both as alibi and as home. It occurred to me as I moved around her rooms and her things that the Dissolution had been a much greater disaster for her than for me. Mornington had been for me the beginning and foundation of my life, but for her it had been its flowering and celebration. The thirty-five years she spent as a widow (though there was a brief and disastrous third marriage) had all been – in spite of the many activities, the war effort, the parties – a diminution and a closing-in. I had forsaken her – how radically will later be seen – and John, hard as he tried, and his wife Dorothy, who tried especially hard, could not do anything that seemed to please her. Even her possessions failed her – of course.

As I sat in the empty pool, my thoughts, though on similar lines, were not of my mother but of how my own life appeared to have come to an end. No vistas; only dirty walls. I believe that, young and sad as I was, I could have wished to die, on that day. But instead I made some rather strange decisions and somehow, from somewhere – possibly anger, possibly something of Blake's indignation – gathered the force, over the years which followed, to carry them through.

The business of seeing, as I have said, came first; of not being able to see properly. It was nothing to do with the unrequired spectacles. The McKenzies' garden was not a patch on ours, but all the same there were surely things to see? Why could I barely be bothered to go and look? When I had thought about it enough I realised that there were two remedies to this depressing condition. The first essential about seeing something interesting was to have someone (suitable) to tell it to and if possible show it to. Why? To show that you loved them, to show that you shared the possession of it, to hear if they could add to the pleasure or interest of it. At the McKenzies' none of this was likely or, I considered, even possible. The only course remaining, the second option, was to make myself more interesting to myself; to have interior discussions. 'You cannot see anything because you do not know anything': it meant 'know a lot more'. What about? Everything. How? Reading, of course, learning, getting about, thinking; especially, finding someone to ask and to talk to.

The only candidate for this last, in my life, was Mrs Hadland; and behind her portly figure I seemed to see in my mind's eye the even portlier figure of beloved Lottie, for I thought it just conceivable that while Lottie and I had been staying together in such bliss at the Sannie, Lottie might have made a friend among the staff of the Hadlands' school, someone who would know where, now, somewhere in Alexandra Township, I might find her – and the little girl, Prudence.

⚞

What followed, during the next year or two, is very difficult for me to describe. I am not going to try very hard to give an account of it because, as I have said, this is not an essay in autobiography. It is a sort of history of the perceptions of a growing (or at any rate a changing) mind, in particular and unusual circumstances.

I did not, of course, find Lottie. Mrs Hadland helped me to ask about her among the staff who had known her, but it was no good. And if I had been able to visit the world, dark and suffering and poor and to me unknown and unknowable, where she lived, Alexandra Township? And if I had found her? Odysseus went to visit his mother in the Halls of Hades and it was not a very satisfactory meeting. '"My child," she said, "how did you come here? This is no easy place to find ... for between you and us flow the wide waters of the River of Fear."' A later wisdom told me that exactly this would surely have been the case, had I by some miraculous means been able to venture into 'the dark township' and find her.

However, I had excellent talks with Mrs Hadland during several days' stay with her, wheedled out of Mrs McKenzie, who, had she known what was afoot, would not have permitted me to go. I told Mrs Hadland that I wanted to study Greek and Latin at Oxford University, and to give up mathematics forthwith so that I should not, as was threatened, go down a year in school, and so that I could, therefore, write the school-leaving exam in two and not three years' time. I should therefore need a private tutor to teach me Greek, and while we were about it, I should also like to learn Italian. I wished to continue as a boarder at school, not move back into the flat with my mother, except perhaps for the holidays; immediately and for ever I would like to leave the McKenzies and for the remainder of the present holiday I would like to join my

friend Kitty on the south coast of Natal where her family had a
seaside house. Finally, it was my opinion that fourteen-year-olds
should control their own pocket money and be allowed to travel
alone on the JMT, Johannesburg Municipal Tramways, and indeed
on the SAR, South African Railways, down to Natal.

Amazingly, it all came to pass! Not all at once, of course, and
mathematics stayed on the menu; but beginning from the day at the
bottom of the dirty and depressing pool. Nor did it come about
without causing irreparable damage to the friendship between my
mother and Mrs Hadland, that between my mother and Kitty's
family, and even between Mrs Hadland and Mrs McKenzie, though
I feel certain that the latter must have been deeply thankful to the
former for taking me off her hands. My mother mostly blamed, for
ever afterwards, the McKenzies; because they had disregarded the
signs of impending breakdown in an adolescent, because even
against their instincts and the trust of their guardianship they
allowed me, in the end, to find my own world and to do what I
longed for and was ready for.

I am afraid that, since Mrs Hadland fiercely protected her
friendship with me, these quarrels pleased me. They did a great
deal to free me from the iron control of my mother; they gave me a
few adult allies – for my dear and chosen friends, being children
like myself, could only listen and try to comfort; they could not
change anything. I felt a bit guilty about Mrs McKenzie, who had
done her best for me, because my mother not only cut her off from
all further friendship but told a number of people how unreliable
and so forth the McKenzies had been, in spite of being appointed
legal guardians. I had always mistrusted that legal bit, the snaffle
and the curb of it, which are so constraining to both horse and
rider.

A wonderfully happy holiday with Kitty and her family in the
house they had built almost on the beach of the Indian Ocean
restored my health and confidence almost from the moment I
arrived. Kitty's mother, Kath, seemed to me a kind of saint, made
even sweeter and stronger by her penetrating and fanciful humour. I

adored her. She helped me back to life without ever knowing that she did, so that I never felt patronised or pitied about my sudden entry into her holiday care. I fell fairly seriously in love with both of Kitty's brothers, who seemed to me so different from my own. When I told Kitty and her sister about what I perceived to be their gentleness and courtesy and understanding, both girls nearly exploded with disbelief and indignation and produced numerous examples of tyranny and treachery. Brothers, I suppose, anybody's brothers, will be brothers.

Those few weeks of summer by the sea even induced in me a modest burst of creativity, so that before starting the next term at school I had two or three stories published on the children's page of the Johannesburg *Star*. They were, of course, set in Mornington, in the beloved home garden that had left me, and were largely about animals, the animals I had lost. I was always amazed when my stories were accepted, and dumbfounded to receive a cheque for them.

18 Queensfield

The real name of my excellent school was Kingsmead. I have called it Queensfield because it was all girls and all women and for those days very 'modern'; and 'mead', though an excellent word, is scented with age, like dried lavender. In those days the school was also all white, except for the servants, though it was among the very first, in the days of apartheid, to admit black pupils.

I want to call it Queensfield because it was there, among and in the care of those women, that I grew up almost unaware of the preconceptions about women in relation to men which prevailed in late colonial society: the belief that success for a female was to be measured first by her ability to attract a desirable husband and forever after by her efficiency in serving him. It is true that this attitude was not, need one say, a colonial invention. It was black as well as white, British, Dutch, French and Jewish and shared by all other immigrants to South Africa; in broad fact a global view, and held by almost as many women as men. It was all her life my mother's view of the matter.

I assume that it was most pronounced in colonial society, on the frontiers of Empire, because that society had itself developed, often very painfully, from the real frontiers of a harsh and dangerous country, difficult for Boer and Briton alike, where labour had to be shared between men and women and it fell to the man's strength to perform the harsher, more taxing and savage parts. The women, of course, were often heroes, but the men as a rule faced a harder physical challenge; and then, again, perhaps the men felt they had to protect and therefore to subjugate their women in case someone pinched them; or worse.

I don't really know the reasons for the extreme and universal male assumption of dominance in all sections and races of South Africa. It is still there in spite of the tremendous advances that women have made in the many years I have been away. Sometimes it seems to me that the very fact of the advances women have made in all activities and professions may lie behind the appalling increase, since political freedom, in cases of rape – now, it is said, over a million a year of *reported* cases – as though the men who feel most challenged could find no other way of asserting their strength.

It is fatally easy to invent reasons for things that you feel in your bones. Over the years I have often discussed the question of male dominance with black women. Many of them find it difficult to account for, in their own society, simply because it has always been woven into every aspect of their lives. It seems to most of them a thing that is given, like menstruation, parturition, lactation; possibly even connected with these functions; therefore, many of them think, it is a topic idle to argue about. The whole continent of African women faces male arrogance, arrogation of power, even though in some African societies, especially in West Africa, women are often the economic mainspring.

Among whites, Afrikaner women would know more about it than people like me, for in the beginning those families had a harder time. Many Afrikaners went on trek from the Cape because they felt threatened; the British settlers, on the whole, came over the sea to what they conceived would be a new and better life, whether they were humble and fearful outcasts like the settlers of 1820 or adventurous, qualified people riding the crest of the economic wave, like my father one hundred years later.

But at Queensfield I was largely shielded from all this male assertion. I saw women as the doers and achievers as well as the carers; it has, ever since, in my life in England, rather unbalanced me (so my children think) in favour of single-sex education, in spite of which they have all thought, and done, absolutely otherwise. The truth is that I feel sure that *boys* should go to coeducational schools, to learn the gentler human arts. But since there are only two sexes in the world I could not say, were anyone simple enough to ask me, what the universal prescription should be. I can say only that I have always been thankful that Queensfield put me among women for my difficult formative years; later on, at Oxford, I was glad at Somerville to be fed and sheltered as well as learnedly and excellently tutored by women; even though in those days and in my chosen field there was not a single female university lecturer among the dozens that we bicycled to to listen to and learn from, in the lecture rooms of the various, numerous, men's colleges.

At Queensfield, quite apart from its being a girls' school, a marvellous sort of natural selection went on. I say 'marvellous' because it meant a lot to me; it improved my life from schooldays onward. In the first place, the school was founded by a brilliant and innovative educationist from England, Doris Vera Thompson. We always referred to her – behind her back, of course – as DV, since she was as powerful a factor in our lives as a benevolent deity, had there been one. Certainly it was she who selected the staff; and, with only one or two exceptions, in my time she recruited staff only from Britain. In addition, she introduced to the country a new method of education which was known in those days as the 'Dalton system'. These factors, or the combination of them, had so great an effect upon my life that I cannot rationally assess them, for I cannot imagine how, otherwise, I would have endured school at all. My home life had, it appeared, collapsed; if I had not enjoyed the final school years which awaited me I would, in some way, have gone under. I can have no doubt of that.

The reason that I see DV's staff selection as, in its small way, a form of natural selection is of course that in Britain – since recruiting in Britain was the policy – only women of liberated and adventurous mind would have applied or chosen to begin, or extend, their teaching careers by travelling so far from home; and only adventurous women who also had advanced and humane views of education would have wished to come and teach within the Dalton system, a regimen which makes very heavy demands on teachers' energy and attention, since it brings about a virtual one-to-one relationship between teacher and pupil.

I feel bound to make plain that one reason for the influence upon me of this wonderful school is that it was partly housed in what, in spite of the Dissolution, I still felt to be my home and garden. In the middle days of my childhood I had attended the junior school, often getting to it through one of Puppy's holes. After my father's death and the sale of our house, Mornington became the private residence for the headmistress, as it still is. Even so, and without any invitation from DV, in my secondary years (when because of the Hadland Agreement, I was the only boarder whose home was in Johannesburg and not in some distant place) I managed to visit Mornington almost daily.

Sometimes the visits were licit. The school was in the beginning rather short of teaching spaces, so Latin and some other formal classes with few pupils were held in our old dining room; and on Sunday mornings after church DV sometimes invited us to bring our darning to her *stoep* at Mornington while she discussed the Gospel or the Epistle or the sermon we had just heard. If you were in for a real parley with DV, something shattering like having tried to run away, or been caught stealing – neither happened often and never, thank goodness, to me – then you would be invited to her private sitting-room, given a home-made lemonade, and asked to reflect upon the affair in relation to your whole life. It might have been worth working up some malpractice.

Then there were semi-licit ways of getting back there, to Mornington. Piano practising rooms were dotted all over the four sites which made up the school, in odd corners and out-of-the-way places. Two of them were in our old summer houses; one of these was my old museum (all it needed, as I had so often hinted, was electric light); two others were down at the stables, one in John's lab! An enormous chart would go up at the beginning of every term saying which girl was to practise where and at what time, so (after persuading my mother that I was suitable to be trained in the piano) all I had to do was to swap the piano places I had been assigned, if they were not at Mornington, with some that were. This simple and honest procedure gave me the opportunity, after a token effort at the piano, of wandering and wondering about my garden, several times a week.

As to the illicit ways I had of 'getting back' (if after some fifty years I am safe in revealing them ...): the two big ditches that ran down each side-boundary of Mornington crossed the road, if you remember, under culverts or 'bridges' and continued up into the main school grounds. All I had to do, when I had a free period or during the compulsory daily siesta (of summer), when we were supposed to be stretched out on our beds, was to arm myself with an excuse to get to the upper ditches; after that, I went underground, or at least below ground. Progress down the ditches and under the road to Mornington was safe and simple, and once there it was also fairly safe to go down the sunken garden, approaching it from the far end. It was unlikely that DV would be walking about her garden in the middle of the day and the declivity of the site was such that, even had she been gazing out from the *stoep*, she could not have spotted a skulker. I even spent many more happy hours, unseen, in my old haunt upon the roof of the coach-house, for the old peach tree with its strong supports was still there to assist. In the early days of these adventures I was mostly hunting for a few abandoned tortoises, especially old Joey. I thought, probably rightly, that no provision had been made for him at the Dissolution, though I remember collecting all I could find of mine before we left, and giving them in a basket to someone with a big garden. I never found any of the remainder at Mornington, or Joey, and never told any friends about these illicit visits. It was too important a secret to risk by sharing, and I didn't need any company. I think that at this time of my life the ditches and the 'bridges' were to me like the catacombs to the early Christians of Rome; or, as to the blind mole, the light of its tunnels.

The essential aspect of the Dalton system was that the child should receive education as a kind of personal adventure, working at her own pace (more or less) and as an individual, and receiving guidance when it was necessary – and guidance rather than correction. There was, therefore, a marked absence of competitive work, since the whole class was hardly ever engaged upon the same tasks at the same time. In all subjects except languages or those in which a girl might be especially weak (me in maths) we were given fortnightly assignments to go away and get on with, in our own time. The staff, on the other hand, had a strict timetable, to be in certain rooms at certain times, so that we could find and consult them there if we wished. But the girls could go anywhere they liked to do their work, alone or in small groups. If the day was fine – and the climate is one of the best things about Johannesburg – we could 'camp' almost anywhere in the gardens (except in Mornington) or go to any classrooms that were empty or the library or the swimming changing-huts or various garden bowers. There would, indeed, be staff or sometimes prefects on roving duty to make fairly sure it was in fact work that was going on; but the system allowed and encouraged an immense degree of freedom and initiative. The idle among us were monitored or paced as a necessary part of the fortnightly system and did not have to be spied upon or hovered over.

It was in my view a wonderful system, but I think it could only be fully practised in a sunny and reliable climate, in a complex of buildings and large gardens such as we had, and by a staff of exceptional calibre. There were some girls with whom the system did not agree. DV, I suppose, sorted them out, in her penetrating wisdom. I never heard of a child who was sent away from the school – perhaps none that was likely to fail so utterly was admitted in the first place – but I recall one or two who were removed by parents who wanted a more competitive edge to the instruction.

There were, though, five or six girls who studied only dog-breeding (they were going to become 'kennel maids') and gardening. We had a lady gardener, a much disputed innovation in those days, since she would have to 'boss' the black male labour by whom the heavy work was done; and she had, also, the care and instruction of these 'special' girls. They did a lot of needlework too, mostly simple clothes for the children at Ekuthuleni, a mission in Sophiatown, which the rest of us also had to do if we finished our Sunday darning in time. I make tiny garments to the same pattern to this day, for my grandchildren and others.

We knew that these special girls were less intellectually able than the rest of us, but their pursuits seemed as interesting as ours. I envied the gardening operations but was not allowed to join. Elizabeth fancied dog-breeding but was similarly debarred. I think, now that I think about it at all, that DV was doing two things: piloting a way of training, a useful and more purposeful life, for those who had certain kinds or degrees of special needs; and by not segregating them in any way except for the demands of those needs, she performed a service for the rest of us, a lesson in insight and friendship.

The school was also agreeably promotive of any special interests we might have. A girl in the class above me achieved a pilot's licence! Half the lower school immediately fell in love with her. Many of us went riding once a week; we were taught bareback at first, dashing up and down the sides of dongas, and then doing the same thing blindfolded; later over progressively high fences. Captain Browning, who used to command in the Cavalry, said we should learn to trust a horse before we learned to master it. Then, whether we trusted or not, we learned the mastering, and played polo if we were good enough, and pig-sticking (into sacks of saw-dust) and drag hunting with the horsy classes of Johannesburg. I am so unathletic that my children have never believed that I used to do all this, let alone that I enjoyed it.

And then – special subjects. I longed for Italian, so Signorina Socci used to visit me for an hour a week and set me translations of fairy stories. Miss Williams, who taught me elementary Greek, was disabled and could not visit, so I had permission to visit her on the same tram that once used to take Lottie and me to the Zoo. One of my friends (Mfanwy) wanted to learn the Welsh harp and went all the way into town by herself. Miriam, temporarily a boarder while her parents went abroad, wished to go on dancing up the Cecchetti ladder but was so young that the matron had always to accompany her to the ballet school in town.

I believe, after all these years, that it was a brilliant school, and I have never come across one to equal it, though when our four children were young Michael and I searched a good deal and tried several types. I was for several years a governor of one of the best of progressive schools in England, but so often was obliged to observe and to accept the limitation placed upon its enterprise by a cold, damp climate, the cost of heating, the competitiveness of parents (especially as there were also boys there, whose parents would expect them to go out and make their mark in a cut-throat world) and various factors to do with its being only a day school; and it was in London at that, where mere space is so costly. So after our two older children had been there a couple of years Michael and I tried sending them to a famous progressive boarding school in the depths of the country, where the space was boundless and beautiful and the amenities superb. Our children were very happy, but very idle, and did badly in their school-leaving exams, and so had to be removed and sent to London 'crammers' in order to get university entrance.

Queensfield suited my newly won independent frame of mind very beautifully. Suddenly, in one term, from being a completely unremarkable student, in fact rather dreamy and ill-organised, I shone, 'as when a sable cloud', my English teacher remarked, 'turns forth her silver lining on the night'. At the ceremony at the end of the first term after the Hadland Agreement I was given some kind of special award – not for achievement as such, which would not have been quite 'Dalton' – but for effort and improvement. But it was not an effort; it was all delight, and after the next term it was agreed that I could, as I begged, be allowed to advance two years rather than one.

What gives me pause about all this is that it has to be admitted that the syllabus and the ambience were in my time wholly and most consciously 'English' as distinct from South African. There were, so far as I recall, only three Afrikaans girls in the whole school – and they were sisters. There was a teacher of Afrikaans and she was a South African, and a few girls took her subject. My parents did not wish me to do so. My father said it would be of no use to me in my life – a self-fulfilling ordinance if ever there was one, since what you have not got can certainly be of no use to you. My mother had some kind of class prejudice against it. She never, for example, spoke of Afrikaans people, only of 'the Dutch element', by this circumlocution putting as much distance as possible between it and herself. I cannot remember if South African history was taught; it certainly was not learned, by me and my chosen friends, for we were all entered for the Senior Cambridge exam, as were most of the girls in the upper school. I should think that the few who were entered for the Transvaal matriculation had to learn South African history, but the fact that I have no recollection of it shows how faint were its features in the school. And of course, in those days, nothing remotely touching upon the languages and history of black people or the continent of Africa was provided. From time to time we went in the school bus to present the little garments we had made to the orphans of the Ekuthuleni Mission, and we played 'In and out the dusty bluebells' with them, and for tea we sat on the dusty playground and shared with them oranges which we brought with us in a sack; and that was it. I suspect that, slight as it was, and condescending and do-goodist as it was, it amounted to more inter-racial contact than was provided by other white schools of the day.

This total adherence to the mother-country culture in my time is my excuse for this excursus into my own educational history. It is not my intent to criticise the school of those times, or Miss Thompson and her founding staff. If there had been more of 'the Dutch element' included in her plans or even a suspicion of a black element, I am sure that there would not have been a school. Her initial funds were raised almost entirely from a group of wealthy parents of the 'English element', mostly of the mining and commercial fraternity, who had been impressed by her personality and her advanced educational ideas. None of these parents, in those days, would have supported any kind of racial 'open door' policy.

That is how it came about that I was not taught to be a South African, either by my parents or by my teachers; and because the prejudices of the former were so strong, and the abilities and regimen of the latter so outstanding, there was little chance that I would ever feel myself to be one.

And yet, and yet ... why should I write only of myself, as though this drop in the immense ocean were a sample or norm? The case is merely that I and some like me were educated out of all the immediacies of this struggle. But I've no doubt that thousands of women who were girls at Queensfield, many Afrikaners amongst them, have become good and sturdy-minded South Africans.

The totally English slant to my education was only one of the reasons why as soon as I could I left South Africa, though perhaps it tipped the balance. The medium of instruction at Queensfield was English, but what was taught in this language (and in French, as regularly taught as it was in England) was based upon the experience and wisdom of a large part of mankind; and it was taught in ways which aimed to make it meaningful to each one of us. Language teaching was taught, for example, almost purely by individual oral and aural means, another way in which the Dalton system was ahead of its time. Because of the oral method we had especially long individual conversations with Madame Mulligan, our French teacher, usually about some literary work and our reactions to it. Sometimes she asked us to memorise and recite a poem. Once, the poem she chose for me seemed to me soppy and juvenile,

about a fawn that had strayed from its mother. So I chose instead
to learn, for my next lesson, something quite different, a poem by
Sully Prudhomme which seemed to me nearer to my own thoughts
than I had anywhere come across (in all of my thirteen, or so, years
of life!). Because I happen, even now, to remember it, I can tell how
deeply teaching of this intense kind entered into one's own development:

UN SONGE

Le laboureur m'a dit en songe: Fais ton pain,
Je ne te nourris plus, gratte la terre et sème.
Le tisserand m'a dit: Fais tes habits toi-même.
Et le maçon m'a dit: Prends la truelle en main ...

In his nightmare, all the work people on whom the poet
depends turn angrily against him until he feels the most hated
person on earth. He asks heaven for pity – but finds lions standing
in his path. In our discussion of this poem Madame asked me: what
do you think he means by these lions? While memorising the poem
I had thought about that for several days. I almost shouted out,
and remember well her startled reaction, 'You can't get by, you
can't go on, the lions will hate us! It's all wrong! It's not a dream at
all!' Madame took the trouble to explain to me that the poet felt
guilty about the fact that he did only brain work and not any
menial work, and that at the end of the last century in France, and
indeed England, there was a very great distance and inequality
between the two even though both masters and servants were
white. I was appalled, thinking how hopeless was the case, then,
when all the servants were also, and for ever, black.

In the poem, everything is supposed to end happily with the
poet's waking from his dream to find reassurance in 'les hardis
compagnons' still going cheerfully about their daily tasks. This also
seemed to me wrong, even if I could share his relief. Queensfield
never for an instant consciously taught us any kind of political, let

alone radical, thinking; but it set us free for our own conclusions, above all in intelligent discussion of the many worlds of literature which we discovered under the sensitive encouragement of Margaret Nethersole, Margaret Morrison, Barbara Baines, Zoë Marsh, Doris Vera Thompson, and certainly Dorothy Pargiter, who memorably taught us Latin, and introduced me to Virgil.

19 Sorry, Frog

⌒

In my final two years at Queensfield I reconstituted world, life and time by being at home in the flat with my mother as little as possible. She was always anxious about my going away during the school holidays to stay with various people, and kept me very short of money so that I could never roam at will but always had to negotiate a subvention if there were any change of plan. But in fact it suited her quite well for me to be away, during the term as well as in the holidays. John had completed his engineering apprenticeship but left in the middle of his first year at London University, which was also the first year of the War, to sign up with the South African Navy. She had consented to that, after a ferocious struggle, only because he would otherwise have joined the Royal Navy. This might have eased her sense of a proper patriotism but on the other hand it would have removed him from her for the duration. So she was alone in a quite small flat, thankful, I am sure, to be free of the clamant self-absorption of her two dissatisfied and confused children. It set her free and enabled her to stand forth in her own right for the first time and make a mark on the wartime effort of Johannesburg, and certainly upon the social scene.

My mother's new preoccupations, and the comparative freedom which they brought to me, were necessary conditions for my salvation, necessary but not sufficient. My absences from home certainly meant a reduction of strife and of continual, crushing, even if caring, supervision by an assertive but insecure parent. The positive reconstruction came almost entirely from my final two years at Queensfield, and in particular from my introduction there to a more meaningful study of English literature – and Latin – and French – and European history and geography – and all the supplementaries which, at that school anyway, accompanied them: visits to plays, and our own productions, and debates and gallery and museum visits and concerts and so forth. All of it was about or from Europe – except on one amazing occasion in 1938 when we were supposed to join with other schools in celebrating the Voortrekkers, for in that year fell the centenary of the Great Trek.

The year before, my mother had been very co-operative and helpful with the costumes when we had done a big sort of dance-pageant (barefooted, on the top lawn of Mornington, where John and I, barefooted, used to play ball at dusk with the *umfaans* and the dogs). That dance-show for some reason celebrated Wedgwood pottery. We dressed up in long wedgwood blue frocks with white wedgwoodian motifs stencilled round the hem. My own and some of my friends' costumes were made by my mother with loving aplomb – anything to do with clothes brought out the very best in her; and we struck slow wedgwoodian poses accompanied by Miss Crichlow wresting Chopin from the piano. Miss Crichlow was a small frail woman, and in order to reach the slow and sorrowful resonances of Chopin, from a tinkly upright piano under a vast blue African sky, she had to put immense physical effort into the playing. She bobbed up and down on her chair, roughly retaining a seated position, stapled to the ground only by the desperate pressure of her little foot upon the *forte* pedal. I think the performance as a whole had been devised by our much-loved English teacher, Mrs Nethersole, an ardent Keatsian, and that we were being foster-children of silence and slow time.

But Voortrekkers! My mother made it sound outrageous by pronouncing the *v* as a *v* and not as an *f*, and the double *o* as it occurs in 'more' instead of 'moor'. And what, she asked, was a *kappie*? 'If it is supposed to be a bonnet,' she said, glancing critically at the school's polite printed request in her hand, 'why not say "a bonnet"?' I have no recollection of the Voortrekker performance. Perhaps I have repressed it; or my mother failed to produce the historic headpiece; or perhaps the school, or the parent governors, recognised in time the essentially political nature of the enterprise and withdrew our school from the celebrations.

By far the most interesting and effective teacher, to me, was Margaret Nethersole. She had been recruited from England where, at Somerville College in Oxford, she had been a friend of Winifred Holtby, and was inspired by her to come to teach in South Africa. She guided my reading with immense energy and devotion; a kind of passion, really, that good teachers have. It was in her tutelary footsteps that several years later, after the War, I went up to Somerville though not, as it happened, to read English. She always tried to impress upon me that an adequate reading of English literature hung upon a knowledge of those of Greece and Rome.

Then there was Zoë Marsh, who later went to Kenya and became a pioneer in the teaching of history in East Africa – not, for sure, in the sense of 'about the pioneers', in the way that South African textbooks used to say that South Africa was 'discovered' by Bartolomeu Dias or the Cape 'settled' by Jan van Riebeeck, or the Victoria Falls 'first seen' by David Livingstone – but pioneering as historiography, in the sense of trying to see the country as a whole and back to the beginnings of time and through the eyes of all who lived there and left any kind of record. At Queensfield it was Miss Marsh's way of teaching the Peasants' Revolt and especially the French Revolution and the rise of nationalisms in Europe which first brought to my mind the mighty insolubles of the South African situation – which, I am bound to add, was never referred to, since it was not on the Senior Cambridge syllabus. I thought of her very often when, twenty years later, I became the first publishing editor of Longmans' Ibadan History Series, a sustained attempt to get rid of the purely European perspective on the history of Africa.

All the same, so far as I was concerned, all of my secondary education amounted to an introduction to what I came to regard as 'the real world' of Europe, especially England, the place I had once feared and disliked as my mother's 'Home'. All my education was, for me, a long-drawn-out farewell to South Africa, an extended parting scene.

Perhaps it was not quite as simple as that. In those last school years I came, for the first time, to make a connection between the plants and animals I had loved as a child and the study of biology. It was the only one of the scientific areas which attracted me; in fact the others repelled, for I did not in those days appreciate the chemistry and the physics of all living things and I was scared of the maths they seemed to involve. A young woman called Freda Wright came out to take over the teaching of biology. She was a graduate of London University and she had recently been in Northern Australia studying something or other under the waters of the Great Barrier Reef, which in those days must have been quite an adventure. She was clearly a very enterprising person, and her methods threw some interesting light on the Dalton system in rela- tion to the teaching of natural science.

I deduce this, in memory, from the fact that while we certainly had to work on assignments about theoretical aspects of the sub- jects, when it came to illustrating them she would not, if she could help it, allow us to copy our illustrations from books. She obliged us wherever possible, in both botany and zoology, to 'go to the life'. The gardens of Queensfield provided quite a lot of the materi- al – especially the insects – and myself with a more solid kind of excuse for visiting the garden of Mornington. I once told Miss Wright about the 'hideous stinkbugs', the ones shaped like tiny violins which it had often been my duty to pick off the dahlias. She bridled at the adjective, pointing out that the emission of a smelly fluid when in danger was a very sophisticated thing to do. But she could not account for the curious fact that the stinks of a stinkbug should be unpleasant to humans as well as to any other creature, including those far more likely to prey upon it than me with my jar of paraffin. Birds, for instance. They often ate the bugs – at least I had several times seen a Jackie Hanger fly off with one. Could birds, then, I asked her, not smell? She appeared fascinated by the whole topic, whereas I had only been airing an old grudge against stinkbugs, and was still licking round the edges of the old worry, that the beauty of the Jukskei River had been so striking to me, of all creatures. The stink business was the reverse of that same coin.

Miss Wright said it would be a personal favour to her if I would substitute the stinkbug question for whatever was on the current assignment, and find out more about it, 'including, for heaven's sake, its proper name'. I was appalled at the idea at first but she had flattered me into considering it and the deciding factor was, of course, that it would give me a season ticket for Mornington, where a few of my father's dahlias were still grown In this way I reintroduced myself, properly by name, to *Anoplocnemis*, the Twigwilter Bug; and discovered it to have certain hidden beauties – most attractive orange underparts and minutely striped red and white feelers. I suppose that I had not noticed them before since my culling had always been done in dwindling light, at dusk; yet there is something to be said about getting to know more about things (and people) when you meet them not as enemies but as the equals which, with a little licence, researcher and the object of study may seem to be.

But the main things I can recall from my Stinkbug Report to Miss Wright were, first, the strange copulation of the creatures. They backed into each other like cars from opposing directions vying for the same parking space, bumping sometimes but not mounting, in spite of the inflated back legs of the male; the copulations went on far longer than I ever had the time to measure. Secondly I was driven to consult a proper book (which became in due course a bible called *Roberts' Birds of Southern Africa*) and after years of rather frightened familiarity with the Butcher Bird, or Jackie Hanger, I discovered that its 'proper name' was *Lanius collaris collaris*, the Fiscal Shrike. There is a lot to be said about that name, 'Fiscal', I mean, and the bird's aggressive and summary modes of execution, often impaling its victims on barbed wire.

The gardens of Queensfield, extensive as they were, could not

meet all Miss Wright's plans for our penetration of the natural
world. When wilder nature was necessary she took us on field
expeditions to an exciting and deserted place, the Melrose Dam. I
don't think it was anything to do with the city's water supply
because its greenish waters were wonderfully fruity, and there was
nothing to stop us from plunging round the banks with nets and
jars. Here I re-met my old friend of the previous year, of the dark
days on the steps of the McKenzies' pool, the bottom of the world:
the African Clawed Toad, now called, in Greek, 'Funnyfoot Slimey'
(as though that would not describe the whole race). We each, about
ten girls, had to catch our own and then, back at the school lab, to
anaesthetise it to death and then dissect it and draw and label its
parts and write about the functions of its parts. I was amused to
come across, quite recently, the following poem, the first poem I
had ever published (the stories for *The Star* must have gone to my
head). It is in the school magazine of December 1939.

ON DISSECTING A FROG

Clandestine croaker, O thou untimely wrenched
From purple shades and lush green slimes and banks!
Dank reeds no more thy supple curved shanks
And palely oozing skin conceal; but drenched
Thy brain in nullifying spirit, dumb
Limbs and clammy feet stretched to blind heaven
Beseechingly, by scientific thumb
Pinned to a sheet of wax, cold and even.

From soft, unfolded abdomen (the sounds
Of piercing steel have made my cold gorge rise!)
Mad, separate reds and blues in slimy harmony
Pour forth; and tubes and unknown fleshy mounds
Must be perused by mine offended eyes.
Where hidest thou, O cursèd fiend, thy renal artery?

What interests me about it now is its revelation of the direction
that my wilful mind was already taking – not the study of the natural world which lay around me and which had, from infancy,
served me with so many delights – but towards Europe and in particular to Eng. Lit.: the strict sonnet form and rhyme pattern, the
Shelleyan invocation, the Keatsian adjectives, the jumble of archaic
diction, the Shakespearian echoes ('untimely ripp'd' as Macduff
from his mother's womb!). I have to think that – allowing for mere
schoolgirl jokiness – the not-altogether-mock exasperation of the
last line was my farewell not only to natural science but, in a way,
to all that South Africa had to offer.

Sorry, Frog. Sorry, Miss Wright. Sorry, I suppose, Suid-Afrika …
yet it was there, in that country, that it all happened to me and was
offered to me. That is what there was, and there was a great deal of
it; and so it must be by choice that I am what became of me.

20 Evasions and deceptions

When I had passed my final exams at Queensfield I was thought to be too young to go to the University of the Witwatersrand in Johannesburg. I'm not sure who it was that thought that: my school? the university? my mother? I had no part in the negotiations; it was decided that I should pass another year at the school, still as a boarder (that was a condition I stuck out for) and do – do what? More of the same, I suppose. I was the only girl doing whatever it was at that level, or who ever had. To mark my advanced status I ceased to sleep in a dormitory with the others, though many of them were older than I was, and instead had a little bedroom to myself in one of the staff houses.

It was a ludicrous decision, and I really don't know how or why it was arrived at. I had passed all my Cambridge Higher subjects in the first class – except maths, but even that was, just, a pass. So it was not remedial work I was going back for. I think it must have been primarily a decision of my mother's and that its object was to keep me away from Michael, who in that same year, the fateful 1939, was entering his third year as an architecture student at Wits.

I had met him a few weeks before this decision. I saw him first in the kitchen of my mother's flat; he was sitting disconsolately on the table, escaping the large cocktail party which, with his parents among many others, was filling our sitting-room and which, by sneaking off to what I thought would be the empty kitchen, it was also my aim to avoid. We fried eggs and bacon and fell entirely in love. He went home with his parents but early the next morning there he was, outside our front door, wondering whether or not to ring the bell. 'I couldn't sleep' was the only reason he offered, and I said 'I know', meaning 'Me too'.

We were both very surprised at what had overtaken us. I was only fifteen, he five years older. For several weeks, although seeing each other daily, we didn't speak of it for fear of being thought simple or inexperienced; or of being unreciprocated, even mistaken. But it didn't, all our lives, blow away. The amazing and sudden, mighty gift of it lies behind everything I think and feel about the human animal.

It had taken a long fight with his parents before Michael had been allowed to leave his apprenticeship to his father's business in the manufacture of wire ropes and to enter Wits and architecture. My mother, of course, may well have been quite right in supposing that if we were together at Wits neither of us would have paid much attention to our studies. All the same, preventing me from going to university at all, when I was ready and longing for it, was an absurd solution.

Lovesick, I paid little attention to most of the Queensfield work and spent nearly all of my time reading Karl Marx in a desperate attempt to become a member of the Johannesburg branch of the Communist Party. The Party would not allow me to become a full member until I knew something about the reasons which made joining it, in my eyes, the honest and essential thing to do. I was interviewed by the great Bram Fischer. 'Indignation is not enough,' he said. The knowledge that they were the only political party which gave primacy to the needs of the greater part of the population – that was not enough, either. I had to understand the processes of history, and what the Party's programme was. He assigned to me a guide and teacher, who in turn set me to reading and observing. They were kind enough not to tell me that I was 'too young' but they may well have thought that I was too unguarded to be trusted.

At home, shortly afterwards, my mother intercepted a typed, business-looking letter for me, which she thought must be a bill, and found it to be notice of an 'appointment' – really just a meeting of the Party – at the rooms of a noted gynaecologist. This was the 'cover' agreed at the time. She rang up the doctor's rooms, demanding to know why her daughter should need such an appointment, convinced of course that it was either for contraception or for abortion, neither of which (alternatives though they are) would she have permitted. The receptionist simply denied all knowledge of such an appointment, which so far as she was concerned was truthful. When my mother then applied to me, I was in a terrible difficulty. If anything would have upset her more than contraception or abortion it was communism. She would not have kept quiet about it, either. I told her some lie about menstrual problems; but from that time on, she didn't trust me on any front at all. She had good reason for her mistrust, then and later, as I'd had for my mistrust of her since the disasters of the Dissolution.

Meanwhile at Queensfield my reading of Marx continued and other books which my communist teachers recommended, especially Sol Plaatje's *Native Life in South Africa*, which explained, at last, the dusty feet that had trudged the streets around Mornington looking for work. All this passed off with the approval of my Queensfield teachers (peering myopically through the wool over their eyes) as intense application to twentieth-century political history. In the evenings I found it fairly simple, if consent had been witheld for '*another* concert, Prudence?', to climb out of a window of the staff house where I slept and to meet Michael at the bus stop.

It was a ridiculous sort of existence. When, in spite of all my entreaties, Michael volunteered and joined the army and went off to camp as a bombardier, I took it all in hand. I realised I was wasting a year of my life and that Johannesburg would be intolerable without him. I applied off my own bat for admission, though a term late, to Natal University to which Kitty, an immensely gifted artist, had won a national art scholarship at Pietermaritzburg. I was able to show my mother their courteous letter of acceptance and she gave up, on that topic; though not in regard to my life in general.

Every move I made after that, coming so soon after the gynaeco-logical mystery, was a cause of suspicion and mistrust; and this brings its own consequences, of course, inviting deception and eva-sion and underhand dealing. My mother and I for at least thirty years, until I had four children and she was entering upon her final illness, had a relationship which can only be called hostile. It sel-dom erupted because we had both learned to keep control, but it underlay nearly all our talkings and doings. I sometimes think that it would have been better for us to have parted altogether, as Abraham and Lot decided to do: 'Let there be no strife, I pray thee, between me and thee.'

In the troubles between us of my childhood, in the house with my mother, I used often to imagine myself enclosed in a bubble of see-through material that was extremely tough and pliable, so that it moved with me and followed my shape, protecting me from her wherever I went and whatever I did. So far as I know, plastic had not been invented in those days; this bubble was exactly like the encasements in which, now, one buys batteries or tools or many other hardware things; their integument protects them so well that you need a laser beam or a tiny chainsaw to get inside it. But the disagreements and spats of childhood were as nothing to the per-manent mutual anger that became a mark of my restless and unhappy adolescence and of her long widowhood. After I had left South Africa and terminated all dependence upon her, both emo-tional and financial, and married Michael, my anger cooled off; but with the sense of this rejection, her own increased. She became a difficult mother-in-law, a difficult grandmother, and I am certain that she found me a greatly less than satisfactory daughter.

Most memoirs say little of quarrels with parents. It is certainly a topic that is painful to write about. I think that accounts of strife in this respect may also be boring to read, unless one had turned out to be Boadicea, or Charles Dickens, or a film star. Why, therefore, am I doing it? Socrates said that the unexamined life was not worth living; and perhaps it should be an exercise in long retrospect, or there would be little to examine as one went about one's ways; and the longer the life and the more extensive the matter for research and reflection, the more likely is its fruitfulness – a sound principle of research.

I am blessedly conscious, now, of almost complete harmony with my own children, though there have been a few rough patches – for them as well as me – which I expect will find a place in their memoirs, if they ever write them. Susie, my eldest child, lives close to me in Oxford, but she works for Oxfam and has to fly about the continents, so her little girl, Sarah, is often in my charge. Sarah thinks that I am fussy and bossy, and I should think that this is correct. The generational gap is very familiar ground to me. But I love Sarah as intensely as I do my own children, and my care of her gives structure to my later days. This is a relationship which, since Sarah is now fourteen – the age at which my childhood came to an end – goes beyond the uncritical grandmotherly adoration I bestow upon the wonderful babies (as they still are) that Vicky and Charlotte have produced; as once I did upon baby Sarah. The grandparents of babies can have a marvellous time, emotionally. It would demean it to call it 'free love', but in ordinary cases it is similar to that: the indulgence without the responsibility. I think that children need to learn, as most African children do, that growing up, even through fussiness and bossiness, you are growing towards a many-fibred bond with the elders of your tribe which is at its best a bond with world, life and time. It can site you and strengthen you and goes far beyond the particular parent or grandparent.

There will always be personal and adventitious factors in quarrels that are recurrent. My problems with my mother arose in large part from my rather wilful and solitary nature but that, in turn, may have been conditioned by *her* difficult London childhood, in almost continuous charge of seven siblings, the cause no doubt of her rather short temper and need for instant obedience as well as the neglect of her education; and that, in its turn, caused by the genteel poverty and Victorian values of *her* parents and so on, backwards. I know that there is a generational matter as well as a personal aspect to all this; but I also believe that there is what can be seen as an historical and especially a colonial aspect.

I know it from Michael, for example, the person I have known best and loved best. His differences with both his parents were not nearly as continuous and destructive as mine with my mother but they were bad enough, especially after he finished at his English public school and followed them to South Africa, when he was 18. In England, apart from his schoolboy desire, which shocked them most rudely, to join the International Brigade, they had rubbed along well enough. Not, however, once they moved to South Africa. And I know the colonial aspect from perceptions of and conversations with very many of my Whitefellows, over the decades.

The divide – the serious divide, beyond the usual frictions – between generations arises with especial force, as we all know, in times of rapid social, economic and perceptual change. In our cases, of course, there was not only that but geographical change as well, the going out to a new life in a new country; to which our parents took all their notions of their own personal and racial superiority, the colonial attitudes and expectations which they had inherited from their forebears since the time, I suppose, of the slave trade (or, as some Afrikaners used to think) the days of the children of Noah. And as we grew up, Michael's and my generation, the great generational divide widened with each instance of the conflict our parents perceived between their group self-interest or personal comfort, and those of the black people who helped us with our lives, upon whose labour and goodwill we were dependent. These instances as a rule touch upon the most basic of impulses and emotions, as I have said before, for the relation between people and their servants involves our approaches to equity, to justice, to care, interest, understanding, compassion, enjoyment, love. Old-fashioned socialism and communism used to lump together, in far too crude a way, all these deep intangibles into a big, strong bag called 'Equality', and they hit people with it, hit anyone who disagreed with them. But there weren't too many socialists anyway in the country of my youth, and many of those who called themselves by that name related themselves only to the working classes of the whites. Many of us were sent to church or synagogue to learn about all those qualities; and European literature as a whole is decked out with them; but home attitudes and experiences were, for so many of us Whitefellows, an entirely different matter.

The evasions and deceits which arose from the clashes between my mother and me, and to some extent between my brother and me, for he was 'of her party', on the whole may seem quite trivial after all these years, but at the time they determined the quality of my life. The principal evasion after the Dissolution, though there were quite a few before that time (the hiding in the ditches, on the coach-house roof, the lovely times with Lottie at the Zoo Lake) arose from my need to be at home with my mother as little as possible. I was thankful to be a boarder at Queensfield, though it was only a neighbourhood away from my mother's flat and must have cost her a fortune in fees; and I was grateful for many invitations from my close friends to spend holidays with them, especially Kitty and her family. Those holidays on the shores of the Indian Ocean, then almost deserted, were close to Paradise for me.

At one time in a vacation from the university, desperate to earn money, I took a job as a salesgirl at the OK Bazaars. Also, it gave me a chance of meeting blacks on a basis quite different from anything I had known; it was even more than equality, I thought, since they were among the customers: it was I who was serving *them*. On three grounds it was impossible for me to let my mother know about this job: she would have considered a 'salesgirl' job to be *infra dig*; and a store that allowed natives in! Never heard of such a thing! But most undesirable of all, from her point of view, was the very reason I had taken it – it gave me money of my own. So I had to invent a reason for leaving home at a very early hour and

arriving back at a late one. I said that I had to write a long essay
for the university, to give in at the beginning of the next term, and
that it needed constant referral to books that could not be removed
from the Public Library. I felt some dismay when she said she
would be interested to read it when it was finished. She didn't press
the point, knowing perhaps that it would lead to more lies.

When Elizabeth was old enough to drive her mother's car we
sometimes went, secretly, to the horse races at Turffontein. We
dressed up in bits of our mothers' fineries, hats and gloves and high
heels, to look twice as old as the adolescents that we were, and we
went to the Non-European enclosure – it was much cheaper to get
into that and entirely precluded the chance of recognition by any
racegoers among our parents' friends. Elizabeth in her quiet and
orderly way studied form and often won something, but I just
guessed or was lured time after time by the false promise of names,
and always lost my modest outlays instead of gaining a little freedom. I published some more stories – under a pseudonym so that
my mother would not know that I had some money from fees. I
secretly sold some of my books and some of my clothes. She
allowed me a generous account at a booksellers and always provided me with beautiful clothes. I borrowed from the cook. I can't
remember all the paths to subvention but I don't think that any of
them involved stealing as well as lying. Misappropriation I confess
to: she gave me money for first-class rail fares to Pietermaritzburg
but I used to travel second (where 'accompanying servants' were
allowed to travel) or even third (for anybody black or coloured),
swear to the conductor that I was coloured, sit upright between
packed bodies all night and so, in addition to saving on the fare,
could pocket the 'bedding money', keeping all the profit for bus
fares for weekend visits to Durban and the lovely coastal places.

The name of all that was freedom – my freedom, my right. I
can't recall ever feeling guilty about these deceptions but something
often warned me that it was a pity it had to be done that way; and
that my father would have been as displeased as I was about all the
untruthfulness.

Something horrible happened about someone else's freedom. At one stage in her small flat my mother employed a maid. Regina was coloured, a sweet-natured young woman. She looked smart and proud in her chocolate-and-cream uniform and apron; was very pretty except for a series of ugly scars which appeared to have been cut randomly across her face. I saw a good deal of Regina that vacation because my mother was away in Cape Town, organising a hospitality scheme of some kind for visiting British troops. What, you may wonder, was Regina supposed to be doing? The answer is: keeping an eye upon me, for the reason that beloved Michael was able at this period to get an occasional few days' leave from camp before the army was to be moved 'up North' to the Western Desert; which is why, for once, I hadn't left home.

Regina revealed to me that she had a violent husband, an unemployed alcoholic, who slashed her – face, arms, anywhere – if he didn't get his way, or her money. I asked her why she didn't report him to the police. She laughed: the police! Out of the question to have anything to do with the police. Anyway, she said, she loved him. I told her about my love for Michael and how wonderful it was to have whole days and nights together, even if so few, even if they were to be the last before he went away. So I suppose Regina and I had a sort of pact about mutual secrecy, though I don't recall formalising it.

My mother returned from Cape Town suddenly, early one morning. Fortunately Michael had returned to camp the night before. I heard, while still in bed, a commotion in the hall. My mother as soon as she stepped into the flat had noticed things missing – things she had treasured from the stables, from Kimbolton, from Home: a long copper post-horn that used to hang on the wall above the Sheffield Plate domed meat covers, of which, she saw with horror, the ornate handles had been unscrewed and removed; a brass chestnut roaster; and two antique flintlock pistols, weapons that could not possibly have been activated for the past two centuries even if one had possessed their complement of powder and shot.

It was the reported theft of these pistols which really engaged the attention of the police, who had been summoned. By the time that I had dressed and emerged from my room the hall was almost filled by two huge Afrikaner policemen, the big Irish caretaker of the flats and his wife, my mother and a weeping Regina, protesting her complete surprise at the thefts. The police annoyed my mother a good deal by going on and on about the pistols – 'Ag, lady, you should not leave weapons lying around for Kaffirs to pick up. Did you even have a licence for them, hey?' My mother ridiculed their ignorance of the antique and English nature of all these objects, especially the pistols. The caretaker was obsessed by the need to exonerate any of the staff in his charge – liftman, cleaners, garden-ers. Regina irritated everyone by sobbing out her innocence, what-ever the subject or allegation. Everyone was standing, of course, and hardly moving. They were standing because each party was seeking moral elevation, defending an interest, and nobody was moving because, in that little hallway, there was no room to do so. It was very like a full-blown sextet in some grand opera, each per-son absorbed by their own agenda, developing their own thoughts and emotions without reference (in the libretto, anyhow) to those of any other performer.

Then the action resumed, and the police asked my mother to see if anything else were missing from the flat which might, in some way, imply an inside job. After a search, it was discovered that in the sitting-room the drinks cabinet, for which only Regina had the key, had been cleared out, lock, stock and bottle. This was the only thing that could not have been pinched by someone just looking into the hall from the front door. It was quite clearly a Regina affair; but the theft of the drink and not of my mother's jewellery, or any of our clothing, made it clear to me that the real thief was Regina's husband, and that she had probably given him the key of the drinks cabinet under immediate threat from his knife, and that she dared not confess her part because it would at once implicate him. So, I'm afraid, I looked my mother in the eye and told her that I had asked Regina for the key, and that Michael and I had had a party the previous week, and apologised that I hadn't yet replaced the bottles that had been consumed. A lie direct, if ever there was one; and I suppose my mother knew it, and it must have been a humiliation for her. Regina was not charged, since it was only the theft of the drinks which could have pinned anything on her, but – from my mother's service, later that day – discharged, and I never saw her again. She, too, vanished into the metaphysical world, the dark and hidden world in which I did not live but the presence of which lay behind, I felt, all my living.

The life from which I have salvaged these fragments was mine, uniquely so. Therefore I am more aware than anyone of the unique personal factors in the struggles and attitudes which I have described; and also of the risk of the deadly hand of total recall, of anecdotage, the proper bane of self-searchers. I have tried to be as honest and particular as memory will allow. The re-searching has not shaken my belief that historically conditioned attitudes and relationships, one race or one people to another, lay at the root of the divisions in the family no less than in the nation. That will not be a surprise to those whose profession it is to study that sort of thing, but it might say something to the many people who think that their attitudes, beliefs, prejudices and preconceptions are based upon various ultimate truths rather than upon their daily percep-tions and the consequences of their own behaviour. It is we who make the truths, just as it is the language we choose that fashions the ideas which guide and rule and so often distort us. This must be why the rejection of the beliefs and attitudes of a person who is near and dear involves an upheaval which may be, as my rift with my mother was, very sad and difficult; and may involve an interior conflict the solution of which, in my case, nearly cost all my life's happiness: that is to say, the leaving, for ever (as I thought), of my native country, the world as I knew it – and the many, darkened worlds I could not enter which lay behind it.

21 Reef of white waters

⁓

It is difficult to write about the most critical period of one's life for the rather tautologous reason that the factors which made that period critical were so – well, so difficult to write about. In my case they were complex and fairly mysterious at the time and therefore elusive in memory. My critical years, when I became more than ever conscious of the pressing need to abandon South Africa, were, exactly, the six war years. They were also my school-leaving and initial university years, when one acquires at least a ground-plan of one's world though not necessarily a route map of the best ways around it – or out of it.

Those six years were overshadowed of course by the war. There was no conscription in South Africa during the war, since the country had been so divided about whether to enter it or not. But Michael (and most young men I knew) and every one of my close girlhood friends voluntarily joined the forces of one kind or another, interrupted their lives and postponed their ambitions 'for the duration'. I could not bring myself to do that. I made all sorts of excuses about it, to myself and to others, but the main thing was that I thought it might bind me for ever – or for a moment longer than necessary – to South Africa.

Even at the time I felt myself to be indefensibly selfish; blind to the fearful emergency which had overtaken the world, from which it might never emerge or, if it did, in a condition crippled and

cowed by evil forces, evil practices – a triumph of death. I never
had any doubt about the urgency of it, the fearful moral need for
doing what I was not doing. My mother excelled herself, as I have
described, in many wartime activities. She was awarded a high dis-
tinction by the Order of St John. Officers of the Order, decades
later, came as the guard of honour at her funeral. My brother John
and I were immensely proud of that, for her sake.

I felt put to shame, also, by John's quitting of his engineering
degree at London University to join the South African Navy. He
joined as a stoker; perhaps he remembered the pictures of my
father stoking the traction engine, against the Boers. Quite soon he
became an officer and was promoted to second-in-command of a
minesweeper, the *Bever*. *Bever* was a very small ship, one of a number of old, weather-beaten, broken-down Norwegian whalers which
had been laid up in Cape Town, taken over in 1941 by the SA
Seaward Defence Force for conversion into magnetic minesweepers,
and dispatched to duty in the Mediterranean. *Bever* was the last-
but-one ship in June 1942 to leave Tobruk harbour where it had
been desperately engaged (small as it was) in the attempt to rescue
as many as it could of the Eighth Army, which Rommel was driving
into the sea or to the prison camps of Italy and Germany. Heavily
laden, braving the shore batteries, which blew a hole through one

HMSAS Bever *is sent to sweep mines in the Mediterranean*

funnel, *Bever* just made it to the open sea and to the safety of
Alexandria. The last ship to leave, just after *Bever*, was another ex-
whaler of the Seaward Defence, *Parktown*, which heroically took in
tow, during the escape, a tug which had broken down, laden with
troops; an act which drastically reduced its speed. *Parktown* was
less fortunate than *Bever*. It was destroyed and sunk early the next
morning by a combination of fire from Italian gunboats and from
German aircraft aiming at survivors in the sea. *Bever* was itself
destroyed, with the loss of all but eight hands, while sweeping off
the coast of Greece two years later. Enemy mines had become more
sophisticated than these little ships were equipped to deal with.

John served for the duration of the war and after demobilisation
he was one of the many thousands, in all countries, who felt unable
to return to the studious or sedentary life of any university. He
took a job in an engineering firm in Johannesburg and completed
his engineering degree by evening study and correspondence – the
hard way.

Middle John died in an Italian prison camp; little John lost an
eye in a flying accident. Philip, Mrs Hadland's son, died in the
Western Desert; Mrs McKenzie's son, Jamie, was killed in the skies
over Germany, serving with the RAF. Five or six others of the sons
of my mother's friends, and a greater number than that of the boys
who had been at school with my brother, were killed. All these
deaths, and the suffering of the much greater number of the South
African Second Division who were taken prisoner at Tobruk and
elsewhere, were a reproach to me. I very deeply felt it to be so.

There I was, through all the war years, swanning my way
through university. I don't remember any particular occasion which
decided me upon this course and thereafter kept me to it, in the
way that the Other had done when I sat so miserably at the bottom
of the empty swimming pool. The Other comes only when one is
alone, and now there were real people who had taken her place as
sources of authority and care. There were teachers, beginning with
some of those at Queensfield, who told me I was clever, or good at
something special, and all of these women urged me to read more

and study more and if possible go as soon as I could to Oxford. Mrs Hadland said it was out of the question to do anything else. That is what she said even though Philip, her son, one of my brother's gang of boys in the garden, shooting birds and bull's eyes, had been killed in the Western Desert.

Fortified because so troubled, I defended myself by studying harder than ever, before or since. When I look back upon it, I am surprised by my industry and the extent of my reading in those days; though I cannot, because I was so young and immature, be proud of any depth in my responses to it. At Pietermaritzburg I had met Mark Prestwich, then a lecturer and later Professor of History, very English, very Cambridge. We became devoted friends and he, a superb and confident polymath, was among those who from that time on took the place of the Other, pointing my nose to the grind-stone as well as into the wind, driving me as well as cheering and inspiring me. In the years of our friendship (of which my mother disapproved too strongly to allow him in her flat) there was interest and amusement to last a lifetime. I also learned from him a good deal about South Africa, for he used to write many of the leaders for the *Natal Witness*, of which for several periods before his death he became acting editor.

When I moved to Wits in the following year, there were many more friendships and in particular, four beloved teachers: John Greig, Professor of English; T.J. Haarhoff who headed the Classics Department; Percival Kirby, towering in his friendly way over Music; and Hilda Kuper, the social anthropologist, who became my lifelong and close friend. Each of these giants, as I still perceive them to be, had such a powerful impact on my nascent mind that for the four years I was there I could not decide which of their sub-jects I intended to 'major' in, so I took them all and a few more besides. I had the time to do it all, since I barely had a home life, and no interest in sport or dances or parties or – as my mother put it – anything normal. 'Why do I bother to buy you expensive clothes', she once said, 'when nobody ever sees them?' She meant that she could not ever see anyone seeing them, since we were never together at any public gathering or private party.

I remember most of that time, though, as a sort of party, in spite of all the tragedy that underlay it. From my third year, when I became a sort of tutor, I shared a spacious, sunny office room at Wits with two other women whom John Greig had promoted to help in the teaching of the large number of first-year students: Zoë Girling and Ruth Nevo. They were, and are, friends of my heart. Both emigrated as soon as they could – Zoë to Canada, Ruth to Israel, both of them after a spell in Cambridge – and almost all of our special friends of those years emigrated too, when the war was over. So a great deal of the like-mindedness which Whitefellows so preciously share, and gaiety as well as gloom, discoveries and diversions as well as depressions, went on in that room.

Also at Wits, until he joined the army, there was Sammy, Sam Liebermann who later on founded the famous Liebermann Pottery near Johannesburg. For the next forty-five years until his death, he was the person I turned to either in trouble or for fun or – the cement of friendships – for no particular reason. About a week after the beginning of my first term I was browsing in the library when Sammy, whom I had not met before, a tall, lean, bearded, sunburned, sandalled, Semitic man came up and asked me to make a fourth at the bridge game which was, apparently, going on in the underground stacks, holy places which the library accorded only to serious students or scholars. I was horrified, and showed it. I

Sammy sombre, Johannesburg, 1969

supposed that he would dismiss me as the priggish swot that I felt, but he said, 'Oh well, never mind. Can I carry your books for you?' When, after a few days, he learned about Michael, he did not drop off as I had expected, but began to attend the Latin and Greek which, unsettled by the outbreak of war, he had almost abandoned in favour of bridge and other diversions. After that we inhabited classical literature together; all those landscapes, shipwrecks, battle-fields, Arcadian meadows, vineyards, court hearings, bloodsoaked palaces, mountain-topfuls of quarrelling deities, symposia, literary salons, Roman *dives* – as well as the real dives and digs of Sammy's bohemian friends, and the exciting literary-philosophic and espe-cially liberal-political salons which were held daily in the 'Greek shops', cafés and seedy bar-lounges of Braamfontein. In the bars themselves women, in those days, were not allowed.

In the months that we were together at Wits, before Sammy joined the army, we had many such colloquies as well as classes together but he could not visit me at the women's residence because there, as he put it, he 'had other irons in the fire'. Nor could he join me on my occasional visits home to my mother's flat because, as I had to explain to him, if my mother saw a Jewish friend the temperature dropped at once to freezing. Sammy had a dreadful fondness for practical jokes, always of a kind which involved a degree of play-acting. He used to torment me sometimes by pre-tending to plan one of these 'jokes' for my mother's benefit. Pretending to expect my approval, he would, for example, suggest that he should dress up as a rabbi and call upon her 'to thank her for transferring so large a sum of money to the synagogue', or for agreeing to allow his congregation to meet in her flat that very morning – '*Shalom, shalom*; we are all very keen to meet you, Madame, and to introduce you to our families who are waiting downstairs!' I would nearly pass out from a weird amalgam of laughter and of dread, for I knew he was capable of doing it.

Sammy had, as I have, so acute a need for alibis of the imagina-tion that the events and places which our reading gave us were about as compelling as our lives. I am bound to confess that we

were also rather glad that they were being presented to us in languages generally thought of as 'dead', for we liked the comparative
secrecy of them; yet there was also a need to share them. In some
ways these semi-secret places of classical literature, which I have
come to regard as proto-alibis, were the foundation of our friendship. He did not like it at all when I went to Oxford to share with
others, and when he returned from the army – he was a D.R., Don
Robert or Dispatch Rider, with the Sixth South African Division in
Italy, from Salerno to the Po – when he was demobbed he returned
to finish his degree but after a while he gave up the study of classics
in favour of the law. He was a far better classical student than I. I
had an allegiance divided between several subjects, but Sammy felt
that Latin was the natural language of mankind. Sometimes, even
from the stresses of the Italian Front, he wrote to me in Latin, with
occasional lapses into Greek. The military censors were rather hard
on passages in both these languages, supposing that they might
convey secret information, so sometimes I had to be content with
the tattered or blacked-out remains of his letters.

After the war and after he had qualified, Sammy came to live in
England for a while. At first he tried to earn a living by purchasing
a motor bike, a Copycat duplicating machine and a raffishly smart
beret (or perhaps he rediscovered the one he had worn in the
army). He called himself, for trading purposes, Don Roberto, and
advertised his services – of copying and delivering office documents
around the City – by affixing to his bike two legends, one down
either side. One said BIS DAT QUI CITO DAT – he gives twice who
gives quickly – and one on the other side said ET CITO DAT QUI
COPYCAT. Business was not very brisk. Later on he had a job to do
with racing pigeons, transporting them on his bike in their little
cages from homes to starting venues; then the bike disappeared and
he found a fixed job for twenty-four hours a day, minding the kilns
of the Chelsea pottery by night and learning the craft by day, an
apprentice potter of great devotion and skill.

Sammy had a hard struggle to find the basis of his later achievement, as did so many of our friends who had chosen to interrupt

their lives in the critical years of their development . After he and his wife Mary, herself a superb craftsman, founded the Liebermann Pottery, he appeared for many successful years to be content with the harvest of his early enterprise. He had a creative, thriving business, a loving marriage and five gifted children, but in his maturity he was afflicted by an intractable depression which led him to his death. The war of our time has prematurely killed men and women years and years, decades, after the Peace. Sammy, as well as Michael and, in some ways, my brother John, was among them.

At Wits a new quality and clarity was brought into my life by Hilda Kuper almost as soon as I began attending her lectures in social anthropology. Like all my generation of whites, I had stumbled through my childhood, close to and yet far distant from the black people and children of my home. The paths of Mornington were swept and trim, correctly drained, Romanly humped at the crest; but the paths of my life were littered with the detritus of colonialism, conquest, exploitation, fear and mistrust. Our parents – all our parents – were both the victims and the perpetrators of these processes, and they gave us, on the whole, and except for the steady straightness and humanity of people like my father, no patterns for behaviour or judgement other than those of the class, society and national aspirations of the foreign lands they had left. A group of South African social scientists, all of whom had faced this conflict and who had been, so several of them have told me, inspired by it to embark upon their chosen professions, had in my time begun to transform the understanding of our world by their extensive studies of our many societies and cultures – Isaac Schapera, Meyer Fortes, Max Gluckman, Monica Wilson, Ellen Hellmann, Jack and Ray Simons, Eileen Krige – and, indeed, Hilda's husband Leo Kuper. There are many others; Hilda was, even in this company, outstanding. Hilda and Leo became less than popular, after the war, with apartheid governments and were obliged to leave the country. They were welcomed by the University of California at Los Angeles and both became Heads of the respective departments of Sociology and Social Anthropology and acquired an extraordinary number of devoted friends and students. When Hilda died, many people in England and America as well as South Africa wrote about her work, the classic studies of the Swazi people, and of the Indians of Natal. Most of her obituarists tried to show how deeply her work was conditioned by her lively and loving mind. I tried too, for she had been by that time my close friend for over fifty years; I tried to show that it was through her that, upon my troubled white-child paths, I began to come across ways of looking at the world which took account of a common humanity as well as the particular insights of social science – the understanding of cultural, social and economic pressures, political frictions, historical processes. During my years at Wits Hilda, her lectures and the warmth and care of her friendship began to make sense of the world I lived in. She helped me to look into the fearful face of poverty and cultural dislocation as well as, on the other side, that of prejudice and self-interest. It began to explain my world to me; it did not make it any easier to live in, nor for an instant deflect my plan to leave it.

John Greig became a particular friend and, as soon as I had qualified, he tried to start me on a properly academic career by appointing me to a junior lectureship in the English Department. I enjoyed that, very much. Most of my effort as a student at Wits was put into trying to improve my Latin, Greek and French, which in those days, before all the modern language-teaching aids and methods, needed great application. Literature, as such, and to the extent that it was separable from 'language', never seemed to me like work; it seemed like life, which I was desperate to experience, so I did little but read for a great part of the day and night. I wrote a lot, too, mostly poetry, but could see that it was no good. It was derivative from literature, not from life. Nobody seems to criticise poetry which is derivative from life, and literature was what I had, at that time, instead of life.

I took trouble over my teaching for John Greig because I cared for and valued him so greatly and wanted to please him and justify his faith in me. His own lectures were so full of knowledge, life, humour, perception – and of whatever is the humane word for 'pedagogic invention'. For example, he introduced all first-year students, including those in the faculties of Law and Engineering, to exercises in Ogden and Richards's *Basic English*, which is a selection of 850 words from the full English register. Used judiciously and as intended by its 'inventors' this is a wonderful teaching and learning experience. It improves the clarity and style of English, and did so throughout the university. It is as good as Latin for the management of English; as good as a short, sharp course in italic script is for anyone's handwriting, and for roughly the same structural reasons.

At John's request I prepared a course in twentieth-century poetry, which in those days I made to mean Thomas Hardy to W.H. Auden, though most time by far was devoted to T.S. Eliot. A course on modern poetry had not been offered by the Department before, so at the same time as there was nothing to guide me I had to make sure of the way. My friends and I produced and acted in Shakespeare in the fine theatre at Wits, wrote and counter-wrote in student magazines, spoke and counter-spoke in debates. I went endlessly to concerts, often with Mark, and to films, usually with Sammy, and began to let communism go, though I taught a few literacy classes organised by Party activists. It was, when I look back on it, and except for the appalling menace of the war, in many ways a golden youth in the City of Gold; but I could hardly wait to leave it.

✌

The 'rand' in 'Witwatersrand' is a series of related reefs of different kinds of gold-bearing rock, reaching about 80 kilometres, east to west, diving sharply at the south towards the centre of the earth, so that some of its mines are the deepest in the world. Johannesburg is near the centre of the Rand. This is why in the garden at Mornington we often heard the rumbles and felt the tremors of the rockfalls, which so greatly disturbed my father.

I have never discovered, however, what the 'white waters' are. There is not much water as a rule in those parts; and as to the colour of it, the Rand lies, rather distantly, between the headwaters of the Limpopo, which as Kipling has told us is grey-green and greasy, and the middle reaches of the Vaal, which is the same though sometimes browner. I cannot suppose that the Krokodil or the Hennops or the few other muddy streams of the Transvaal which have just made the grade above *spruit* contributed anything to the naming of the mighty Rand – or even the Jukskei, which ran past Elizabeth's childhood home, even if it did give me my first glimpse of the splendours of Creation. But when I think of the University of the Witwatersrand and the hectic, scrambling, racing, bubbling flow of the life and times that I spent there, it gives me an image of a long stretch of turbulent, rocky river, 'white water', shooting and stopping and reeling and rocking, rushing and gushing, and however else the water comes down at Lodore. For me, that, and not something geological, is the Reef of White Waters. What made the water so eventful, always so challenging, often in its quieter moments so beautiful, was of course the presence, dangerously near the surface, of the unremitting rocks, the insoluble, immovable facts, as I considered, of a country founded upon greed and fear, force and hate, self-interest, injustice and resentment, and which, together with most of the rest of the world, was itself being challenged by a state that was far more evil and immeasurably more powerful.

I realised, after keeping afloat for a while on the torrent of those days, that I would have to work out a strategy for reaching, somewhere, somehow, the safety of a dry bank. I had most passionate feelings about racial equality but I was not made for a life on the political barricades or spells in prison, or any kind of detention, and almost certainly I was a coward. But how could I be sure that there would be a place of escape? How could I be sure Oxford would accept me? There would certainly, after the war ended, be a greater pressure than usual on places in the women's colleges; and unless it were to go to Oxford or some such approved place, how could I hope that my mother would allow me the necessary funds? There was a good chance that she would give generously in order to remove me from Michael, but I wasn't prepared to give any promises about that. So I began to write a long essay which would please me by putting together all the writers whom most, at that time, I loved, Greeks and Romans and the English of the eighteenth century; and which might at the same time persuade Somerville College that I would be worthy of a place to read Classics – Literae Humaniores, as Oxford so proudly terms it. With John Greig's and Theo Haarhoff's somewhat conflicting guidance I made a study of the classical sources of Dryden and Pope, Swift and Addison, and a few of the others whom the brilliance of these four put into the shade. It took several months, allowing for all the other activities, until my mentors thought it fit to submit in application to Oxford. I would have written it in Latin, if they had told me it would help, or in my blood.

I saw little of Michael during this time, though we wrote nearly every day. He was with his regiment in East Africa, training for the day they were needed in the Western Desert. He rose from the lowly status of bombardier, though that always sounded so powerful, and became an officer, but before the South African forces set off from Kenya for the front he contracted rheumatic fever and came home, desperately ill, with a failing heart, on a hospital ship sailing from Mombasa. It took him, as it does, many weeks to recover, and it left him with heart trouble from then until he died of it thirty years later. Part of the problem was that he was a very large man, not bulky but very well built and tall – six foot eight and three-quarters, as he was always careful to say when strangers approached him with the inevitable query. So his physical heart, I feel sure, had to work harder than most, a burden even without the weight which I cast upon his emotional heart.

For I could not give up the idea of going away. Michael on his recovery was given a staff-training job at a large camp not far from Pretoria, therefore not a great distance from Johannesburg. Life and especially weekends began again. He didn't much enjoy teach-

ing others what he had learned without any personal experience of
warfare. 'Those who can, do,' he used to quote with Shavian mal-
ice against himself, 'and those who can't, teach.' All the same, he
imagined that even before the war ended, because we were both
earning, we could have some kind of life together in Johannesburg
– marriage even, or marriage after the war and when he had
returned to architecture and, in two years' time, qualified; but if
that were to be the plan, what I imagined, with increasing convic-
tion as the war drew to its close, was that the pressures to stay in
South Africa would become insuperable: good professions, enough
money, security, servants, comfort. All of these were considered by
others a great attraction, and certainly known by all, including me,
to be an extreme contrast to what might await us in England –
even though Michael was as clear as I that England was the ultimate goal.

Whatever the indices, the prospect of further involvement with
the insolubles and inequities of South Africa seemed intolerable. I
did not trust myself to deal adequately, or at all, with the conflict
within myself between aesthetic and intellectual interests and my
longing to be of some use in allaying the suffering I saw around
me. I think this dilemma exists in many young people in most societies. My own daughter, Victoria, has faced it squarely, growing up
in England and, a little, in America; dividing her life and effort into
the two streams – social service and the study of literature – and
successfully riding on the tide of each. She has shown me the bifur-
cated way which, perhaps, I should have chosen. But I was not
strong or clear or courageous enough; and full of fear. The war had
done nothing towards reducing racial frictions or reforming attitudes between black and white and it had placed even greater stress
between English and Afrikaner, since very many of the latter had
hoped for a German victory. Indeed, the years before and during
the war saw an alarming resurgence of militant Afrikaner nationalism. It was this as much as a sense of hopelessness about black–
white issues which fostered in me the desperate need to escape. I
feared the violence of these people, the intensity and the narrow

channels of their hatreds which made their emotions and grievances seem to flow with directed force. I cannot claim prescience, but it happens that I had good reason to fear them; for as things turned out, they very nearly cost Michael his life.

Under the military mesmerism and the pseudo-scientific race doctrines of Nazi Germany, an extreme strand of Afrikaner nationalism blossomed, if that is the word, into a paramilitary body with its own stormtroopers, known as the Ossewa-Brandwag, 'the sentinels of the ox-wagon'. These men wore Voortrekker beards and leather-girt uniforms (as their political descendants still do, the latter-day 'Bitter-enders'). Nobody doubted that they were armed, and at the beginning of the war they were often to be seen marching and drilling in small, tight groups in the streets – stimulated to this display, no doubt, by the presence of uniformed soldiers of the South African Defence Force.

It is fair to stress that only some Afrikaner nationalists supported the Ossewa-Brandwag, and not all of those actually joined it. To hear some of the English speak, even today, one might suppose that Afrikanerdom as a whole supported the Nazis. This is possibly because no one of older generations can forget that on 4 September 1939 General Smuts took South Africa into the war by a margin of only 13 votes out of 147. The long animosity between Boer and Briton dates at least from the British abolition of slavery at the Cape and was enormously boosted by the Boer War and the terrible suffering of displaced Boer women and children in the concentration camps. These are the deep undercurrents which brought the dissenting politicians of 1939 into parliament – into politics at all. It does not follow that on the issue of Nazism and Hitler's war they were necessarily representative of their constituents or of the Afrikaner people as a whole.

At the university, however, we became gradually aware of yet another manifestation of resurgent Afrikaner nationalism and the threat it posed to all that most of us held right and true. This was the formation in 1939 of the Nasionale Instituut vir Christelike Onderwys en Opvoeding – the National Institute for Christian

Education and Instruction. Its aim was to reinforce and widen the basis for 'culturally separate education' in all schools and colleges. It was an elaboration, in some ways a sort of intellectual upgrading, of the separatist doctrines which have had a history among Afrikaners as long as there has been white settlement. Afrikaans language and literature were to be given the greatest emphasis and there was to be insistence on the fundamentalist, racist and anti-Darwinian doctrines of the Dutch Reformed Church of that period – and all that was implied by that for the teaching of the natural and the social sciences. One-third of its members were said to be teachers and all were Afrikaners. In the Arts Department of the university, most of us were teachers too, or teachers in training, or anyhow unwilling to be brothers and sisters with teachers, or anyone else, who thought like that. We felt threatened and we felt the whole population and the future of the country to be threatened. We were not mistaken: apartheid descended upon the country, and who could have foreseen when or even whether it would be lifted?

So the attractions of staying on in South Africa seemed to me bound to be, at best, short-term. I could not believe that the country had any future other than an agonising approach to an appalling, interminable war between white and black, probably preceded by a smaller war between English and Afrikaner; both of them wars which none of the parties could win since in a modern state none could properly exist without the goodwill of the others.

I had to leave – and yet Michael was there. He always regarded England as his home, since he was born and grew up there, but when war broke out he was with his family in South Africa and there he meant to stay 'for the duration', bound to the army and bound by his sense of where an evil lay in wait for the entire world. On every count I felt torn and trapped, like a netted animal. But I never doubted that I had to go; and I had also to leave my mother and her unremitting hostility to Michael, which made it impossible for me to stay with her even when – especially when – he was on leave in Johannesburg. And when it gradually became clear that (thanks to the efforts of almost everyone except myself) there would be a recognisable Great Britain to go to, the longing turned into a compulsion.

So even before hearing whether Somerville College had received my application I engineered the first really serious alibi and resigned from my job at Wits and indeed from everything else, acquired a permit to leave the country and went off to stay with Elizabeth in Cape Town, to wait for any kind of ship which would take me to England. My mother, glad to get me away from Michael, had given me enough money for the fare. With what I had saved from my salary I hoped to get by until it was clear whether she might also give me a small allowance and pay my College fees. She would not commit herself in advance about this, since she saw my dependence, as always, as a useful sanction if the need should arise. My hope was to get to Oxford and finish there as soon as possible and make a home for Michael to come to, in London, or somewhere – anywhere, but not Johannesburg, not anywhere in South Africa.

I called it, to Michael and everyone else, a 'devoted desertion', but of course it hurt and humiliated him. We did not, exactly, argue about it. He saw, I believe, that I could not accept South Africa, and to a certain extent he shared my feelings about that. But he thought that if I could only postpone my Gadarene rush we could have more time together. He told me, much later, that he thought this each time he felt his physical heart to be wavering in its function. It would not have been in character for him to have brought that to my attention.

Anyway, I went. I have no recollection of how I said 'goodbye' to him. I remember Mark's tearful eyes on the station platform in Johannesburg as he weaved about among other people, trying not to be seen by my mother, who was also in tears. I remember Zoë and Ruth giving me a beautiful leather purse, and John Greig a copy of Blake's Dante illustrations; a few other friends. If Michael had been there, surely I would have remembered that? It's no good arguing with memory, for if it has let you down it will never tell you. It is not a confesser, even if you pose as its confessor.

Elizabeth had been demobbed and was working in Cape Town. She kindly put up with my sorrowing but determined presence and I hung around for some weeks for a place on a ship; and at length, shortly before VE day, I secured a passage on RMS *Andes*, serving as a troopship, and three difficult weeks later arrived in Liverpool. I went to stay with my Aunt Mary in Surrey, one of my mother's sisters, whose address I had given, of course, to Michael; but there were never any letters from him until the end of that summer, nearly three months later.

I wrote to him very often. It felt like sending out messages in bottles upon the ocean. Rather reluctantly, but hoping that a few glimpses of those extraordinary times in post-war Britain may interest 'those who live now' (as, some 2500 years ago, the greatest of ancient Greek historians conceived his readership!). I will put into the next chapter some extracts from letters I wrote him at the beginning of this most embracing of all my alibis. Months after his death I discovered that, so far from destroying them unread, as I had many times imagined, he had carefully labelled and dated them in a little brown paper concertina-file which, again confined for many weeks to hospital, he had made himself.

22 Not exactly Union-Castle

～⌒～

Waiting for a ship, I had no idea of what kind of ship. I would have gone (I thought then) on a submarine, had it been offered; or a little caravel under tiny sails – a virtual fishing boat not 100 feet long, which was all that Bartolomeu Dias had (though he had three) for discovering the southern continent. Sometimes I indulged the foolish hope that, in spite of the total disruption of the world's transports, one day I would see, nobly steaming into Table Bay, the well-known and much-loved, beautiful lines and colours of a Union-Castle mail steamship, such as those on which I had often sailed Home with my mother.

Out of Elizabeth's kitchen window I yearned, like Madame Butterfly, to see this wonderful ship approaching, even though from my personal Pinkerton it was to take me away. From Elizabeth's kitchen window in Claremont one could not actually see Table Bay since it is on the other side of Table Mountain, but I had only to gaze at the mountain to envisage it brooding over the flat, blue waters of its bay beyond; and there would be (one fine day ...) in its lee, coming slowly towards me, a towering lilac hull, its dignity enlivened by peeping scarlet petticoats at the water-line, broad scarlet funnel, black-topped (to mask any smoke-stains – what careful dressers they are!), softly steaming, its fires abated for the land-fall ...

I sent Michael a sheaf of poems before I left Cape Town. All except one were about the misery of leaving him, which of course he couldn't have found very impressive. The one about something else was a sort of long and undisciplined *haiku* addressed to the Union-Castle liner which seemed never to come, comparing the tantalising glimpses of its red petticoat with the red flanks and lower wing-coverts (which I called 'the linings of its sleeves') of the Cape robins, which they flash as they make their impulsive little ascents. And, I'm afraid, likening the black rings which mask the smokestains on the funnel to the black rings round the eyes of white 'native' cattle, which the Chief once told me were specially prized because these black rings fooled off the flies from their eyes. Michael thought this poem was comically grotesque. So do I – now.

My departure, my voyage, did not happen in any poetic way, of course.

◢

RMS ANDES April 27th 1945. At sea. As to my whereabouts, that is all that I know, and certainly what I feel. Somebody said, this morning, 'near Buenos Aires', but it cannot have been a reliable person since proper people do not, as you know, 'talk about ships or shipping'. Which is why, my dearest, I could not let you know that I had finally got a passage.

Anyway, we are in convoy, going rather slowly. The ships certainly talk to each other, in their shiply way, especially at night. They sort of moan, in what they think is a gentle way, though it wakes most of us up. So what, if not shipping, do they talk about? I wonder if submarines would be able to hear them? Or aircraft? No lights of any kind are allowed on deck, not even cigarettes, which suggests that there could be unwanted aircraft. So perhaps the ships say nothing interesting, just make noises so as not to bump into each other in the dark. Could we be taken for whales?

It is very, very hot, especially as most of us were all togged up with woollies against the English Spring. Well, we South Africans were, I think about thirty of us. In my dormitory, F1, which holds about 200, all the rest are women coming back to England from Australia, many of them with quite small children. They do not have winter woollies, or anything much else. They keep very much to themselves, in different groups that have formed during the weeks that it took them to get as far as Cape Town.

We sleep on narrow iron bunks four – four – high, and this, apart from a small suitcase, is the only personal space we have; so everyone hangs up their garments all round their bunk on every available space, and this keeps out all vision and light and air, and it is smelly and close. The clothes sway all the time, but only with the rolling of the ship, not with zephyrs. The children play hiding games in these endless corridors of clothes, some high, the tots low down, and they get lost, and howl, and the mothers can't find them quickly enough and get ratty and anxious.

Apart from the dormitory, and the seething crowds on the decks and in the lounges, and the inability to wash etc. properly, things are not too awful. Not exactly Union-Castle, but an experience I shall not ever forget. Anyway, the food is good and the tables are clean and the meals are punctual – at rather uncongenial hours: 6.30 a.m., 11.30 a.m. and 5.45 p.m. We have, or are, the first sitting, because of the children, I suppose. The feeding of the multitude on this huge and crowded ship must take a miracle of organisation and endless work for the modern galley slaves.

Darling! Because of the hot weather we, the women of F1, have now been given permission to sleep on deck! We are guarded by the RAF on board who, together with many soldiers and sailors, occupy the lower decks. The soldiers and sailors we never see and know nothing about. There are always RAF sentries on the ladders that lead up from the lower to the top deck, where we are, so that there shall be no comings-up or goings-down (goings-on, in short). The deck is a very hard lie, but at least one doesn't fall out of bed if one rolls over, and it is cool, or cooler. It is wonderful to lie on one's

*back and look up at the stars. If you were here beside me – well for
one thing you would know, astronomer as you have become, where
we were, roughly. I have never seen stars so bright and various, and
also variously coloured. I did not know that, before. I've always
been rather scared of looking at the stars at all, but now I can see
that there are not only silvers or whites but yellows and blues, and
even a couple of pinks! I lie and watch the mast, or rather the tall
black line where one knows the mast to be, sway stiffly from side
to side as the ship rolls, briefly blacking out sequences of stars as it
moves; and you can hear the swish on the sea of the ship's
progress; and there is no women's clothing confining one's outlook
to an arm's length. I try to secure a place on deck that is near the
railings so that I can also lean over and see the phosphorescent
flashing as the ship cuts through it. Whatever it is. Sometimes it is
very bright. If there were any of the Luftwaffe above us, what
would they make of the ship-shaped bright arrows in the water, all
pointing the same way in strict formation? With the cigarettes and
every other light so carefully blacked out …*

⌐

May 8th 1945 VE day!
*The Captain told us so, over the tannoy. Everybody became
emotional. We have no way to express joy or relief, or to celebrate
in any ordinary way (a dry ship, of course). I have a few friends –
Anne, Peggy, Mae, Boris, Dave, and we began to tell our life
histories, with amazing frankness, for comparative strangers. We
certainly, the tellers at the time of telling, wept a little. What an
amazing day. One was aware of the approach of it, Victory I
mean; but anything could have delayed it. Without any news bul-
letins, how is one to know. And before it happens you cannot
imagine it, like someone you love being dead; I cannot think of a
joyful simile. Giving birth to a child perhaps, something that
changes the entire world from that moment onwards. I long for
you all the time, and have felt, most dreadfully, so sad, so unreal,*

in such pain, that you were not with me on this day.

☞

We have been parking for a couple of days outside Gibraltar. From early in the evening it is all lit up! Every torch and candle, I should think, after six years of blackout. On the top deck I sat under a gun turret, for shade, and began a drawing of the Rock, to send to you, since no photography is allowed. The Captain (no less), who looks like Mr Punch, came and stuck his long nose and chin over my shoulder and said that it was illegal to make drawings, but that mine didn't matter as it just looked like a doodle. Sensing that he might have hurt me, he altered that to – no, well, it does look like something; it looks like a muffin. That is what he said.

☞

Dearest M – something so wonderful! We were guided through the Straits by an American airship. How do they have the courage to use them, after the terrible fate of the Hindenburg? *Do you remember those pictures of it on fire, tethered to its mooring tower in, I think, New York? At Gibraltar we saw in the sky not very far above us this enormously long and elegant silver fish, mackerel-shaped, more-or-less, and suspended from it a long, transparent cage or gondola, or whatever they call it, in which were dozens of pink men; that is, entirely naked American airmen. I suppose it was built for downward observations; anyway, when they saw our ship-ful of women they became quite excited and jumped about, waving; whether from joy or embarrassment, who knows? Not many naked people, I guess, like to be looked at from beneath.*

Mysteriously, for after all we have had VE day, even if only for a few hours, we had to join a much bigger convoy which came out of the Med., with several more Destroyers, and for a while the sky was full of strange white *aircraft. Do you think they were Red Cross or hospital planes? If not, why are they white? It feels bad*

*and dangerous to say all this shipping and aircraft stuff; but it will
be ages, I expect, before I can post this; and perhaps even the
Japanese war will be over by then.*

May 24th. Sanderstead, at Aunt Mary's
    *This will be a short letter, because I'm nearly asleep; just
climbed into my first proper bed in three and a half weeks. It is bitterly cold. I have climbed in with a hotwater bottle which I have
named Luke, since that is what it is. Arrival at Liverpool was total
chaos, everything. That was three days ago. Luggage from the
ship's hold was dumped, forming a mountain range, on the quay.
To prevent real mayhem we approached it according to instructions
from a loudspeaker and according to first letter of one's surname. It
took nearly two days to get to the Ps for Pryce. If I had known, I
would have travelled as Fanny Adams. For those two days Anne
(Sproat, therefore even later in the queue) and I just hung about the
docks, living on hot tea from kind ladies with an urn and sleeping
wherever we could stretch out. The cold was indescribable. Boris,
who is a W, disappeared to some barracks or other with some airmen, apologising for the unusual (so he said) advantage of being a
male.*
    *How to handle one's trunks? We ogled soldiers, I'm afraid. I
ogled two but one of them smashed his thumb and went off.
Somehow the remaining one and I got the stuff – all my worldly
goods – onto the right van of the right train. The real trouble began
when, hours later, we arrived at St Pancras. It was 9.30 p.m. No
soldiers to ogle. We hoisted trunks and pushed trolleys, and other
people out of the way, and broke fingernails and tore our clothes
and hair. I spent pounds in twopences for the phone, trying to get a
hotel room, but the receptionists laughed tiredly. At midnight Anne
and I were trying to make ourselves a little cabin of trunks on the
platform so that we could huddle up and not die of cold, when an
incredible thing happened. A lorryload of people drove slowly
along the platform and shouted to us to get in, and said a following
van would get our luggage. Without a second of hesitation we did*

so; could easily have been white slave traffic; and it took us to a London County Council Hostel in Bloomsbury! Now I know what Heaven will look like: a converted school gym with rows of bunks that are only two high; and trestle tables with hot food dished out by more kindly ladies, calling one 'dearie'. They were superb. Nobody would take any money, and probably they, and the LCC, saved our lives, for it was so dreadfully cold outside.

In the morning – this very morning, in fact – I got through to my Aunt Mary, who works at a solicitor's office in the City. She was so kind and welcoming and within an hour or so she and I were on a train to Sanderstead, with all my luggage. It was, and is, hard to believe I am here.

It is very hard, too, not to find a letter from you. It takes a bit of the gilt off one which has come from Somerville saying they will 'with great pleasure' give me a place, starting at the Michaelmas term. If you know when Michaelmas is, please will you write and tell me? Please will you write and tell me anything; any blessed thing?

23 The promised land

In the summer and autumn of 1945, before going up to Oxford for my first term, I wrote to Michael nearly every day. The letters from London written during that crucial summer after the war are for the most part a pain to read. It could have been a marvellous time to write about, as the world woke after a long nightmare to find itself free; a time that people would want to know about. Well; sorry, people. I was so unhappy, so guilty, so angry, most of the time, that what mostly they reveal is only me and my continuing struggles with the difficult thoughts, emotions and relationships that I had brought with me from South Africa.

I cannot merely excise, as I have done from those in the previous chapter, the many passages which in various dosages express devotion, longing, guilt and concern. Some of these London letters of 1945 do describe some things which may be of interest to 'those who live now': what London was like after six appalling years, and when the American programme of Lend–Lease had stopped (the day after VE day!) and not enough people had yet been demobilised to look after the essential services or even the shops, and tens of thousands of people had descended upon the capital to start new lives (like me), and the American soldiers and airmen had not yet departed from it, 'over-paid, over-sexed and over here', and all that. But except for the first few, written before I had heard about the terrible thing that had happened to Michael, these descriptions are not at the heart of the letters.

Now that I read them through, these decades later, I can clearly
see the conflicts which caused me so much pain and depression.
Had I been able to do so at the time, I might have found a way
through the suffering and written more entertaining accounts of a
city which was celebrating, in spite of its wrecked appearances and
all the grief at its heart, a victory as telling for our world and our
beliefs as that of the Greeks over the Persian Empire two and a half
thousand years before.

It's obvious that I should have begun to feel more keenly than
ever the fact that I had in no way contributed to this victory – had
declined to do so. It's obvious that without Michael I should have
felt lonely and deprived, and that I was sad and guilty at having left
him. All these themes were brutally reinforced by the news that
only a few days after I had left Cape Town, Michael had been savagely attacked and left for dead; he was found with his skull
smashed in, spinal fluid leaking from his nose, one eye almost
gouged out. It happened one evening while he was with a small
group of friends at an open-air function in aid of 'the war effort',
an Air Force fair. His attackers were a group of about fifteen bearded and uniformed young Afrikaners of the Ossewa-Brandwag,
roaming about looking for ways in which to express, I suppose,
their manhood and nationhood. They spotted that Michael, in his
officer's uniform, was wearing the red shoulder tabs which showed
that a soldier had volunteered for active service beyond the borders
of the country; so they tried to kill him, and very nearly did, and
when he was down on the ground they tried to finish him off by
smashing a large stone into his skull.

He was so seriously ill that no one, not my mother and not, for
some time, his parents, wrote to tell me about it. Meanwhile I was
writing letter after letter and getting no replies. I heard about it,
almost a month after arriving, at third- or fourth-hand from a
friend in London, and cabled to Mark Prestwich to get me a full
and proper account and prognosis, which he did with characteristic
thoroughness, rushing up from Natal to see him and to interview

the doctors. It was a protracted and harrowing story after that, with many operations to repair a fractured skull and broken nose, reposition an eye, and at the end of all that several rounds of plastic surgery and eye and jaw and dental operations. He was in and out of different hospitals, according to the expertise required, for many months. I could not get back to be with him for I had, almost literally, no money. All I could do was to write, which I did in every spare moment; but was so distraught that, as I have said, most of my letters are too full of misery to reproduce. When he was able, he began to send rather brief replies. Each one shot me into joyous overdrive for a few days during which I was able to observe the world around me with something like clarity and confidence.

The cold struck me most, as it was bound to do. There was no fuel to spare for heating in homes, hotels, shops, trains, anywhere except where the armed forces or the government required it to be: getting the army and the prisoners home, by air and sea and road; getting the supply ships going across the Atlantic and to – and especially from – the Commonwealth; rescuing the building industry, repairing shattered cities.

After the cold, the greatest burden was the shortage of food. With the ending of Lend–Lease food had become scarcer, it is said, than at any time during the war. I am writing this chapter in South Africa in 1998, a country of thriving agriculture and, at the same time, for Freedom does not of itself fill pockets, of extensive poverty and malnutrition; so I shall not dwell unduly on how scant and unappetising was the food in post-war Britain. As most people know, owing both to generous food provision from the United States and the strict and fair British rationing of it, the national nutrition during the war was in fact better than it has ever been, before or since. Immediately after the war, it lurched downwards. In London, while I was responsible for my own feeding after I left Aunt Mary's, I became fairly ill from lack of food. It was largely because I spent what little money I had (my mother cut off my allowance when I left my aunt's) on theatres and concerts, queuing for hours to get the cheapest seats, and ate little but dry bread and raw cooking apples. The small weekly rations of eggs (if any), cheese, bacon (called 'American belly fat'!) and meat were eaten in a meal or two. After a few weeks I told Michael with great dismay that I had become bloated and pimply and that he would do better to find some other woman; but he sent me some money instead.

Another topic that my early letters were full of was dirt; not only in the streets. I was a young, white middle-class South African and in addition to complete ineptitude at cooking (although I considered that I knew all about laundering and ironing) I simply did not know that rooms had to be dusted and swept every day and dishes properly washed and dustbins emptied. I thought that all that side of life, which in my home the servants had performed, was more or less due to my mother's setting such high standards and having such a big establishment. It is time to give a picture of the very small flat that I found.

June 6th 1945

Dearest M,

Still no letter from you. Why, why, why? You could have told me you were going to ditch me. I have been here three whole weeks and it feels like three years. I can't blame all of that on you. Staying at Sanderstead is really impossibly empty. Did I come here to moulder? I go to London most days on the horrible trains and the worse undergrounds and by the time I have found my way about among all the crowds it is almost time to catch the train back. My aunt and uncle are out working all day. So if I stay here until I go to Oxford in October, there is only my old grandfather's Complete Leather-bound Dickens Edition, and old Tapioca who sleeps on my bed purring at his own dreams. Did I tell you about Tapioca – dear old tabby with fat cheeks and square paws?

June 8th

I will do so later, since now there is real news to impart! I have found a little London flat! It sort of fell into my lap, being discarded by a complete stranger. It is almost small enough to fall into a lap, too.

It's in quite a grand neighbourhood, though. It's the basement of what looks (from the outside) like quite a respectable Georgian terrace in Manchester St, just behind the Wallace Collection, not far off Baker St. Manchester St is trim and wide and has a large, old notice up, saying ' Organ Grinders and Street Criers are not Permitted'. What a pity! The grinding and crying would be something to tell our grandchildren about. I will have to stress all the socially acceptable aspects when I tell Mother about it, because the flat, in itself, is extremely small and dark. Quite a good place to hide, anyway. I am reminding myself of something I came across this very morning in grandfather's Dombey and Son: *'Perhaps there was never smaller entry and staircase than the entry and staircase of Miss Tox's house. Perhaps, taken altogether, from top to bottom, it was the most inconvenient little house in England, and the crookedest; but then, Miss Tox said, what a situation! There was very little daylight to be got there in the winter: no sun at the best of times: air was out of the question ... Still Miss Tox said, think of the situation!'*

Well, I suppose my 'entry' is alright since it shares it with the whole handsome house but, once in, you dive down a sneaky, creaky side stair to a small space in which there is a telephone on the floor and a leather pouffe. That is the Hall. There is one bedroom – Ann and Mae from the boat are going to share with me (which is why I can afford it, though the rent is amazingly low) so two of us will have to sleep on the floor. We are used to a ship's deck, anyway. A small living room, for small living, and a kitchen and bathroom which are one and the same, sharing their plumbing. It is all extremely dark, dirty and dingy and we are all delighted.

We will in due course try to clean it, even re-paint it; but somehow one gets used to dirt. As you can imagine, London streets (when you can see them for the crowds) are filthy. No street cleaners. There are rubbish bins and there are Pig Bins, and one is supposed not to confuse the two, but there seem to be people who think pigs can eat tins and rags and things. Quite often I have seen people, usually old people, poking hopefully in the Pig Bins. This morning, struggling with the latchkey of the flat for the first time, I was a few feet from a very ragged old lady who was grunting and fishing in the Pig Bin and urinating the while, down her thick wrinkled stockings.

The streets in London which seem the cleanest are those which have been extensively bombed and then, some time after the Heavy Rescue, I suppose, cleared up. There are broken bits of walls standing, with rough edges and exposed interiors with shreds of different-coloured wallpapers, and many have marks of burning. They are quiet and still, some of them sprinkled prettily with the long shoots and pink flowers of 'bomb-weed', which is Rosebay Willowherb. They are deadly neat, in the way that graves are. Last week I plucked up courage and went to Finsbury Park – Ossian Road and Ferme Park Road – where two strands of Mother's family were bombed out, before they moved to Sanderstead. I have not told her that I went. She gets very upset at it all. Anyway, that is what those places looked like, where I used to stay as a child. My dear old Grandfather was killed there. They say he would never go down to the Shelter but just cursed 'the Boche' from the comfort of his bed.

Round Sanderstead though, and the Croydon district, after they moved out there, the bombing became very bad. My Aunt says they had more of the 'flying bombs' there than anywhere else. You can still see some horrible shambles, gaunt and shattered wrecks of houses and people still live in some of them, crowded into the basements. She says that every night when the sirens went Tapioca, who was brought with them from Ferme Park Rd (shut in the meatsafe), used to dart down to the shelter before anyone else. I was going to tell you about Tapioca but now I haven't the heart.

⤙

June 20th

Darling M, still no letter from you. I have been trying to paint the flat before Ann and Mae get here and spread their stuff all over it. It is depressing to have to do it so badly – not sandpapering, not cleaning out cracks, just smearing white gloss over it all. Thinking about you, I flung down the brush, like Mole, and said 'Bother Spring Cleaning' and caught the tube and the train down to Sanderstead to see if there might be a letter from you. I had forgotten I no longer had a key. Tried peering through the letterflap to see if there was post; there was, upside down on the floor, illegible. It alerted Tapioca who sat in the hall mewing. He is lonely, too. I went round to the back door – locked of course; tried the fanlight – bolted of course. Tappy kept going in and out of his cat-flap, to show me how easy it was. In the end I climbed onto the roof of the kitchen, which sticks out at the back, and found my old bedroom window unlatched.

There were letters, none from you so none of interest. I feel so sad and exhausted, I can't face travelling back to London. I will stay the night here, start another Dickens, talk to Tappy, best friend.

Later:

Dear God, dear Michael; you will not believe –

When my Aunt came home she told me that Mother had written to tell her to tell me that if I didn't give up the flat and return to Sanderstead, she would cut off my allowance and write to Oxford to cancel my place! I feel sure she can't do that, the cancelling. I am, after all, 21. And a half. But it will make a real fool of me, won't it. And of her. And, even if Somerville ignores her, what on earth shall I do about their fees? They are not going to ignore those. I really can hardly believe that this is happening; nothing

worse than this could happen, could it? Could it? What about why
you are not writing to me?

Do you think you could go and reason with her? I suppose that
(even if willing) you might be the wrong person. Mark, as you
know, she will not let inside her door. I feel I cannot possibly
involve Greig or Haarhoff in my family affairs, so ridiculous and
shaming. So I will look for a job, for the present, and try for a
scholarship for the future – though I doubt if scholarships and
grants etc. have been started again …

I have reached the promised land, but the promise seems
broken, or missing or some other negative. I suppose it was only I
who promised it to me. Whatever sort of job can I get? Have own
typewriter and that's about it. Poetry will not get me far.

But curiously enough it was, in a way, poetry that led to my ascent
out of this pit. At Wits, as I have said, John had invited me to give
a course of lectures on twentieth-century poetry. In the course of
the research I had come across several volumes of *Poetry London*,
edited by Tambimuttu. So, stranded in London and in life, as I supposed, I went to see Tambimuttu to ask what sort of job a stranger
might ask for.

He was very beautiful: brown and soulful, exactly like the
famous portrait of him by Augustus John, and very helpful too. In
addition to gentle and intelligent advice he gave me a letter to the
editor of an international literary review called *Adam*, who turned
out to be a surprising, enterprising, volatile, restless, histrionic, lov-
able and unpredictable Romanian intellectual called Miron
Grindea. Tambimuttu said that Miron always needed help since he
organised, from no base at all, ambitious and resounding schemes,
not only the monthly issues of *Adam* but all sorts of meetings and
performances besides, and was constantly in touch with all the
great ones of English, American, French and general European literature and music. That's how it was, too.

July 28th 1945

*... I found this Miron in the library of the London
Philharmonic, where, in some way, he works. The minute he read
Tambimuttu's note he flew into his temperament, very nearly
embraced me, said he couldn't think in this pigsty of an office
where he earns his living: (what, if without thinking, at ?) and
pushed me downstairs into the Philharmonic Library, which
seemed in an equal mess – only its temporary quarters, though.
Begged me, very courteously and ceremoniously, to be seated; but
there were no chairs so he tore upstairs again and brought a minute
camp stool, such as one queues for theatres upon, and he sat on the
floor. I cannot possibly record the conversation which followed. It
was disjointed and mostly in French and continually interrupted by
comers and goers, musicians and the like, manoeuvring big,
unwieldy instruments. After a while we repaired to a café, more
talk, poetry, music, food. To judge from what followed the next
day, he thinks I agreed to become 'secretary' of the International
Arts Guild, 'co-editor' of* Adam, *'editor' of an anthology of S.
African Poetry, about which he seems to have been in correspondence with Haarhoff. I feel certain I did not agree to any of this,
but the next morning he appeared at the flat – he refuses to work
in his 'pigsty' – with a string bag full of papers and confidently said
we should get down to work! Well, he is keen to get* Adam *revived
with a series of Big Names. My part is in fact simply that of secretary, since I have a typewriter and have at least heard of all Great
Ones he talks about!*

*What he does, in rapid spatterings of English, French and (I
suppose) Romanian, is to tell me the sort of letter he wishes to
write to so-and-so and roughly what to ask them to do and to
apologise for not being able to pay them for any contribution they
may be kind enough to make. He rushes off. I compose and then
type these letters, in either French or English, and when he returns
he seems pleased and signs them. Would you like to know who the
'so-and-so's' are? Well, the first day it was T.S. Eliot, Cecil Day*

*Lewis, Denis Saurat, André Gide, Pablo Casals and Jacob
Epstein ... He insists that, whatever the language, or their national-
ity, each should be addressed as 'Cher Maître'. The only one for
whom I have refused to do this is Viscount Samuel, at the House of
Lords. I felt sure it would get him a bad name; but at the same
time had not the faintest idea of the wording due to him. I decided
to be full-bloodedly Johnsonian: 'My Lord, Your Lordship may
recall that ...' etc. etc., and ending with 'I have the honour to be
Your Lordship's most obliged, humble servant ...'. Miron was lost
in admiration; he thought it éblouissant and signed it with a flour-
ish. I bet the noble Samuel will be amused.*

*The next day Ann and I were still at breakfast when he arrived
with more letters for me to do. He gives me no more than a sort of
poetic impression of the effect which each letter is supposed to create: to Georges Duhamel (you know how much I admire him – he
nearly wrecked our first weekend in Pretoria; or was that the pur-
gatorial Dante, as you put it?), Benjamin Britten, Augustus John,
Louis MacNeice, Stephen Spender. It is all to do with the International Guild thing and a reading by Cecil Day Lewis of his translation of Valéry's 'Le Cimetière marin', at which Eliot is to take the
chair, or so we hope; and he is also canvassing articles and poems
for the magazine. Drinks my cup of coffee, kisses my hands, says I
am the blotting paper for his tears and rushes off.*

*Half an hour later he is back, thundering on the door in
extreme agitation. Ann and I groan. I have not yet finished my
replacement coffee. I open the door and he yells at me the astounding news of the Labour Victory! We embrace feverishly and fall
down the stairs together, smashing the 'phone. He stays to lunch,
several other friends come in, all bubbling with political joy and
astonishment. Miron is rather rude to them; we all go out, bursting
with glee, talk too much, drink too much. Miron gets jealous, says
I must go home and get the letters done, I refuse, he fumes off.
First thing next morning ... guess what.*

The celebrations of the Labour victory (when 'The Red Flag', as I told Michael in breathless wonder, was sung in the House of Commons) were as nothing, of course, compared with those in the following month, of the victory over Japan: VJ day and night, which went on for several days and nights. On the day that the first news of the atom bomb broke, 7 August, Miron and I, unknowing, were travelling in a bus to the Ministry of Information press room which was then occupying part of University College. The streets seemed normal; not many cars (even for those days) or undue numbers of people. When we arrived, we had obviously just missed something enormous. It was not lunch time yet the great press room was empty and all its rows of phones deserted. The correspondents, whom we quickly joined, had all filed their reports and were jabbering to each other, in many languages, in the foyer of the refectory, desperate not so much to eat as to talk about what Hiroshima could portend.

August 8th 1945

There was no hope of lunch, and Miron had to file his story, so I caught a bus to go home. By this time the news of the Bomb had trickled outside the walls. Showers of torn paper were beginning to flutter down from the windows, odd groups, very many Americans, were beginning to gather and to jig on the pavements and quite soon all over the road. After about ten minutes, the bus had to stop, so thick had the crowds become. I got off and tried to walk down Oxford St to Marble Arch. It took more than an hour to get even half way! The paper from the windows became a snowstorm, lay thick upon such corners of the pavement as could, for the crowds, be seen. The crowds were grinning and gabbling like lunatics. Aeroplanes began to tear about the skies making smoke patterns and dropping queer green floating lights. I was snatched by an enormous American officer and lost the scarf from my head before I managed to escape. I tried my best to assume an air of

jubilation and agreed with him, as he bobbed me up and down in
an insane sort of dance, that it was certainly the greatest day in his-
tory. His kisses smelled of beer and the buttons on his chest hurt
my nose which was jigged up and down the vertical of them. I was,
of course, tired and very hungry but mostly felt stunned and
appalled, thinking only of the Bomb.

I did not think it meant the end of the war. I had not taken in the
extent of the annihilation at Hiroshima but even if I had, I thought
that nothing on the earth, even if it came blasting down from the
sky and then blasting up again, to cover the earth with its destruction, would make the Japanese surrender. Well, everyone else in
Britain, so it seemed, all those screaming, foolish crowds, that crazy
great American soldier, knew more than I did.

The following couple of nights I would not go out. I could not
face again the frantic crowds, the panic from firecrackers, the
drunken men, the lurching women with paper hats which said
'Hello Yank' or 'Kiss me, Honey', the squeakers and rattles and
streamers. The little flat again became a mini-centre for everyone's
friends and in turn for their friends; we were nearly all South
Africans, several of them soldiers returning from prison camps.
When our supplies of beer, as a rule fetched in saucepans from the
nearest 'jug and bottle' department, ran out, most people moved off
to 'see the bonfires in Piccadilly' and so on. I was as thankful as
any non-combatant can be that the war was finished but it seemed
to me a time for sorrow and reflection as much as joy. I stayed at
home, with the quieter ones. With one of these, an old Johannesburg friend, Tom Bright, of cherubic face entirely inconsonant with
a fierce nature – wide blue eyes and flaxen hair under the assertive
red beret of the Parachute Regiment – I went to a Promenade concert on the day the news came that the Japanese Emperor had, in
fact, withdrawn his country from the war. It truly was the prayed-
for, fought-for, died-for End.

August 15th 1945

It was an amazing evening at the Albert Hall. A Mozart–
Schumann evening, as full as ever, no room for the promenaders
to promenade or to sit down, even at the back. Tom and I had
Miron's press tickets (foolishly I'd said I'd write tonight's review
for him) so at least we had proper seats for once, even if almost on
top of the percussion. Before things began, a loudspeaker
announcement said that at 9 p.m. there would be a break between
the first and second movements of the 'Jupiter' for the relay of a
speech to the nation by His Majesty. This was astonishing enough,
but even more incredible, we thought, was the fact that the
announcement was greeted by an enormous murmur from the
crowd – which quite clearly resolved itself into boos and hisses!
Everyone knew, by this time, of the surrender, of course. All the
same, I and even Tom the Tough felt the need for the King to say
so; though God would have been better.

When the time came, Basil Cameron having made a superb first
movement of the 'Jupiter', conducting without a score, and all the
hundreds of people exhilarated and entranced – when the break
came there was for a few moments almost a riot. 'Carry on, carry
on!' from many quarters of the hall, especially the promenaders.
Cameron was very angry, though he said nothing. We had a close
¾ view of him. His face turned red and he walked stolidly to the
empty piano stool and sat down, glaring at the crowd. When the
Anthem came from the wireless a few moments later, all the thou-
sands sprang at once to attention and there were no more distur-
bances. Except at one stage when H.M. said something about the
biggest fruit of the Peace being prosperity. At that there was a dis-
tinctly scornful rustle, or so we interpreted it. I found all this very
significant. What do you think that rustle was about? Perhaps
everyone has got used to hardship and poverty, so that 'prosperity'
seems a tastelessly exaggerated promise.

Life went on, for about two more months, in that dear and squalid little flat. I had to work hard not only for *Adam* but at Greek. I had been to see my tutor at Somerville, who received me very kindly and said they would allow me to do Honour Moderations in one year instead of two, and then knocked me down with a list of the preparatory study requirements. So I found, through the College, a superb tutor in London.

She is a tall and masterful woman married to a Russian (I think) scholar called Zvegintzov. How she drives me! And how I need it. Each day I have to give in three or four proses. At Wits we had one a week, and Sammy usually did mine anyway, as I had too many other subjects and their homeworks. The first time I went she gave me high marks and praise, until I told her that it had taken me the whole night, looking up almost every word either in the Dictionary or in the Grammar. She was very triste *about that and for that entire session rained upon my skull hard blows of passives and supines and duals and optatives. She suggests in all sobriety that I lie in a cold bath (she thinks I have a bathroom!) and sing the declensions and conjugations, inventing tunes to correspond with the intonations, until I know it so well that the next time I go under an anaesthetic, that is what I will babble ...*

Dear one, when I am dying, or similar, I do not want Goodwin's 'Greek Moods and Tenses' marching through my head. I want your beautiful voice in my ear, saying that you will not forget me. She says that when she was at Somerville she was lovesick all the time (she says I am lovesick) but she was lucky because after that she went straight 'e manu her mother in manum her husband'. I only wish she could instruct me in this risky manoeuvre, help me to weather the whopping hiatus which is my lot. Anyway, in addition to some useful Greek, she has taught me how to make a macaroni cheese. A whole family's cheese ration (she has two sons, and the mother and the husband) does well just for flavouring the sauce.

Miron was a trying taskmaster, being so disorganised, but one cannot doubt his editorial genius; he brought out *Adam*, full of the good and the great, for years and years. I had to leave him when I started at Oxford but for the time that our strange understanding lasted it greatly enlivened my life. He always seemed to have tickets for concerts; he procured me a reader's ticket for the British Museum (for research into the South African anthology) which I treasured until its expiry, which was a long time, I confess, after the idea of the anthology. After his very attractive wife, a wonderful pianist, and little daughter came back to London from the country, where they had been staying for safety, I became a 'house friend' and went there many times for a meal to discuss the 'Proms' we had all seen together.

Most of my letters of that summer are about the exhibitions, theatres and concerts which seem to have filled my days and nights and certainly emptied my purse. My mother, defeated by my intransigence but maintaining her own, had offered to put me on 'half-pay'. But John Greig, to whom I wrote all my troubles, had entered me for a generous scholarship when once again they had started up at Wits, and it had most luckily been granted. So I thought I might last in London on my own resources until Michaelmas, if I was amazingly careful. I declined the 'half-pay'.

When the war ended, London had blossomed, burst out, poured forth all the artistic triumphs which could at last be shown and staged and mounted on a scale at least adequate and often with insights and interpretations I felt to be inspired. I felt a little hesitant, I can see, about telling Michael so much about all these delights, even about the incredible richness of the music and talks which the BBC brought, free, right into one's home – a source of wonder which has never left me. After all, Michael could not in spite of my rhapsodies share any of these miracles (as they seemed to me). He was ill and I did not know how ill; facing one operation after another, writing rather seldom, and the writing wonky because he could not see very well. Also, other people's pleasures, like their dreams (or their love letters, I'm afraid), are not the compelling and vivid things they are to them, to the teller. A reader is at even greater remove than a listener so I think I will add only my account of my meeting with Eliot, who was, and is, to me so much the greatest of the 'modern poets' I had tried to encompass for my lectures at Wits.

August 10th

It seems to me that this Valéry memorial thing cannot possibly come off. It is 2 a.m. Miron went a few minutes ago. We have been sitting on the carpet since tea-time among piles of French newspapers with Valéry obituaries, trying to compose a few paragraphs which will be, Monsieur insists, not only informatifs *but also both* discrets *and* émuants *– a difficult conjunction. Not to mention* une bibliographie des oeuvres. *It is for the programme notes for the function* TONIGHT. *Until today, I did not know there were to be any. I thought that all the info and the scene-setting would be down to Prof. Saurat, who is giving the lecture before Day Lewis' lecture of the poem. But thank god this impossible task has been completed – all that remains is for me, tomorrow – no no today! – to blackmail both the paper and the printing trades and get a hundred programmes done; as Monsieur himself will be busy at some job he has at the Ministry. In the evening, he will conduct M. Saurat to the hall, so it falls to me to conduct the evening's chairman thither. Who is Eliot. All I feel is terror.*

August 12th

... the typesetter knew no French, was laboriously slow, and seethed with indignation with Miron who called in with cables from Paris and last-minute alterations to the actual facts! M. kept adding bits in his quaint English and I had to correct and alter them in the teeth of the machine and almost of the man. Meanwhile the necessary paper had not been procured or even vouchsafed. M. darted off to change – to change! I had to hover

and catch taxis and push and wail to get it all done and then rush off to Fabers to usher Eliot. I was tired, bewildered and dirty. I thought with longing of our funny little shower at the flat – a saucepan, really, kept by the hotwater tap, and a basin to stand in. And the clean dress hanging up, that I had mended and ironed for the occasion, unworn by sad and vain me.

Fabers or at any rate their building seems a battered and neglected place. I think all London offices still are that, even amid the grandeur of Russell Square. I climbed up the stairs behind the porter with no sensation beyond extreme weariness. The porter opened Eliot's door, on the first floor, and then vanished. Eliot rose quickly from his desk and came round in front of it. He was silhouetted against a big window in a small room and I could see only a very tall person offering me a hand to shake. He moved a pile of papers from a well-worn armchair, took from me the pile of programmes I was carrying, and offered a cigarette. These entirely usual courtesies nearly stunned me.

I'm not sure what I had expected. Perhaps a spiritually intense American facing me from the opposite side of an imposing desk. But this was an ageing Englishman – or so he seemed – apologetically re-arranging his room for what might have been a friendly visit. He did not go back to his desk but sat on a hard chair near me and we began to cope with the business. I had to hand him some cables (one from Duhamel, who is the president of the Guild) and other things. When he took them to the window, for the daylight, I saw again his tallness, and that he was lean, and has a 'distinguished stoop'. His face is firmly formed, rather long, cheeks somewhat hollow, a large mouth, straight across, with deep folds at the corners of it. His hair is dark, thinnish, a little grey at the temples. He has long hands, elegant and trim, almost as good as yours.

He asked questions or made comments from time to time but while he read the letters etc. I had opportunity to look around the room. Extremely untidy, covered with books and papers, on the walls many small pictures, mostly engravings of (I think) saints and

*medieval objects. A large map of Harvard University. When he had
finished reading he asked a few more questions – he was rather
vague about the evening's proceedings, or what was wanted of him.
I thought he had a fine and even voice, the only American in it a
fullness of tone. He speaks rather slowly and hesitates a lot, but
always chooses the right (or an interesting) word; as one would
expect.*

*When the business had finished he offered me another cigarette,
took one himself, and began to speak about Duhamel – what luck!
– which we were still doing when it was time to go, to walk to the
hall. He was so detachedly companionable, so quietly communica-
tive. It was raining, gently. I was ashamed that he had to carry the
programmes which, there being no suitable bag, he had wrapped in
his mackintosh. Neither of us had an umbrella. I was so absorbed
that we walked right past the hall but he was quite amused about
that, in spite of the rain.*

*Day Lewis' reading of the Valéry was superb. It was indeed a
moving occasion, as M. had hoped, because Valéry was buried, in*
le cimetière marin, *on that very day.*

*After the meeting we went to a scruffy little café near the
Museum. M. wanted to propose a toast to Eliot (in lager) but he
avoided it, covering his embarrassment by saying he was too thirsty
to wait for his first gulp. Miron, suddenly a stickler for ceremony,
transferred the toast to Day Lewis, who enjoyed it and was the
moving spirit of the meal. Eliot ate little and spoke little yet seemed
at ease and laughed a lot; smoked incessantly. I think he did not
speak much because he is distressed by the profound attention
everyone pays to his remarks; which for this reason he often ended
flippantly, to take the charge out of them. I spoke to Day Lewis
about Virgil for a long time, of whom he is an incomparable trans-
lator, and rather nettled him by strong protest when he said something foolish and derogatory about Homer. What a weird thing for
a poet and a sentient man to do! Since Homer is not a person, or
one person. Why try to belittle a mountain?*

People wonder why Eliot writes poetry no more. I can suppose that he would not, if he doesn't feel the need. He did not strike me as 'a literary man' so much as a learned man both deep and simple. If it were not for the over-smoking, I would say he was at peace.

24　The Cheshire smile

It was spring when I had arrived in England, and the cold, as I have
made plain, was the background to all experiences; but the fuel
supply was no better, the cold much worse and the food shortage
even shorter when towards the end of the year I went up to Oxford
to face the winter, let alone the rigours of the university, at
Somerville. My first letter to Michael from College recounts with a
sombre sort of pride that each person was allowed hot water for a
bath twice a week and, according to a severe notice on the wall
signed by the Bursar, no more than an inch of it. By the time an
inch had settled into the bottom of the large Victorian bathtub, it
was refrigerated, so this was a problem with no hope of solution.

Most of the rooms had a little iron grate in them, and once a
week each inmate was given a few sticks of kindling and two tiny
cakes of firelighter. Unless one went on Port Meadow or to the
Parks to collect odd bits of fallen tree, which there was never time
to do, this supply would give a meagre blaze for two or three hours
– once a week. All the same, a real, live fire warms a whole room.
Some rooms had a small electric fire in them, and the notice from
the Bursar said 'One bar, never more than five hours in twenty-
four', but they made little difference anyway. Their main function
was to lie on their backs ('as you may take turtles or women', some
brutal character in Ben Jonson remarks) and to heat enamel mugs
of water for the infusion of whatever milkless and sugarless drink

one could buy. In my letters to Michael I thought all this worth
mentioning not only to elicit his sympathy but to show what the
natives had become, over the years, entirely accustomed to. I tried
to fall in, not to complain, not to shiver. Anne Welsh – who had
been at Queensfield with me and is still among my closest friends –
Anne (not to be confused with London Ann) and I used often to
discuss strategies for Not Minding. It was embarrassing to be
caught minding and out of the question to be thought complaining.
We were both aware, all the time, that we were among people who
had lived through six terrible years, people to whom the discom-
forts of the peace were a relief and a freedom.

Because of the intense cold the custom in College was to work,
in the evenings, in small groups, in the room of wherever a friend's
real fire was being lit that night. The owner of the room was
expected to provide snacks and drinks, and that might take a lot of
research, for our food coupons were naturally handed in to the
College at the beginning of term. I once invested in a bottle of
British sherry but it made everyone feel sick. Sometimes there was a
food parcel to share from my mother or from Mark, Zoë, Elizabeth, other kind friends who were beginning to get the message:
tinned ham, sardines, condensed milk, bars of chocolate (always
turned grey in the post but only Anne and I could remember proper
chocolate) or dried apricots and, at my special request, strips of bil-
tong – and Oxo cubes, the ideal beverage for the rape of the electric fire. The study evenings in my room used to be well attended.

If you live in Europe you have to learn all the agreeable things
about the winter, and learn to look forward to them so that the
approach of what is disagreeable becomes easier to bear. You have
to attend and attune to the sounds and sights of it, the treats of it:
fresh snowfall which cleans and clears and simplifies, improving the
essential shapes of town and tree; the slow and fearful putting-forth
of leaf buds, so timid in the cold, so rash to try it at all. And there
is always the hardiness of the birds and the beasts to admire. Even
frogs and some of the fish learn how to let parts of their body
freeze while they go on living; I have always found that a difficult

thing to do. In all of the first year of letters to Michael, this is almost the only example I can find of a sturdier approach:

January 21st 1946

There has been the most severe frost known for some large number of years – more than my age, anyway. The cold excruciating but the sight so ... wondrous. That semi-religious word is all I can find. The trees and bushes in the College garden gone feathery and fantastic; the spider webs, even, over the rotting vegetable garden, frozen into sparkly symmetries; in the town, the dirty houses smart and white, the blackened colleges like pearly castles. And because of the cold, it was all dry, no slush or puddles.

Anne and I went this afternoon to Port Meadow, which is an enormous flat almost-marsh which stretches as far as (in the mist, anyway) you can see. We walked to it over the railway bridge and looked down to see all the electric wires frosted and the rails showing up like veins of silver. The canal runs parallel with the track, and usually looks rather muddy and bedraggled, but today was like a shining, silver glacier. There were hundreds of people on the Meadow – usually only a few cows and horses. Dons skating placidly round in academic circles, children on sledges, people falling, people dancing, big young men in College scarves playing ice hockey. Not everyone had skates on, not A. and I. It wasn't slippery to walk on because of crisp frost over the ice. Like a Brueghel winter scene, such a vast stretch of white and so many variously occupied people; in the background only white mist and grey shapes of more people.

We came back and had tea in my room: boiled eggs (illicit, from the Principal) cooked on the electric heater (illegal) and honey (from my mother) and half an orange each (saved from breakfast), and lit the real fire, and crouched around it, the getting warm again as exciting and exquisite, in its own way, as the thing itself, the Great Frost, as it will surely be known.

That winter of 1945–6 was not as terrible as that of the following year, when snow fell for months on end, fell and froze. Oxford's plumbing seized up for weeks, and people had to go out at night, into gardens or parks, with torches, to defecate, digging careful holes in the frozen snow and then covering them, like careful cats. But '45–'46 had been my induction, and I was in any case unhappy and lovesick and obliged to work very hard, which did not suit me as I had no ambition to become a scholar. I was also very poor. Anything that Michael was able to send me I had to save to live on during the vacations. The stresses were such that in due course I inevitably became ill, in addition to all these problems.

There were, of course, many delights. Somebody lent me a small radio and I spent many happy hours listening at night to my new and most valued friend, the BBC, usually under the bedclothes for warmth (as at school one had read, in the same way, after 'Lights Out', for secrecy), marvelling as usual at the extraordinary wealth of offerings in music, literature, talk and sheer information. If only, I used to think, if only something like this could somehow be offered, in their homes, to South Africans, especially black South Africans. There were also many excursions, usually on bicycles into the countryside. One day Enid Starkie, Fellow of the College and famous, at the time, for her work on Rimbaud, drove a friend and me out to a sale of the contents of one of the great houses of England. Very sadly, only six years after this sale, the house was destroyed by fire; but so sacred is the memory of the Inigo Jones house at Coleshill, especially to architectural historians, that the ground it occupied, the actual house-space, at least of the ground floor, has been turned room by room, stair by stair, into a sad and evocative gravel garden. When I went to revisit Coleshill a few weeks ago, I felt that I was visiting a lovingly tended grave. None of its walls remain, not even the chimney stacks, although you used sometimes to see these sticking up from the ruins of blitzed and burned houses. All, all was either burned or subsequently pulled down, and the site became, before the garden was made, the crest of a green hillside, a meadow. When I first saw the house at Coleshill in the summer of 1946, the days of its dispersal, as distinct from its destruction, had come – the dissolution, a sale which was to last a week or so, of the family life that it had sheltered for about 350 years. I thought that its dignity and pride seemed enhanced rather than mocked by the marketing display of all its contents.

Enid Starkie was an expert not only in the more obscure French poets but in antique glass and china which, that day, she was after.

June 20th 1946

She always looks the same: brisk, foursquare, rather like a businesslike terrier, and yet merry, bright blue, sailor's eyes and always a pert and bright beret on her head. Today it was scarlet, but not the same scarlet as her scarf or her gloves. Perhaps bright blue eyes are colourblind. She was full of the sort of china she hoped to buy and only with difficulty was led round to Rimbaud, of whom I would guess she is rather tired having just, she says, come upon, too late for her book, some amazing new evidence. We could not worm it out of her.

Darling, Coleshill is a miraculous house, in Oxfordshire, or on the border with Berkshire. Starkie says it's the last domestic building which Inigo Jones designed, in 1660, and is said by many to be his finest. I think you will be fed up that I cannot give you an adequate description. But you could not go inside, unless you had bought something and wished to pay. The goods for sale today were all outside under makeshift canvas, as was the doubtless noble entrance door and steps which, also covered by canvas, we could not see. It was raining all day and after examining all the amazing contents that had been poured out of the house onto trestle tables, we spent a long time in Starkie's little car, eating buns, Starkie scribbling in the catalogue and waiting for her auction numbers to come up.

I can only tell you that it was a huge house, grey and rectangular and tall. Along its length, on three floors, are nine perfectly identical and symmetrical windows and emerging from the roof seven smaller ones ('Why should servants –', I suppose, 'need as much light and air as their masters?') and on top of the roof a little cupola topped by a huge golden ball on a stem. What a strange device! Is it famous? What does it mean? I know that you would have found a way of deducing the plumbing (if any) and the staircases and where the fireplaces were and all that.

I can tell you a little about the contents, though, or the bits that interested me. Just listen – from the catalogue: 'One dozen dressed moleskins, 200 feather beds and bolsters, oak napkin press, two officers' dress swords, 12 evening fans, 18 Ladies' evening kid gloves, assorted night commodes and fittings, seven-leafed draught screen, terrestial globe on stand, Sheraton card table ...' The name of the people who own it is Pleydell Bouverie and (Starkie says) it has been in the same family since it was built. Handing down all those things ... In South Africa we did not even have houses, to speak of, while the Pleydell Bouveries were flapping their fans and their servants pressing away on the napkins.

Some of the lecturers at Oxford were brilliant scholars and some were brilliant teachers as well, and to two or three I accorded both distinctions. Some were largely unintelligible but even among those there was one whom I found charming and whose lectures I seldom skipped:

Dr Pflutter looks like a bird. It is hard to see what or how big their bodies are, under their voluminous black gowns, but his head is an almost perfect sphere except for a long, straight beak, and the back of it (only) covered by small fluffy feathers. He is the one, you remember, who made Homer so unintelligible to me last term. This term he is (hoping for help from us!) reconstructing some fragments of Sappho and other poets whose oeuvre has been torn to shreds by time. Part of the way to do this is by reconstructing the metre of the whole from the evidence of what remains, and then guessing what thoughts and which words in that poet's register and period might complete the broken thoughts of it in that metre; and after that you can begin to wonder whether sense, let alone poetry, has been made. Everyone supposes that you somehow know, already, what all the possible metres of Greek lyric are, so no time, I fear, is wasted on that.

Well, I have learned by now hardly even to notice the German accents of several scholars here. The wonderful Professor Eduard Fraenkel, for example, seems to me like the voice of Wilamowitz himself, his meanings perfectly clear even when in a state of scholarly rage. The problem with Dr Pflutter, though, is not so much his accent as the fact that he is never for a moment silent or still. I wish to clap a large butterfly net over him, stroke the back of his feathers to calm him, make warbling noises back at him. All the normal pauses between sentences or quotations are filled in with sounds of meditation, or doubt, or mirth, so that the total effect (accompanied by waving of hands, nodding of head, little runs about the platform) is something like: 'Zair ist in er der Griechische Metrik er ah konseederible room vor er hee hee hee! vor der Monkey Play and Beezniss und er ha ha ha vor der Messing Abowt mit der – ja – mit der metrik vor er scholars, vot is Showink Awf and er and er such dings.' He is always merry – indeed, sometimes dances about waving a long rod, singing, ' Tum ti tum la la – nein, tum ti la – nein, tum ti ti tum ti la – ist der anapaestik kataleptik, nein? ' I took Anthony Price with me the other day, up from London for a few days; stuffing him into a scholar's gown. I shall never forget his astonishment at Dr Pflutter. I was so afraid that he would laugh, and betray his illicit presence.

But the whole woman of me, as distinct from the student, was kept together and comforted by Somerville's new Principal, Janet Vaughan, who was not then a Dame. She was in several ways my salvation and, until her death at a very great age, a beloved friend. She was also a doctor and most distinguished research scientist, a haematologist, famous for her studies in the biological effects of irradiation – she published her last paper in this field when she was 89.

A few days after my first term began – which was also Janet's

Janet Vaughan in her nineties

first term as Principal – we were all invited to an address in Hall, after dinner. We expected some kind of pep talk, I suppose, about 'winning the Peace' and women's role, or something like that. She greeted us warmly, but then – the rest of her talk was about Belsen. Five months before term began she had been sent there, with a scientific team, as soon as it had been liberated. Her purpose was to try to find a substance which might help those who were dying of starvation – a matter of great urgency not only for those remaining alive in the German camps, but for those returning from the hands of the Japanese.

She described the unspeakable and revolting conditions, sights, smells and sounds – of the sounds the most terrible, she said, was the screams of the starving who, when they saw anyone of her team approaching, in terror cried out, 'Nicht Krematorium! Nicht Krematorium!' Syringes before, it seems, had meant not careful starvation-feeding but benzene injections, for more efficiently burning alive. I am certain that not one of us who were there has forgotten that talk, and the news it carried about the depths to which the latent savagery of mankind may sink.

15th November 1945

The Principal is such a lovely person. I have not been well, and spent all of yesterday in her house, which is next to the College. Most of the time I spent on the floor, by the fire, doing proses. No. Just one prose; putting into Greek, if you please, the Cheshire Cat episode from Alice. *The things they choose ... It's a relief when it's a solid, logical Latin passage, Caesar or Cicero, Romanly and rationally collecting wood for building palisades or explaining why it is undesirable to murder a parent. A few days ago it was a scatty episode from* Don Quixote – *in Elizabethan English. Why not Rabelais, I wonder. It would, by lowering it, greatly extend one's Greek vocabulary.*

The point about this Cheshire smile, or 'grin' as Carroll calls it, a tougher word than 'smile', is that there is no Greek word for the noun of it; it has to be a participle of the verb, an adjectival participle attached to a noun; so you will at once appreciate the difficulty of dealing with a smile which remains after the cat has vanished and which cannot therefore be attached to anything. So the verbal adjective becomes what is known as a 'hanging participle' (because, for sure, in Oxford they hang you for it) and you are forced by logical absurdity into grammatical impossibility. I put it into Greek as 'the cat, smiling, was no longer there'. No good. It implied that he was smiling somewhere else, which naturally was not the point. You try it.

Janet has two lovely, playful, pig-tailed daughters and a silent though very kind, nice husband, who brings the firewood and eggs and other goodies up from their country place in Surrey. She is vivacious but untrivial, beautiful, a powerful presence but simple and friendly – friendly, at any rate to me, thank goodness. I am told she can be hostile and sharp. Some boring people came to dinner, which I helped her to cook. When they had gone we relaxed over whisky and (hot!) water and held a rather hostile and sharp post-mortem.

I think that what I am trying to trace, in re-reading these Oxford letters, is whether there was a moment, or interval, when I came to consider that England was, really was, my 'home'. The boiled eggs after Port Meadow in the frost had seemed a little beginning, 'a melting, a madrigal start'. The first day at home with Janet (and there were many that followed, over the years, both in Oxford and at her home in Surrey) brought me nearer to it. But I believe that the comfort I found in Janet may be in part because she was taking the place where my mother used to be; where, I thought, my mother had ceased to be but the place, in me, remaining. Perhaps what was remaining was the *need* for a smile. Perhaps the Cheshire's disembodied smile was not such an impossibility, after all. And this search for a Home – perhaps we just have to change the grammar of our experience.

As to my mother, my difficult mother and my difficult self: a few weeks after our rupture, the most wonderful food parcels began to appear, wrapped up in stout unbleached calico and strongly sewn along the folds and seams to keep them safe. (From these wrapping cloths, written all over, franked, stained and battered by weeks in a ship's hold, I made the first pillowcases and teacloths of my married life!) She took an enormous amount of care with the contents, too, choosing my favourite things. For example, she even sent fresh eggs. To preserve them she did not use the usual thing, which is isinglass; she put them into lidded tins, as though for that, but then filled up the tins with quantities of melted bacon fat; not just lard, but home-rendered bacon fat, which itself was a treasure, a means of turning tired slices of bread into magical little crispily fried platforms – pedestals or plinths to enhance the glory of fried eggs.

I always wrote to thank her and to give her carefully selected bits of news. In the beginning I knew that because the mails took so long, these first parcels had been dispatched before our rupture; so they were blameless, motiveless parcels. But what about the ones that were sent later? They were in a way Cheshire parcels, a friendliness but – nobody, I thought, really there. I was especially riven by a parcel which contained not food but a pretty bowl, a bag of dried compost and some tulip bulbs. It seemed so personal to me and to her knowledge of me, needing to grow things. Before I had my own children, I did not know how desperately discriminate, how forgiving, how absurdly prone to guilt, loving mothers may be. Whatever their sins and whatever their wounds, they do not push off like Cheshire cats. As for me: I was willing to accept love, if I thought that was what it was, but not power. Since one could not tell which parcels had been sent before the rift between us, and which after, I just continued writing thank-you letters and so a bridge of some sort was kept open.

⌇

I saw, in Oxford, a noble medieval city which, although modernised around its ancient edges, was uncrowded, calmer and more open than it is now. It had not been damaged by the war but it was very dirty and badly in need of repair and maintenance in all the respects that a city and its buildings have; it was (and it is) in the winters cold and damp; it was not (and is not) as elegant and orderly as Cambridge; it was, and is, more lively and more various than that place. It is a small but international city and is therefore a wonderful place to be and to live, with no narrow provincialism and plenty to do, day or night. For those who love it as – completely unpossessively – I do, I would like to find in my memory, and in my letters to Michael, some things about Oxford rather than about myself.

But all of Oxford is still here! The chief difference is that there is much more of it now, including one of the most beautiful of all the buildings that it has, from any period, which is Arne Jacobsen's St Catherine's College. So it comes down to people, really: apart from all the distinguished scholars and teachers, many of whom were returning from war service, there were many wonderful people of my generation. They flitter through the pages of my letters to Michael. There were many, many others of the nascent great and good but I did not get about much, or know them as well as others

who have written about them. So I'm picking out somebody whom
person-to-person I did not know at all, but who seemed to me, at
the time, like Homer himself.

January 26th 1946
  ... Sir John Myres – his lectures at the Ashmolean, and not just
because they are now so rare, a great experience. He is extremely
old and ill. He walks almost doubled-up, and uses two sticks and
has a man with him all the time, to carry his books, open doors
and so on. I suppose that Homer went about just like that. He is
tall, except for the stoop, and very thin and, naturally, sits down to
give the lectures. A long, white pointed beard, and moustache, but
the hair of his head, of which there is a good deal, is hardly grey at
all; and one of his enormous, bushy eyebrows is black and the
other white! The whole time he is talking – altogether without
notes – he pulls fiercely at the white eyebrow, which probably
explains its colour; and by the end of the lecture its environs are all
reddened, poor thing.
  He has a glorious wit and makes the topic of ancient mineral
deposits as exciting as a treasure hunt. This is because he has done
so much of the search, and the research, himself. Especially thrilling
– the deciphering of the Minoan tablets! It's rumoured that he has
got pretty far in deciphering the script and is desperately working
on it, before he gets too ill. As you probably know, he has inherited
the care of these tablets from Sir Arthur Evans who died in 1941,
having rather kept them to himself since 1900! Myres passed a
dark hint today, remarking that the Knossos tablets throw a certain
amount of light upon the question of iron ore deposits in Crete.
Well I don't suppose anyone there got excited about the iron. There
are only four of us, anyway. One of them is a rather strange
American colonel, I mean strange to find him there. He is a known
archaeologist and at the hint about the tablets, as distinct from the
iron, emitted gasps, as I did. However, the lecture was about iron,
not about the history of the world.

In later years the man who really did decipher 'Linear B', the script upon these tablets, Michael Ventris, became a good friend. He was a young architect who worked with Michael at the Ministry of Education, which was at that time asking its architects to devise new and better means of building schools, to meet the desperate post-war need. He was, Michael said, a very gifted architect with a particular power of analysing the complex sets of data which school building requires and the many constraints which in the difficult post-war days it had to observe – all the unseen things which architects have to attend to before the design process can begin.

This gift was also shown by Ventris's invention – together with his friend and fellow architect Oliver Cox – of a strange architectural drawing aid. It was made of a transparent plastic and resembled a young giant sting-ray, with a broad, rounded head and a long tail. Its edges were calibrated with figures which were incomprehensible to me. It is an instrument which enables draughtsmen with instant accuracy, instead of sheaves of calculations, to draw perspectives of the insides or outsides of buildings. In his wonderfully neat and controlled handwriting Michael V. had etched the figures on a prototype model he gave to my Michael. Some people say that the minute and unfailing precision of his script and his drawings were factors which contributed to the decipherment of the baffling maze of short strokes and slight curves which Linear B presents. He enjoyed them, the very intricacy and obscurity of them, the endless possibilities of conjunction one with another.

During the war Michael had served with the RAF, choosing to become a bomber navigator (aged 20 ...) where, I suppose, the same kind of complex and instant intellectual skills of analysis and co-ordination are crucial needs. I have heard that he used to take his own typewriter with him on the bombing flights. At first I found the thought of that somehow grimly amusing – this careful, well-prepared, meticulous boy, travelling to Hell ... but of course, how else in a vibrating, roaring vehicle, dark within, and a moonless night, and a blacked-out land below – how else could one ensure that calculations and notes were, to his high standards, instantly legible, intelligible, reliable?

Michael was such a skilful and hardworking architect that for a long time none of us took too seriously his interest in the Minoan tablets – which, it appeared, had occupied much of his attention since as a schoolboy of fourteen he had seen some of them, and heard Sir Arthur Evans speak about them, at an exhibition in London. We all knew he was 'working on them', and I was electrified to hear that he had been in correspondence with Sir John Myres – and, indeed, before that with Evans himself. But we thought of it, in Michael, as a sort of hobby – rather as, at Somerville, it had seemed rather amusing that the brilliant philosopher Iris Murdoch should be 'trying' to write a novel.

One evening early in June 1952, Michael and I were asked to dinner at the Ventris's beautiful modern flat in Highgate. Lois Ventris, whom we always called Bets, talked amiably, apologising at fairly frequent intervals for her husband's absence – he was in his study, she said, and would come as soon as he could. We grew a little hungry, and a little drunk on the pre-prandial sherry, and Bets a little anxious and embarrassed. After what seemed a very long time Michael burst into the room, full of apologies but even more full of excitement. 'I know it, I *know* it,' he said, 'I am certain of it —.' I thought he must have confirmed an earlier idea that the language was Etruscan. But what he had proved, of course, was that the language was an early form of Greek, Greek of the Homeric Age, recorded on the earliest known documents of European civilisation; and settling for ever the dispute among historians about the course of it.

That evening, after dinner, Michael took me into his study and showed me the particular piece of work which, added to what he had developed over the years, had led to his conclusions of that evening. He had shown me his worksheets before and I was to some extent able to follow, in those distant days, the complicated businesses about vowel frequencies and phonetic values and syllabic variations and inflectional endings and other ancient languages in other ancient scripts, all set out on cross-referenced grids as challenging to me, in their own way, as the Minoan labyrinth to its victims. But I hung on, knowing little about the methodology but enough Greek not to doubt that if Michael's complex positionings and suppositions were valid, then the revealed language was indeed a form of Greek. At last (I thought later) my reward for suffering the ghastly regimen of Mrs Zvegintzov and the whips and scorns of my Somerville tutor; a reward, especially, for attention to Cretan place-names which had been such a feature of Sir John Myres's search for ancient metals; for it was some of these place-names – Amnisos, Tulissos, Phaistos, Luktos, Knossos itself – which provided Michael with important correspondences, rather in the way that the names of Cleopatra and Ptolemy had provided vital clues in deciphering the hieroglyphs on the Rosetta stone. Michael's work still had a long way to go, but the road he had travelled entirely persuaded me, on that strange evening, of his achievement.

The point of this story is that (hotly pursuing my love affair with the BBC) I had become, soon after leaving Oxford, a talks producer for the Third Programme; and at the next week's editorial meeting with my colleagues I managed to persuade them, incredulous though they were, that Michael Ventris should be invited to announce his decipherment on our cultivated part of the air. No, I had to tell them, he did not work in a university, or a museum, he happened to be a friend ... a young architect. They were sceptical – rightly so, for I too was very young; but they gave in, I suppose, to my fervour. Michael himself, a shy and inward man, also needed a little persuasion. But his purpose had always been to share what he knew, and to seek the advice of others. He was always conscious that he himself had only schoolboy Greek (proficient though he was at a wide range of modern European languages). It was his habit to send out worknotes to several scholars, asking their opinions; and he realised that an announcement in the brief compass of a twenty-minute broadcast might be more effective for his purpose than a delay of several years while he struggled to develop the material to a length and complexity suitable to learned publication.

That is exactly how it turned out. His broadcast was an essay in modesty; and of a complexity which would not today, long after the demise of the Third Programme, be tolerated on the air. It was not an easy assignment – this was radio, not TV – and in our preparatory search for an approach which would be intelligible in spite of the complexity, Michael gave me a copy of a letter he had recently written to Sir John. That letter in itself is a miracle of modesty: after a detailed answer to Myres's last letter, and some related intricate matters, Michael ventures to say, 'During the last couple of days I have been carrying on with the phantasy I discussed in my last Note, and though it runs completely counter to everything I've said in the past, I'm now almost completely convinced that the … tablets are in GREEK. It's a pity there is not a new language to study.' There follows, in the letter to Sir John, two closely written pages of detailed evidence, some of which he had shown me on the night of our dinner, and the letter ends characteristically, stressing what he considered his amateur Greek, 'It may still be an hallucination … But the thing that staggers me is that whenever I go to the Greek dictionary to check a word I seem to have found but which is unfamiliar to me, it generally seems to exist and to make sense.'

When he came to write the final script for the broadcast talk, I tried, in spite of the enthusiastic publicist in me, to respect his innate inability to make any grand statement of claims, even to preserve his rather surprised and grateful air of its being a revelation which had somehow or other happened to him. He begins by praising Champollion's work, goes on to show the advances made in the last hundred years in the decipherment of early Middle Eastern texts, outlines the sad lack of advance in that of European languages, introduces the work of Evans, Myres and others, discusses decipherment systems and problems … and halfway down the seventh of its eight pages, briefly though firmly announces his new conclusions.

Most fortunately, the broadcast – on 1 July 1952 – was heard by John Chadwick in Cambridge, then at the beginning of his distinguished career as a specialist in ancient forms of Greek.

Chadwick had never heard the name of Ventris, so he consulted Sir John, who lent him a copy of the letter from which I have quoted and of the preceding Note which had adumbrated the 'phantasy'. Chadwick studied them and wrote with much enthusiasm to Michael, who promptly invited his collaboration. Their great and lengthy work, *Documents in Mycenaean Greek*, was published four years later. Shortly before its publication, Michael Ventris, at the age of 34, was inexplicably killed in a car smash, driving himself home alone at night.

⌐

For me, the real moment of acceptance, of transfer of allegiance, or whatever it may be called, from South Africa to England, could not arrive until Michael came from South Africa to join me. But by the time that happened I had been forced to realise that unlike my parents (my mother, anyway) I did not need a Home; that this long-ing for a country called Home was a product of Empire, or banish-ment, or exile or overseas service, travel, deportation, anything that takes people from one country to another for any length of time, whether they want to go or not – but especially if not. Talking about Home is like hanging your harp upon the willows; it is a term for use only in the most dire and painful situations.

So the point of going on about Oxford fifty years ago is not to show how I acquired a new 'home'. It reduces, again, to an effort to talk to 'those who live now', *hoi nun eontes*. But apart from what is now a much higher standard of physical comfort and the admission of women to men's colleges and vice versa, I suppose that Oxford in those days was in most important respects very sim-ilar to what it is today, at least from an undergraduate point of view. What was different was our lives, the lives of those who were there at the time. And I can only speak for mine.

One day in February I received from my bank the information that £100 had been paid into my account 'from South Africa'. Supposing it could not have been from the South African

Exchequer, I wrote rather crossly to the bank to ask from whom it had come. They replied that they were not at liberty to tell me. I have never found out who sent it. I know it wasn't Michael; he would have no reason to conceal it, for while he was on army pay he often sent me sums of money, hoping they might buy me food or warmth. It was almost certainly from my mother, for I had refused money from her for about a year. She would have known I would return it if I knew it came from her. But since I could not find out – or before the donor could write and tell me what to do with it – I made and paid for the bookings to spend the Easter vacation in Sweden.

Madness, really. My tutor, Mildred Hartley, was more shocked than anyone since in June I had to write stiff language and litera-ture exams, Honour Moderations, before I could proceed to study for Greats, the big finals in history and philosophy, two years later. I bitterly regretted the privilege – which before I went up had seemed so gratifying – of being allowed to sit for Mods after three terms instead of five. Miss Hartley could hardly believe it when I told her my travel plans: 'But nobody, NOBODY, imagines you can spend any time at Easter except in Preparing. You have a lot to make up, as it is [I had been ill a great deal in the winter]; and you should have considered my [meaning her] position. I have given you a lot of time and effort [she had, indeed] and I don't want any-one to think I have not.' I didn't really care what might be thought of her; Mildred Hartley seemed to me safely among the immortals; but I was very depressed by what might be thought, if I failed, of me. You didn't get a second chance.

Janet thought I was not well enough to go anywhere. Michael thought I should save the money. My mother wrote to say I should stockpile essential food. John Greig wondered why I didn't choose Greece. Mark said I should do whatever my tutor told me. Miron thought I should go and do things for him in Paris. Everybody was fed up with me – except London Ann, who to my great pleasure came with me.

I had to go, and went ahead with the boat and train arrangements – Harwich, Esbjerg, Copenhagen, Stockholm, then north to stay with the Nordenfelt family at Fagersta, the big steel works. They were an engineering family. The father, Lennart Nordenfelt, was a friend of my father and he had often stayed with us in Johannesburg when the stainless steel linings for the rockdrill bits were being developed, and had many times invited us to visit them. He was a tall, thin, strong, fair man, older than my father but much more light-hearted, even whimsical, which small girls adore.

The link with my father – that, of course, is why I had to go. England, Oxford – it was not a new Home I wanted; it was the love, however removed by death and time and space, of my father. Home depends upon where in life you are, not upon the wheres of cultures or countries.

Denmark and Sweden were thrilling to me and to Ann. The Nordenfelt family overwhelmed us with fun and love and care.

Fagersta, April 11th 1946

Last night after dinner Lennart's wife said there was going to be a 'show', and chairs and tables and things had to be got ready. I prayed it would not involve live performances; but it was home movies, and of films Lennart had taken during his last stay with us in Johannesburg! And after a bit of mining and engineering stuff – of our garden, a tennis party at our house! There was I, aged nine, running round with dear Puppy, our best fox-terrier! She had pinched the ball I was playing golf with, on the putting green. Albert was there in his high hat serving icecream from a wooden bucket. My mother in a grotesque – fashionable, I am sure – long white tennis-dress. John tearing round on his bicycle. And, of course, my father, the only one not dressed up for tennis, limping on his bad leg. I could hardly bear all that sad excitement and was thankful for the darkened room. Hurled in a moment back, all those years, all those miles, from the top of the earth to the bottom of it. Lennart came and put his arm round me.

I wrote to Michael using many superlatives about the Nordenfelts,

and about the beauty of the snow and ice in Sweden – which
puzzled him a good deal since in England the same phenomena did
not, as a rule, earn my kind words. But I had not seen or imagined,
before, such things as the glorious moments during darkness when
the furnaces of the steel mills were opened for the emission of the
rods and the huge, white landscape and the snowy forest and the
night sky were emblazoned by fire as though from the Harrowing
of Hell. 'Encarnadined', I'm afraid, is the word I used in writing to
Michael – as though Macbeth's murderous hand could compete
with that magnificence. And Spring was approaching.

April 17th

*Lennart has been driving us round Dalecarlica, which he says is
the most fair of all the provinces and, since he was born in it, by
far the most important. Lake Siljan seems as huge as a sea, completely frozen over as well as snowed upon, blindingly white but
with promontories of dark green pines and very pale green larches,
and in the distance the bare trunks and drooping branches of thousands of birches, purple with the approach of spring. You couldn't
possibly paint it, for nobody would believe it.*

In my garden, the garden in Oxford which is my last garden, I
planted some years ago a fine Swedish weeping birch, *Betula pen-
dula dalecarlica* – it even comes from the right province – to remind
me of Lennart and to thank him for the break from despair which
he afforded me. It has grown as high as my house, and the doves
use its branches for queuing upon as they wait each morning for
me to bring out their corn; as the pigeons used to wait, in eager
queues along the iron struts of the windmill, for my father and me
at Mornington.

No work was possible that Easter vacation; but for several
weeks, back in Oxford, I felt rejuvenated before succumbing again
to melancholy. My spirits had a kind of alacrity in sinking, as
Falstaff remarked of his great girth. I managed to do enough work
to scrape through the exams; but in spite of Janet's care my illness

continued, a strange sort of undulant fever. I didn't get over it until one day during the summer vacation, staying very gratefully with Philippa Foot, I had a completely unexpected cable from Michael, who had been boarded out of the army and, between fearful bouts of eye surgery, replacement of much skull and jaw, then of extensive plastic surgery, had been writing architecture exams. He had another university year to go but had suddenly been granted permission to complete his degree from afar.

His cable announced in strips of confident capitals 'ARRIVING FIVE THIRTY SUNDAY HEATHROW SPRINGBOK SERVICE REJOICE GREATLY ENORMOUS LOVE MICHAEL'. For a royal fanfare, who needs punctuation?

With Michael on a visit to Johannesburg, 1961

We were married that Christmas, after Michael had found a job in an architect's office and after my mother, who had flown Home with the intention of destroying our project, had failed to find the way – for I had cut the power link. She tried to forgive us, and came to the Registry Office, but sat at the back of the room, and cried. The snow fell generously down upon St Giles, the beautiful wide road outside, to her a sign of chill defeat, to us of the transformation into brightness of some dark months.

I believe that I was the first woman at Oxford who was allowed to be married while *in statu pupillari*; not as any form of favour but because several women who had been up before the war had returned in the married state from military service, to complete their degrees. So whatever the case had been before the war, it had been altered, like everything else, for ever.

25 The trunk

⟶

I said that I thought this sort of writing, memories of this kind, needed a biographical structure, however frail, upon which one could hang the leaves and buds of memory, so that a reader would have some idea of the nature and history of the 'I' which starts to burst forth as it re-experiences all the impressions. A twig or two may be helpful but I cannot justify any great time spent on trunk, or main stem. That is something readers need if they have picked up a book because the writer is famous; because they have read or heard in various places, seen in various pictures about, or read the works *of*, or the opinions of others *upon*. Almost any preposition is apposite to fame because almost everything you read or see about the famous is concerned with the fame rather than the person.

I learned about the more repellent aspects of Fame long ago, at Queensfield, when Miss Pargiter introduced us to Virgil with the touching love story of Dido and Aeneas and the tragic ending to it which was brought about not only by duplicity but by public opinion and nation-wide gossip. *Fama*, Virgil calls it, a great, sickening, female bird, 'quick of foot and swift on the wing, a huge and horrible monster, and under every feather of her body ... there lies an eye that never sleeps, a mouth and a tongue never silent and an ear always pricked.' Virgil goes on and on with this simile, as the ancients expected, since they understood most of life (as I do, lacking any scientific training) in terms of its similitudes.

Of my life, the trunk is made up of my thirty years with
Michael, of being mother to our four healthy and intelligent children, and of doing what that entails while coping with an exciting
job which often took me abroad. Those were the nourishing channels of my life; the trunk, if I am a tree. It's not like an oak tree
though, with a single trunk, one vascular bundle with various
extrusions towards the top. It is more like the banyan, of which the
original trunk is soon obscured by the adventitious roots which
grow down from its branches, seeking the earth, themselves becoming trunks crowding around and supporting the older structure. As
I grow older I feel increasingly like *Ficus benghalensis* and rejoice
in it. My children and their families are, of course, my chiefest
roots, now fellow trunks; but I am also thankful for sturdy and
supportive friendships, both at home and in the countries where I
travel; and a surprising number of old friendships in South Africa,
seeing that I uprooted so early.

But as I've said before, my life as such, trunk or trunks, is not
what I am writing about. Some years ago, when I found all these
letters that Michael had kept, I had for a short while a grandiose
scheme of extracting and mounting a few chapters mock-hubristi-
cally called 'Comedies, Tragedies and Histories'! Reading these
letters now, I have enjoyed remembering most of the experiences
they recount; certainly not all of them; and the letters are full of the
pangs of worry about him and the children and the *au pairs* and
about whether the burden which my absence put upon him was not
interfering with the architectural practice he had gradually built up;
of guilt when I was enjoying myself and dolour when I was not.
Arising even from the parts which were not enjoyed I have acquired
opinions about Mothering, Women at Work, Attitudes of Men
(black and white) towards working women or any woman, deteri-
oration of intellectual standards in most broadcasting *pari passu*
with (though not because of) immense technical advances, and so
on, which I could use to stir things up in various kettles of fish. But
wisdom, and idleness, have prevailed.

Forty and thirty, even twenty years ago, not many women flew alone about African countries recording and reporting upon views and news of upheavals and all manner of things. Apart from the excellent Hella Pick of *The Guardian*, I did not ever meet another woman journalist or broadcaster doing it, so far as I remember, in the many countries I visited during the 1950s and 1960s. There have been a few exceptions to the masculine rule, from the time of the distinguished correspondent of *The Times*, Flora Shaw, at the turn of the century, but in general it was thought that women were too vulnerable and therefore, in a world of deadlines, too unreliable to send – as though women travellers of other kinds, anthropologists, historians, missionaries, nurses, aid workers, had not been venturing about Africa for very many years at the time when I began, and black women since the dawn of mankind. The British idea of aggressive promiscuity in the African male, based upon incomplete understandings of polygamy, was partly to blame for this; but so was the male British stereotype of women as creatures weak in mind as well as in muscle. For years and years women were not employed as newsreaders (let alone foreign correspondents) for the BBC because it was thought that they 'lacked authority'. I had a dear, elderly, gentlemanlike cousin who, when women newsreaders first came in, used to switch off if the newscaster were a woman and hope for better luck with the next bulletin. He seemed to find no difficulty in explaining to me, with his usual elaborate courtesy, that he could never attach any weight to what a woman said, or even remember it!

But now if there is a place in a state of war, genocide, massacre, famine, it is certain that women as well as men will be there reporting it. I was not sent out to cover that sort of thing, though a few times it overtook me. I went out, each time for several weeks, as part of my duties in the robust, eager youth of the BBC Third Programme to make programmes about the cultures and societies of Africa that, in the wake of Indian independence, were either clamouring for political independence or, in the case of white South Africa, legislating at home and conniving abroad to ensure that such a thing never happened. Of course I came upon difficulties and dangers, but time after time was helped and encouraged and indeed on occasion rescued by African friends and acquaintances and even strangers. My mother, who sometimes came to England to help with the children while I was away, could not believe that I was not in permanent danger being so much alone among black people, and she did not hesitate to pass on her anxieties to Michael and the children. But it was not so; I did not feel it to be so. I suppose that I might feel differently now that so many African countries are riven with factions, rebels and irregulars who are supplied with Western armament, arms, landmines, and all the desperate insecurities and hates and fears that go with them.

It was very important to me at the time, when country after country in Africa was reaching towards political independence, to travel as widely as I could and to report upon what ordinary men and women were thinking, as well as recording the opinions of their leaders, traditional or political. It was important to me as a person, let alone as a journalist. One thing I discovered was that it was far, far more difficult to get the views of 'ordinary', poor and struggling people, the majority of anywhere, than to record those of the confident and powerful.

I arrived in Kano, Northern Nigeria, in February 1959, for the celebrations of the independence of the Northern Region, which was a separate affair from that of Nigeria as a whole, which happened in the following year. The disparity in the dates was due to the wish of the rulers of the North to have their independence celebrated precisely on the fiftieth anniversary of a painful event in their long struggle against the British forces under Frederick Lugard. The symbolism was important to them in spite of the inconvenient fact that the celebration therefore had to take place during Ramadan, the holy season of fasting.

The ceremonies were extensive and splendid, all the same, as was right for the largest region of the most populous country in

Africa, and – except for India – the largest territory of which a British government had ever relinquished control. All the rulers of the North took part, inheritors of the desert kingdoms where Islam had first penetrated Africa, giving a fresh stimulus to the vast trans-Saharan or Northern slave trade which had existed centuries before the Southern or Atlantic trade and of course indigenously, within Africa, for centuries before Islam.

The Emirs and Viziers and other Chiefs, with lavish, magnificent robes and turbans, arrived in long black Cadillacs followed by bearers of their huge honorific umbrellas, trains of jongleurs and praise-singers, musicians, and the famous horsemen of the North whose fathers and grandfathers had cost the British army dear in many fierce and desperate encounters. The horsemen performed, time after time, the traditional salute to their rulers, galloping up to a yard or two from where the Emirs (and by courtesy I) sat, and then stopping dead in their tracks, the horses steady and composed while the riders fired volleys of salutation into the air. I dined that night amid a different kind of magnificence, the colonial splendour of what had been Government House, where the guests were all members of the outgoing culture and administration. I found it an equally moving occasion; particularly when, at the stroke of midnight, the new flag of Northern Nigeria was slowly raised up the flagpole where, until nightfall that day, the Union flag had listlessly twitched in the airless heat. At the moment when the new flag reached the masthead the band of the Katsina Native Police, wonderfully turned out and waiting at prime attention in the courtyard, struck up, with instant precision and the vigour of a march rhythm, not any victory song or newly forged anthem but – 'Auld Lang Syne'. I have never heard it sound so brisk, even merry, yet it reduced most of us to sorrowful tears.

The following day I set out to make contact with Mallam Aminu Kano, a leader of the chief party of opposition. From the elite, black or white, I could not expect to have any help with this, but I'd been in contact with him through an intermediary and was warned he would be hard to find but would send a man to guide me if I would, in secrecy, wait with a car at a certain place at a certain time. It came to pass, though I grew uneasy for a while at the length of the journey through the city and its endless streets of trim Saharan, desert houses, made all of ginger mud, and crowded markets to the outer perimeter where the houses were much smaller and closer together, the streets narrower and the air hotter and hotter as we drove towards the desert itself. At length the guide told the driver to stop and to wait at that same place for me to return, and he took me down several more streets where there would not have been room for a car, and showed me into a small room of a very small mud house. There was no furniture of any kind. The floor was entirely covered by sleeping bodies of robed men in various attitudes of exhaustion. But one of them sprang up as I entered and welcomed me to his home with great warmth and kindness – Mallam Aminu.

He took my heavy recording machine (in those days the so-called 'midget' portables weighed almost forty pounds) and placed it on the floor, between two bodies. He apologised that he could not, in this holy month, offer me any refreshment, and asked me to sit down. I could not see where or how to sit until he arranged two of the bodies so that they were lying on their sides, so he and I could face each other by sitting on two robed pelvic girdles, not putting pressure on any fleshy parts, and begin our talk. Throughout the recording the bodies made no stir. He had wanted me to see how the poor lived, how thin the line between poverty and starvation especially in a season of fasting. I have never forgotten it, or the humanity and concern of Mallam Aminu himself. When the interview was broadcast on the Third Programme, a few weeks later, there were strong protests from officials in both British and Northern Nigerian governments.

During an earlier visit to Nigeria I spent some time with my friend Molly Mahood, who was for several years Professor of English at the University of Ibadan. There was a conference there of African historians and Molly's boundless hospitality made it simple for me to meet them and record various interviews and discussions for my programmes. When it was over we set out in Molly's car on a long journey to the Eastern Region. Molly needed to visit various schools and missions on the way and I had arranged appointments with traditional leaders – the Oni of Ife, the Oba of Benin – and politicians of both Western and Eastern Regions. I wrote to Michael nearly every night recounting it all.

One letter, which I had to ask him not to show to my mother, was written on the evening of Easter Sunday. We had spent the night at a mission station near Umuahia, north of the Niger Delta, where there was a hospital and settlement of people suffering from leprosy, and together with the patients we attended Holy Communion that morning. The patients, identifiable only by their copious white bandaging, mixed freely with the staff but we noticed that they were reticent about coming near visitors. Although I'm so atheistical, I have attended very many church services in Africa and am always deeply thankful (never more than on this occasion) that they exist and for their works, the care and love they give to their people and the stability and continuity which they uphold in the darkest times. But it was not leprosy which I thought might upset my mother.

To Michael. Late, Easter Day.
   On this Sunday all the countryside seemed to be rejoicing – the E. Region is very Christian, hardly any Islam; but the risen Christ was celebrated in the villages with the most joyous amount of pagan paraphernalia: big 'ju-jus' (what sort of word is that? But Nigerians use it!) jumped about, many of them on stilts, shrouded in raffia, with terrifying masks, followed around by frenetic drummers. Whenever we got out of the car they would rush round us asking for an Easter 'dash'. I saw no women but there were very many children. We would pretend to be frightened of the masked men, which sent the children into ecstasies. We photographed them as best we could in the milling throng, doled out pennies and were given most vociferous and flattering send-offs. It is quite an odd experience for a big, fierce ju-ju to wave and shout, through his

alarming mouthpiece, 'Bye-bye, God bless you, Madam, bye bye!'

I have grown bolder with my driving and so thankful that I finally managed my licence before leaving! The roads were full, over the holiday, of those murderous lorries with big, painted names like 'God Help Us' which try to force you off the tarmac and have no brakes or steering to speak of. But the only trouble we met was when we saw a big, turbulent meeting taking place in the forest and left the car to investigate. We went to read a notice stuck on a tree which said 'Agricultural Recruiting Agency'. Molly said it was a notorious organisation which transported hundreds of Nigerians to underpaid labour on the plantations of Fernando Po. Then for some reason she and I went off in different directions. I photographed the notice and went to join the meeting, consisting only of men, but I was spotted and surrounded by an angry group who told me I must wait and speak to their chief.

When the chief came, a very large, berobed man, speaking pidgin and wielding an ugly iron bar, he wanted to know why I was taking pictures. I said, cleverly I thought, it was because this big religious meeting showed what good Christians were doing on Easter Sunday. Perhaps it was the church service and the masquerades which put this into my head. So he said (he was clever too) I should pay £1 for each photograph to 'his Church'. I should have paid, and departed, on the spot; but I felt annoyed, probably because guilty of intrusion. I said that if 'his church' behaved like this to strangers, then it must be a very odd church. He got angry and raised his iron bar as though to strike. I don't suppose he would have done so, but in any case his own people restrained him, with loud reprimands. While they began to quarrel among themselves, I edged nearer to the car, to find Molly next to it but surrounded by what appeared to be a rival crowd, for each side began to shout at each other, over our heads – differing views, I assume, about what should be done with us. So I told the chief I would pay him £1 if I could photograph him and that I would send him a copy of the picture as soon as I safely got back to Ibadan. While fresh argument broke out, a young man whom I had not

seen before quietly took my hand and led me round to the passen-
ger door of the car. Molly was already at the wheel. As we drove
off a large group ran after us, shouting excitedly for the few
moments they could keep up with Molly's acceleration.

I am not at all proud of my wilful straying into that episode, whatever may have been in my head when recounting it to Michael. It
was an inept nosiness, a mistaken foray out of my sense of voca-
tion. I truly wanted to mingle with, consort with, understand what
I could about people who were poor, struggling, exploited. The barriers between black and white during my childhood had always
been so entire and extreme (except in the domestic childhood
scenes I have described) that I was sometimes, as on this occasion,
led by chance and inexperience into folly, trespass, impertinence
and it might well have been into harm. All reporters of disorders in
foreign lands have this problem to sort out. By what right are you
there? And if not by acceptance or invitation, how will you get to
an understanding of what might be grave dangers or wrongs? No
use in waiting for horrible old *Fama* with all her spying eyes and
clacking tongues. I have come, over the years, increasingly to value
the reporting (it cannot be called 'simple') of what is seen, when the
view is clear enough, rather than – when the situation has already
quaked up into crisis – the desperate gleaning of vox pop opinions
to gather into some kind of master opinion or headline for the next
bulletin. Radio, the classic foreign correspondents' radio essay
which has flowered in the last decade or so, often does this better
than television can, because if there are pictures it's often assumed
that words and the thoughts which make them would be redun-
dant; which is not the case.

The world has been deeply shocked by the massive genocides in
Rwanda and Burundi since in 1994 the Hutu rose against their
Tutsi masters, the slaughter continuing in retributory wave after
wave, spilling over national borders, until the profound and bloody
disorder today in the Eastern Congo. In August 1954, forty years
before it started, I visited what was then called Ruanda–Urundi,

joining a party of anthropologists as guests of the Belgian administration – successor, after the First World War – to that of the colonising Germans. The Belgians did us proud, with lavish entertainments and transports to wherever we wished; and what we mostly asked for was visits to the settlements of *indigènes*. What remains in my mind are pictures of a kingdom as deeply divided as any that can be imagined. The Belgians, of course, in those days, were up there at the top, like the Olympians who presided over Homer's world. What has stayed in my mind are indelible pictures of the black kingdom, of two completely different peoples, the Tutsi and the Hutu, who had arrived, from different quarters of the vast, surrounding continent, centuries before the Germans from over the sea. I described it all, at enormous and here compressed length, to Michael.

The Tutsi are extremely tall and long-boned, their skin the darkest, I think, that flesh could be, and – at the time I saw them – the soft and flowing robes which many of them wore, as blindingly white as finely spun cotton can be. In the countryside, never very close to the immaculate Tutsi homesteads of rounded huts within closely woven precinct walls, were the ragged, disorderly settlements of their virtual slaves (who far outnumbered them), the Hutu; a brown-skinned, rather stocky people with the poor and minimal clothing of labourers.

The Hutu were all hard at work, the men smelting and hammering fine metal tools or shaping pots or binding strong reeds into fences; the women at work in the fields or washing the fine white cloth and spreading it on the bushes to dry. Our Belgian guides introduced us to the Tutsi, who clearly expected it, and greeted us kindly and very graciously showed us how they lived. But the Hutu were not expected to interrupt their work. We were left by our guides to stare at them for a while, till we backed off under the pressure of their evident and justified resentment.

I could not divine, I told Michael, what powers or provisions kept this inequitable kingdom together or what might happen when the Olympians departed – as they did, in 1961. There were troubles enough between Tutsi and Hutu in the years after that; but for all my foreboding, I could not possibly have imagined a million deaths since the start of the genocide in 1994; the tally, it seems, unfinished; and, as with all war, the suffering unfinished, throughout the decades which are to come. It has been a fate which, for even more than forty years, I felt was bound to overtake my own country.

On the occasion I've described I was not (I don't know whether to say 'thank God not') on a broadcasting assignment. And if I had been, would I have known what to say? And if I'd had a television crew to help me, what a peaceful and orderly, lying scene would have been shown: a rural idyll, in the heart of darkness.

Compared with the limitless forays and commissions that women journalists and broadcasters do now, what I could write about this sort of life and its delights, difficulties and dangers and the ancient problems it freshens up about love, duty and the pain of leaving husband and young children – for the views I could offer about that, 'the time' (as Mehitabel the cat puts it, that great *connaisseuse* of what is wanted and what is not, *doyenne* of the dustbins of New York) 'the time for that is not ripe, it is rotten.'

26 In the heartland

～⌒～

The first time that Michael and I went to Italy, before we left Oxford, before my final exams, was the most amazing and exciting of many, for it was also the first time (apart from Scandinavia, which was an emotional rather than a terrestrial journey) that either of us had visited mainland Europe. Michael was preparing an essay on Roman Baroque to complete his degree at Wits and I had a College travel grant for pursuing 'Etruscan origins', but we were both so overwhelmed by being there at all that we tried to see everything and do everything that each wonderful day presented to us. Our money would not stretch to much, so we tried to do it, all the same, by a fearful policy of hardly eating and travelling in railway cattle trucks. We were inspired and refreshed by our adventures, but the real research, apart from copious photography, was done quite adequately later, in the library of the Ashmolean Museum.

In the Baroque photographs, I had always to appear as a stander-by, to give the scale; for my Etruscan photos I considered that Michael could not perform such a role since – because of his giant stature – he would have reduced, rather than illustrated, the massive proportions of Etruscan building. So in fact he was the photographer throughout, and I have hardly any photographs of my beloved husband on what was virtually our honeymoon. I had to do the accommodation research, since I retained a little of

Signorina Socci's fairytale Italian from Queensfield. Many a slum Italian landlady had her heart, or else her mirth, touched by my pleas for a bed ('but very large, please – *molto matrimoniale*') for me and my '*innamorato*', or '*fidanzato*' or '*sposato*' – fairytales do not seem to have a word for mere husbands. They were not equally charmed, though, by our reluctance to engage for any breakfasts, which we could not afford.

As years went by, we joyfully afforded more comfort and the last holiday we had before he died was blissfully spent in a Rennaissance hunting-lodge which we had rented in the hills over-looking Lake Garda. The older children sported in or on or around the lake; the younger remained content to stay with us, in a pleas-antly wild, terraced garden. We spoke very often about finding our own modest place whenever he should become well enough to spend time and energy in the search for it. So, when he died, what I wanted, needed, was to carry on from there. It seemed to be the sort of alibi in which, for once, I could take him with me.

I saw an advertisement in *The Observer*: 'Small, old convent for sale, village outskirts, unspoiled Umbria. Twenty hectares olives, vines …' I thought: that is just what we need, another home. The one we have in London has lost its heart. London will have to do, for office and school, but we – the children and I and Michael in all our minds – will start to make another place, an alibi we can share, and make a wild garden there. I thought: there must be, in twenty hectares, besides olives and vines, the wild things we need: trees and rocks and banks and – if we are inconceivably lucky – a stream. No matter how run down the land may be, we can in parts retrain it and in other parts set it free. In its natural forms and graces it can be a reassurance, a proof that in spite of the disaster, there can be peace and order in the world.

But the 'convent' turned out to be a sort of rural punishment block for disobedient nuns, in appearance rather like the tall brick tobacco-drying towers which disfigure the modern landscape. The earth under the sparse olives and dried stands of corn was dead and lumpy, mashed by inexpert hand-ploughing. It was a touching sight but far from pleasing. I had to go much further, over several visits, deeper and deeper into Umbria and away from the blandishments of Tuscany, into the now almost deserted heartland of Italy, before I found Le Buffaie.

The first moment that you see Le Buffaie, you see almost the whole of it, because it lies for the most part on a rocky spur which juts out into a wide valley. You come around a perilous corner and suddenly you are looking down upon it, from the height of the hills. Over the groves of gnarled olives which march down the hillside you see a low, square farmhouse perched on a rock; beyond it a steep valley and, over a small river, the opposing hillside covered with forest. Such are the convolutions of this landscape that this view from above is the only one which will reveal more than a little at a time. Seeing the whole of it, on the first occasion that I saw it at all, revealed to me, instantly, that I had at last found the right place.

Yet it's a place that rejoices in surprises, which start immediately. There is a little road leading down to the house, but it is more like the rocky bed of a dried-up stream. You could not call it a 'drive'; more like a *donga*. You plunge and scrape downwards, through a mighty olive grove, and when the slope lessens you come to a shallow ford over a little stream (stream!) which is fed by a modest, secret waterfall threading its way down the hillside forest. After that, you must do an almost vertical take-off to get up another rocky slope – and are suddenly welcomed by a wide walnut-bordered path which urbanely welcomes you to the homestead.

The farmhouse was derelict and long abandoned, and the site of habitation very old indeed. The people who last built upon it had used, as is customary, any rocks or large stones lying about, and piled them up to make walls that were very thick and lumpy, with many buttresses, since with such materials, and building on a rock, you cannot rely upon deep foundations. In the ruins of the massive bread-oven in the courtyard we found an egg-shaped, roughly chiselled little rock which the museum in Perugia revealed as an Etruscan stone to mark the grave of a female. In the usual manner

Le Buffaie is built on a rocky spur which juts out into a valley

*The courtyard of Le Buffaie. The magnolia was bought
instead of bathroom curtains*

of small farmhouses, the ground floor had been used for beasts, the upper floor for people, and they were connected only by an exterior staircase – of great size and solidity since it too was built of found stones.

In the very core of the house a huge stone mound, or excrescence from the rock, thrust up through both floors; the building has grown around it like a living thing, so that some of the smaller rooms on the ground floor, at least until we put in arches and windows, felt like caves; and even then some of our visitors were surprised to see that the walls of the inner rooms were of solid rock. The floors of these rooms were at differing levels and the relationship between them was, you could say, organic. I could indeed hear Michael's voice saying just that, as I took the decisions on what to do about it; for no architect could have *designed* this huddle of spaces for the shelter of man and beast. In spite of Michael's canons of architectural ease and order, which themselves echoed my father's love of foresight and precision, I decided to do nothing whatever about the floor levels. It was sufficient that the new windows let in light enough to guide your feet. There were no steps or sudden drops, just undulations. The workmen protested in favour of modernisation, rationalisation, flat and reliable floors, but I pointed out that hundreds of years of trotters or hoofs had managed all right, even in the dark.

The children and I especially loved the large main stable, or byre, for the milk-white oxen which work these hillsides, now as in Virgil's day. The floor of this room, which became our living room, was of smooth-worn, closely fitted stone. Down the middle a narrow channel had been carved, a runnel to take the beasts' urine out of the lower door and down the hillside. To facilitate this the floor on either side of the runnel was slightly raked, forming a gentle declivity on either side; while in the opposing direction, the floor as a whole was tilted from the higher ground to the lower. And the room, several feet below the modern ground level, was entered in a manner appropriate to hoofs, that is, down a wide, smooth slope of dressed stone. It was out of the question to alter, in any way, this far from rude, rather V-shaped floor, sloping in several directions, or its entrance which caused you to slide or totter if you did not wish to be tilted headlong. All that we humans had to do was to alter our gait.

We tried to change as little as possible in this beautiful, careful, ancient stable, so Virgilian in its sturdy, tender, practical provision for the working beasts. But since stables do not, by definition, lead anywhere, an archway had to be made through to the adjacent rooms. I found a sketch I had made of an Etruscan arch thirty

years before, on our honeymoon! On the ceiling huge, rotten beams
had to be replaced by long, whole trunks, and stained dark with
instant age. The house was exquisitely cool in the intense heats of
the summer when we went there for the long school and university
holidays, but Easter and autumn were also favourite times to go,
for shorter spells. The hardier children and their friends, or lovers,
or both, sometimes even braved the winter snows. So central heating pipes had to be concealed inside the rocky walls and, as
Michael, in my head, vainly pointed out, they lost thereby most of
their efficacy. About the hideous great radiators to which the pipes
had to conduct the struggling hot water, I could do nothing. We
had to have them. I had mentioned this in a despairing letter to
Sammy; he kindly cabled back from South Africa that I should
have the radiators at once replaced by gladiators; the nearest thing,
he said.

The radiators were ineffective, anyway, and after a few months I
decided we must embark upon a great fireplace; so a flue was with
very great skill tunnelled upwards through the central rock and out
through the roof in a squat little chimney. The local blacksmith
made some mighty firedogs, the forests were generous with dead
wood, and the result was wonderful, for the rock retained the heat
long after even the biggest logs had fallen to ashes. It was a novel,
possibly 'organic', kind of central heating; rather like a giant hotwater bottle placed in the centre of a big cold bed.

The only sadness about the fireplace was that the opening for it
had to be made in the middle of the great stone-built feeding
trough which ran the length of the interior wall. This trough was
surmounted by a long plank, a sliced tree ('fashioned', as Virgil
directs, 'from one tree-trunk') so venerable that it felt like stone. In
twelve places there were bays in it where pendulous dewlaps had
rubbed the wood to a patina bright as bronze; chafing away at it
all night, I suppose, as the ruminant jaws chomped and shifted
from side to side. Virgil, in the Third *Georgic*, praises, in a cow at
any rate, 'a generous neck, and dewlaps hanging from jaw to leg'.
The bays of our trough had certainly been very thoroughly pol-

ished, though 'jaw to leg' seems more than is needed for such a purpose. Two of these bays, in the centre, and the trough under them, had to go, to make room for the fireplace, but the rest of it remained. The two halves that were left, coursing down the wall at oxen-mouth height, displaced a certain amount of furniture, but it turned out that large troughs are a wonderful facility for a rural living room. You can safely stack them with wine, oil, logs, kindling, books, discs and tapes, cameras, newspapers, fruit, nuts, flowers, boots, walking sticks, car parts, *objets trouvés*, sleeping babies ...

There was a good deal of work to be done on the rest of the house, both to save it from further decay and to do such alterations as seemed essential. It took a team of five or six local men, under the direction of Siro, the contractor and village carpenter, almost two years to complete. At this time I had left Longmans and was again working for the BBC, at the Open University, in a great rush for the opening of it, and could get to Italy only a few times and for short periods during the year. In the intervals there always seemed some reason why the men had been deployed on some other local project; but I was glad that the work proceeded in fits and starts because it enabled me to have frequent consultations with Michael in my head. It often seemed as though both of us were monitoring its progress, supervising the details. In the same way I was glad, in the end, that my 'gardening' went fitfully. Michael had never expressed any opinions about gardens and anyway the point is a different one: each time I visited there was some astounding trope of nature which, had I proceeded on a plan formed on the previous visit, might have been spoiled or lost.

I had given a great deal of anxious thought to the floors of the house, both to those which I had insisted on leaving in their primitive undulations and to the beautifully built slopes of the main stable – and various lesser points, upstairs and down, inside and out, where the battle was between poetry and prose. Siro and the workmen were always in favour of the prose. I do not know, even now, what my father or my husband would have counselled. I know I could not have decided otherwise than as I did. My wonderful friend Nuala O'Faolain came with me a few times in the early days, braving the cold and the mud and cheering my grieving spirit. Nuala wanted things to be done in ways that would please me; so it was a matter, for her as well as for me, of finding out what it was that I wanted to be done. This is a sensitive and entirely logical way to go about such things, but there are certainly people whom I respect, architects and engineers among them, who would look upon such an empirical proceeding with dismay and disdain.

Shortly after all the building work had been completed, Dick Sheppard, the distinguished architect, said he would like to come the next time I was there. I felt nervous about that, though of course I readily agreed. For two years Dick had heard from me all about the worries as well as the splendours of Le Buffaie, never gave advice, never complained of my monomania or expressed boredom with botany, or Virgil, or Darwin. I was worried, of course, that a great architect – for he was that, as Churchill College in Cambridge and many other fine buildings show – would be able to point out all the opportunities for improvement that I had missed. I was also worried because Dick was a great man in size as well as spirit and, at the same time, a severely crippled man, a polio victim since late childhood. He had a specially adapted Mercedes in which he drove about like Jehu, but walking was a very difficult matter. I had told him about the floors, of course, but I could see that he underestimated the problems which, to him, they would present. That is what he did to all problems, which is why he achieved so much.

But he could not even have entered the living room, the old stable! There was a door and not just a cattle ramp at its lower end, but the floor here was about a metre above the ground outside and there was no step. Only one thing to do, before he came: I took a weekend flight out, drove up from Rome, met Siro, and intended, with him, to scour the Umbrian countryside for huge stones which could be turned into wide, strong steps. But Siro took me straight to his yard, and there among all kinds of useful bits of

wood and iron, doors and windows, were three or four perfect
stone steps. He had acquired them from an old building that was
being demolished. I could have phoned him (he pointed out) and
said 'Siro, *per piacere*, put in some steps.' We measured the steps;
they seemed about right so we drove out with Siro's workmate and
they dropped them into a bed of sand; they were so heavy that
there was no question of cement. I brought another of Siro's steps,
a smaller, slate one, home with me; and now it forms a little flat
bridge over a stone stream in my Oxford garden. (You will think
my garden is a sort of personal museum. Well? So are most gardens.)

Dick, when we got there, and apart from asking a few questions, said almost nothing about the house until he had looked at it
from every angle and into every corner, except on the top floor,
where he could not get to. He even laboured up and down the site
inspecting various little outbuildings which I had merely caused to
be tidied up and repaired. He observed, with an accusing glance in
my direction, that the steps up to the stable had only very recently
been placed there; there were still some traces of the bedding sand
on their surface. He manipulated himself on his crutches halfway
up the hill at the back so that he could get a view of the roof; and
down the hill again, a far greater trial of strength and patience.
When at last we sat down to lunch he gave me – *he* gave *me* – an
account of all the problems and possibilities I had been faced with,
and the decisions I had taken, and the manner and the workman-
ship with which they had been carried out. Long before he got to
the end I began to have a struggle with my tears, for in each respect
he said he could see no way in which I could have done otherwise,
or better. He said finally, 'Thank God you didn't have an architect
to tell you what sort of person you are, or what you ought to
want.' What a friend!

The following morning I rose early and took the furniture onto
the grass outside the stable, and began to sweep away all the dust
and detritus that had gathered in the room since my last visit. Dick
came up to the door, leaning on his crutches in the courtyard, and

said, 'You are, for an educated woman, remarkably dim. How do
you think the cowherds have been cleaning this stable for hundreds
of years?' It had not occurred to me before that the whole align-
ment of the place, the ramp at the top, the V-shaped rake of the
floor, the runnel, most of all the slope from front to back, had been
devised so that a stream of water directed down from the top
would carry away all the dirt until it emerged in a rush out of the
lower door. It was not just the urine of the beasts, as I had supposed, that went that way. I felt even humbler when I recalled that
even as a child I had known that this was exactly the way in which
Hercules had cleaned out the Augean stables, though he was
obliged to borrow the entire flow of the river Alpheus.

In the beginning the children and I were both thrilled and comforted simply to contemplate the hillsides and the ancient groves and
orchards, two little forests, the banks of the river, the little waterfall, the pool. The thought that this beautiful place had become a
part of our lives fell like a balm upon the fearful wound we had
suffered in Michael's death. It pushed back the prisoning walls
which had seemed to close in when, for so many months, years
even, we had been able to help him only by our love and care; and
it had not been enough, nor all the skill of the doctors and sur-
geons and nurses. We were almost physically crushed and
oppressed by the weight of his death and it had not seemed likely
that any view beyond, or ever any lightness of spirit, could come to
us again.

We loved especially the little waterfall which dropped delicately
down through the forest, became bolder as it crossed the ford,
bouncing on and over the rounded stones and then vanished downwards into a hanging thicket which concealed, to judge by the
sound of the falling water, a deep pool. But the slope was so steep
and the thicket so thick that we never penetrated it or saw this
pool. If it was a pool. Benedetto the roadmaker, who had a cottage

on the road above, said that there was a big stone tank down there where, long ago, the village women used to do their washing. *What village; and how did they get down the bank; how long ago?* He did not know. What is certain, as I found much later after a certain strange happening, is the presence down there of standing or slow-moving water; not just the stream rushing down to the river.

I kept putting off the decisions about the 'garden' – that is, the land immediately around the house and all such slopes as were not under olive or vine: how to help it to become a wild garden, or a better wild garden, or a garden rather than a wild place. My objectives were never very clear. I went on though, visit after visit, making preparations against the time when I would know what to do. For example: if there were to be planting or earth moving, labour would have to be found. I kept thinking of Mornington. But here in Umbria were no dusty feet coming to ask for work, no Chief, no *umfaans*. I wondered, at first, though not for long, about Girolamo.

I met him shortly after we had moved in to the house, settled in with most of the furniture, spreading ourselves generally and with much delight. The only slight worry was the amount of sheep droppings, bringing flies around the building. I had been glad to see, that spring, that the hillsides were dotted with large, brightly white sheep, their clean fleece proving how far we were from the haunts of men and motors. It is a long-bodied, long-haired and long-legged sort of sheep, the only sort, I imagine, under which Odysseus and his men could have clung as they so amazingly escaped from the cave of Polyphemus. The thought of the heroes clinging to the fat, woolly bellies proper to a Welsh hillside is not to be borne. These big and noble sheep, and their hardy shepherds, are Sardinian, come to central Italy over the sea from pastures which have become too dry and restricted to support them.

One fine morning when I heard the distant chink of the bell-wether I asked one of Siro's boys to go and find the shepherd and invite him to come to the house for some refreshment. I wanted to introduce myself and my family, so he could register our recent

arrival, and perhaps leave him to divine that we should not want
sheep droppings near the house. After a while the two of them, boy
and shepherd, came hurrying back. Girolamo's brown and weathered face was tense with some kind of anxiety. He would not sit
down for a drink. He poured out words in the Sardo language that
I could not understand. I was slow enough in understanding Siro's
boy's efforts to translate it into Umbrian. Eventually it became clear
that Girolamo, who supports a wife and nine children, supposed
that I was going to ask him to pay rent for his grazing. For many
years, since nobody had been there to observe them, his sheep had
safely grazed, and free. When I assured him I was not, and that his
sheep (in the right places) were a pleasure to me, he fell down on
the ground, seized a nearby stick, made as if to plunge it into his
heart and uttered many emphatic Sardo sentences, followed by a
death rattle. Siro's boy did not share my alarm. 'He says, Signora,
that he feels so happy he will lie down and die.'

I thought I would never feel comfortable gardening with such a
histrionic person and that in any case I should never master the
Sardo language. I tried five or six of his sons, on modest clearing
jobs, but – they are shepherds. They are fine young men, highly
skilled at the many jobs and the hard life which the rearing and
transhumance of sheep entail; but none of this relates to gardening.
After the first clearances round the house, to sanitise it against
snakes and sheep droppings, the only garden help I ever had at Le
Buffaie was from Benedetto the roadmaker.

With Benedetto contracted I set forth more purposefully to the
nurseries. But I have to record that in the ten years that Le Buffaie
was mine I bought, apart from a few herbs, only five plants. Three
of these were blue Atlantic Cedar. They are, historically and aes-
thetically, completely unsuited to the region. It was wrong of me to
buy them, and I had to struggle with myself to do so. I bought
them because they are of surpassing beauty and grandeur and I
would never have a garden in England big or grand enough for
them; more specifically I bought them to be planted in a triangle so
as to hide, among their copiously sweeping skirts, the newly

installed oil tanks for the heating and hot water. I could not find
any native Italian trees which had skirts of this amplitude. Even the
females of the great *Cupressus sempervirens pyramidalis*, which
grow blowsy with age and childbearing, thus ruining many a grand
columnar sweep up a noble drive – even these, once they 'let go',
do not develop skirts.

    The story of the remaining two plants will show the total of my
disasters and triumphs. There was only one of each, so it will not
take long. One was a white oleander. Guilty about the cedars, I
thought this would not be too out-of-place since it grows freely in
the wild places of the Mediterranean. I thought it might serve to
grace and soften the rather stark little guest building which used to
be *stalletti* for pigs and formed one side of the courtyard. Benedetto
came to dig the hole. He brought his roadmaker's pickaxe, for he
knew that the ground under the growth was solid rock. When this
became too apparent I suggested that he could with honour give
up, but he went doggedly on with the pickaxe, saying that this
plant would grow anywhere in Italy, even out of marble. While he
picked and delved Charlotte and I laboured up and down a steep
bank with buckets of ancient manure, from the pit into which we
had saved it. The oleander looked lovely for a week or two and
then died, in its little sepulchre in the rock.

    We had success, though, against even greater odds and in the
same courtyard, with the *Magnolia grandiflora*. I did not think it
was suitable for a wild garden, any more than the cedars were; but
what it was exactly suitable for was screening the upstairs lavatory
window. This little room had been contrived out of one of the
peculiar spaces between the main bedrooms; anyone seated there
had a wonderful view of the largest olive grove as it marched down
the hill and of any approaching motor car as it plunged down the
drive. These views were too important, in their differing ways, to
be obscured by some trivial curtain. On the other hand, anyone
outside the house, especially if walking on the hill immediately
behind it, had an intimate view right into the lavatory. The solution
was to plant an evergreen tree outside the window, an airy and spa-

cious tree, one with broad but not too numerous leaves.

Charlotte and Vicky came with me to buy the magnolia and we spent a long time choosing the grandest and most flowerful. It was dusk when we brought it home, carrying it in relays down the rocky drive (which we, in the family, knew better than to drive upon). We laid it against the wall where it was to go. It had seemed so big in the nursery; here, it reached only halfway up to the window. 'Never mind,' we all said. 'It will grow quickly.' Though after the oleander I had secretly to doubt if it would grow at all.

Next day, Benedetto was asked to bring his pickaxe. When he came he looked both amazed and scornful. 'You cannot plant it there, Signora.' This seemed a shameful turnabout after his insistence on planting the oleander. 'Why?" I asked. He looked embarrassed. I pressed on: 'It was bought for this place and for no other. This time we will make sure the hole is big enough.' He sighed at my stupidity and, I suppose, lack of delicacy. 'Signora, this is the place of the *pozzo nero*, the septic tank. *Naturalmente.*' He pointed up to the lavatory window; then he tapped on the ground with a spade; it made a hollow sound. He scraped the weeds aside, delved a little and with great satisfaction revealed a thick, plastic, circular cover. 'Well,' I said, 'perhaps a little to one side? ... After all, the branches will spread.' 'Signora,' he said firmly, 'we cannot plant it anywhere along this wall. It is where the drain goes. *Naturalmente.*' I had supposed, and he knew it, that a septic tank was just a deep, round, separate thing. He softened his heart a bit and suggested planting the magnolia in a pot in the middle of the courtyard. Not wishing to lose momentum by considering this awful suggestion I put on a vatic air and gravely asked him to dig a little and expose this *cloaca maxima*. With tired snorts, he did so, and when the fat, plastic pipe of the drain appeared I saw with relief that, in order to lay it, the workmen had excavated a deep trench in the rock and had then filled up the trench, around the pipe, with rubble. So what we did, and why there is now a wonderful magnolia, reaching up to the roof, what we did was simply replace the rubble with our fine, antique compost, support the pipe with a few flat stones, and slip in the little tree rather deeply, so that its roots would not annoy the pipe. For some years now, from inside the *gabinetto*, you can see and not be seen. It makes you feel like one of those secret people who peer out from among the stone leaves of Southwell Minster.

You may think it a matter for shame for a self-professed gardener to have planted, in ten years, in that wild place, only three Atlantic cedars and one magnolia, all of them solecisms. To make an even cleaner breast, let me tell you what happened to the small collection of herbs that I mentioned. A herb garden, I had thought at the beginning, was not merely essential but would be a suitably modest way to start, before all the major decisions were made. I planned to plant it a little way up the hill at the back where, under a leaning, old cherry tree, there was a depression filled with lush grass and therefore the promise of soft and fertile earth. The next time I visited, my son Matthew was with me. We flew to Pisa where I had left our little Fiat, and Matthew, newly licensed at the minimum age, drove us through Tuscany and over the Umbrian hills to the farm. We stopped at Pienza for the dark, wild honey (and the town architecture) and at Montepulciano for the *vino nobile* (and the church) and at a wayside nursery where I bought some small plants, in tins, of rosemary, sage, oregano, mint. But when, the next morning, I went up to the cherry tree with a trowel and my little tins, I found all that lovely, moist depression filled by thousands of fruiting wild strawberries! It was a sort of defeat, of course, but Matty and I celebrated that evening with bowls of *fraises des bois* glistening under a light sprinkling of the wine, of which they were entirely worthy, and a drizzle of the honey, and a dressing of finely chopped mint.

A few days later Emilia, wife of Girolamo the shepherd, came with a Paschal lamb from their flock. It was a whole, skinned, newborn lamb, cleaned and ready for the pot with its legs bound under its belly, its blind head raised up in apparent attentiveness. I was upset by the creature, which apart from any other matter reminded me of my beloved dachshund at home in London, but very touched

by the gift. The big Easter egg I had brought her family as a
Paschal gift seemed, by contrast, so trite and worthless. I asked
Emilia the best way to cook the lamb. She said, plucking vaguely in
the air, 'Oh, with this herb and that herb, in the pot.' I showed her
my pitiful little tins, the mint all gone on the strawberries, and she
said '*Pouf pouf*' and strode off down the drive, beckoning me to
follow. She turned off down an almost vertical sheep-path and her
robust figure slid down the green and springy slope and there she
lay, panting, and thumping the ground in a curious way. *Is she
going to lie down and die, is this a Sardo custom?* I slid down after
her; and from the crushed herbage around us rose up the paradisal
scent of wild thyme. It was a whole hillside of it, several kinds of it.
In other spots we were later to discover banks of *mentha*, *salvia*,
lavandula, *rosmarinus* and the excellent summer savoury *satureia*,
and many other herbs never diagnosed or named but often trustful-
ly put into the pot. Up to the time of Emilia's sliding the only culinary plant I had noticed was a patch of giant fennel; and the only
thrill about that was the reflection that Prometheus used its hollow
stem for carrying the fire which he stole from heaven.

It is important to me to say something about the animals. When
the children were with me, the animals were a grace and favour;
when I was alone, which over the years was about half the time,
the animals and the plants were what I had as children. Whatever
the case, there is no accounting for Paradise without the beasts.
Every Hindu or Buddhist painting that I know of the Himavant,
and every Christian painting of Eden that is not a Creation,
Temptation or an Expulsion, makes a point of showing the animals
living along with humans in the amity which, in time, Adam and
Eve wrecked; as on a far mightier scale their descendants continue
to do.

At Le Buffaie we were not always sure about the amity. Outside
there were certainly adders. I put pictures of them on the wall of
the stable so there should be no mistaking them for any harmless
sort of snake. Inside, there were small, black scorpions which often
caused the smaller girls – Charlotte and occasional friends – to

shriek and sob. If Emilia was there she used to exclaim '*Gamberetti!*', the diminutival suffix expressing her scorn not of the creatures but of our fear, as she cuffed them into her plump hand and threw them out of the window. Nobody would listen to my assurances, derived from much anxious research, that the only European species of scorpion to be feared occurs east of the Carpathians. Perhaps at a moment's notice no one can be sure of the longitude of the Carpathians.

We did not doubt the amity of the field mice, though they were awkward friends: forgivably, one winter while we were away they became house mice, making free with the cushions and mattresses. And moles and bats and hares – I once saw, hardly believing my eyes, hares boxing in the moonlight – and green-enamelled scarab beetles and an old toad who hung about the kitchen door, disguising himself as one of the stones we had put round the root of the magnolia after a fox, or something, had tried to dig it up. There were all these and more, of the beasts which are so lovingly described in the *Eclogues* and *Georgics*, which made their friendly presence the more wonderful. There was even, from time to time, 'an old boar who comes to muddy my spring' as Corydon complains in the Second *Eclogue*; only with us it was an old sow who belonged to Giuseppe up the hill, and whenever she escaped from her pen she made a bee-line down through our land to the river for a wallow. Sometimes I used to think that Giuseppe set her free so that he could amble down after her, passing our courtyard, to join us in a glass or two. Once, a swarm of bees settled and built their town against a window pane so that we had a privileged, inside view of their proceedings. Nobody has written about bees with the love and wonder that Virgil shows in the Fourth *Georgic*; and that summer I was able to study their 'tiny and admirable republic', as Dante referred to the Underworld, with Virgil as my guide.

In the early summers the nightingales sang all night in the trees on the hill behind the house. In the daytime they, or something else, made a coarse, coughing kind of chirp: is this what Eliot, or the old poet he is quoting, meant by 'Jug jug to dirty ears'? There were very many other birds at Le Buffaie, of course: I tried to name them as I saw them, because only by seeing them properly (as with plants) can one give them their name. What is important is the properly seeing. I remember the Barn Owl and the tiny Scops Owl, as hard to see in the dusk as the Nightjar with its curious drooping wings, as though they were too heavy to carry in the usual manner. In the daylight there was often a small, grey shrike to be seen, sitting on a fence or an isolated stump or post, in the way that they have, looking around to see if there is any tasty kind of thing moving about the grass. They pay little attention to mere humans. In South Africa we call them (or at any rate their smart, black-and-white relatives the Fiscal Shrike) 'Jackie Hangers', who often impale their prey on twigs or barbed wire, as they eat it. That is the bird I saw at Mornington eating stinkbugs. And sometimes we saw, rising up from the grass, a family of little quails, crying sweetly and sadly at their disturbance. The Italians, inveterate Jackie Hangers, catch them in nets and roast them on skewers.

One evening when Joan Bennette, who takes such knowledgeable delight in plants, was staying with me, we went for a walk down a steep part of the hillside, towards the river. Suddenly we both cried out and ducked, and covered our heads with our hands; for it seemed as though we were being dive-bombed by a great number of small and speedy birds with wings like little scimitars and excited little battle-cries in their throats We sat down on the grass, for safety as we thought, though the hill was so steep that it was easier to lie. Only then could we see that the birds were not interested in us at all. It was a crowd of swifts which had, it seemed, just caught sight of a swarm of insects rising up from our hillside; they swooped, with their scimitars and battle-screams; a windfall for them on the long flight to Africa. Their hunting could not be more unlike that of the shrike, which has proper feet, not just hooks for hanging on, which is all the swift has. The shrike can therefore sit on a stump and calmly wait, giving humans the mistaken impression that it is a companionable sort of bird, like the robin, hanging about for a favour. The swifts cannot retire to the nearest trees if they see that someone has preceded them to their hunting-ground; for they cannot sit or stand on anything unless it presents a vertical surface; they cannot even walk or hop about upon the ground.

But the loveliest winged creature there, which I saw only once, was the largest of the European moths, *Saturnia pyri* – identified only weeks later with the help of David Pears in Oxford. They are as large as a child's hands hooked together by the thumbs, making a 'butterfly'; soft and downy, Ovaltine-brown with a deep topaz-and-purple 'eye' on each wing. I found them one early morning when I opened the upper door leading to the outside stair. A drift of them had settled, like a soft, dusky, pale purple coverlet, against the steps where the sunlight lay. There was no jostling or crawling or even overlapping; only a barely perceptible thrumming as they rested there in the weak sunlight, trusting me. I stayed looking down upon them for a long time and, since there was no using that door or getting downstairs except by those stairs, went back to bed. An hour or so later they had gone.

The comity of animals – I don't feel that it was amity, in the way that I felt the mice made themselves at home and the moths trusted me – I met once again, in a strange way. There was a time when the small pool near the drive, which caught the waterfall, was in grave danger from me. I liked the tiny enamelling of the bright green weed round its edges but would have liked to move some of the patches of it to make room for some irises, or reeds, or water-lilies. This little fall and pool were after all one of the many ultimate sources of the Tiber – 'Tiber, Father Tiber, to whom the Romans pray'. I had discussed it with Sammy from Johannesburg and we agreed that something a little special was due to it. For two summers the pool could not be dealt with because the workmen kept cool in it their food and wine, floating plastic bags and bottles in it, incongruent growths among the duckweed. By the late summer of the third year the men had gone and I thought the time had come.

A certain evening I drove down to it with various buckets and dredging and pruning implements. As I approached the ford over the drive, it seemed more turbulent than usual. Why should this be, in these dry, hot days of the dog-star? But it was not water; it was flowing the wrong way. It was a swollen stream of struggling, leaping frogs, a pouring, eager mass of them coming up the steep slope from Benedetto's wash-tubs or whatever ancient dam lay in that secret place. The upward flow of frogs continued as the light declined, never changing course. Believing, if frogs believe, that they had a common purpose, they disappeared up the forested sides of the waterfall until, in the dark, I went home.

I had to drive home backwards; there was no room to turn, since I couldn't cross the ford and the frogs. Not only backwards but almost vertically upwards, up the rocky slope to the walnut avenue, in the total darkness, the headlights uselessly blazing away at the wrong end of the car, the reversing lights showing only a bank of rocks. I longed for Matthew, who was in London; who with his masculine assurance and co-ordination would immediately know in his mind what to do and with his nerve and muscle execute it perfectly, as I have gratefully known on so many occasions. The next morning I walked down to the ford. There was no sign of frogs; just the usual, silent pool and its proper weeds, and that is how it stayed.

In the late autumn of that year the struggle of the gardener in me came at last to an end. The hill at the back of the house, though steep, was easy to climb because there were many trees and shrubs to give one a hand, from the leaning cherry near the courtyard through droves of tall sweet broom, past a huge dying chestnut (victim of another killer disease that had swept through Italy), up through many sapling oaks to the parent oak whose trunk had split under the weight of its enormous boughs, but which continued in abundant leaf and fruit. I climbed the slope in gardening mood: *could one not do some evergreen planting; isn't it all, in the winter, rather dull?* Then I saw the broomrape, many stands of it. The broomrape is like no plant I had ever seen. *Orobanche ramosa* has no green, in any part; no leaves, even, since they are reduced to scales of the stem. Its handsome, flowering spikes (if 'flower' is the right word) stood in stately groups in no apparent relation to light or shade – or to the broom, which, raped or not, looked calm and well. Its appearance was so adventitious that it seemed more akin to a group of garden statuary, except that by its texture and colour it seemed to be made of flesh, pinkish flesh. I did not know at the time that it was parasitic upon the broom, but even so recoiled from the thought of disturbing in any way its secret life, or even from touching it.

On a later day that year I climbed the hill, avoiding the broom-rape, and reached the top. Giuseppe the sow-follower had told me that the previous winter the old oak had been struck by lightning. I wondered: did it need any help? When I looked up into its branches I saw a great ball of fire, a golden presence of mistletoe high up among the black boughs. The mighty Aeneas, guided to his sight of it by the doves of his goddess mother, had taken this revelation fairly calmly; but for me it was overpowering. Sir James Frazer took thirty years and twelve volumes to address the mystery of the Golden Bough – and, very curiously, seems himself never to have encountered it. Near the end of his great work he asks why the mistletoe was called the *golden* bough. 'The whitish-yellow of the mistletoe berries', he wrote, 'is hardly enough to account for the name, for Virgil says that the bough was altogether golden, stem as well as leaves.'

We do assure you, sir, Virgil and I, that we have seen it wholly golden.

At Le Buffaie we pruned and harvested and pressed the olives, which were excellent, and the vines, which were a disgrace, and we enjoyed the orchard fruits and nuts and the amazing and endless passage of all the wild plants and the peace and quiet (enhanced by the occasional Saturnalia) and the comity or amity of all the beasts. It was for me a ten-year alibi and alternative to a world which had been made untenable by Michael's death. I learned there how to feel alive although alone, which is the most valuable thing I have ever learned.

It was not only the beauty of Le Buffaie which brought to me, in the end, a quietened and reconstituted spirit. Behind it, there was Mornington and all the people and the things which, there, had brought me, so long ago, to the love of beasts and birds, soils and seasons. I withdrew from all hubristic plans by gardening arts to 'improve' this ancient, numinous place; and set off to try to repay a lifetime's debt to the great ones of my childhood, in Africa.

27 Thanks, Kalulu

At the BBC I had the chance to learn more about 'black' Africa than I could possibly have done had I stayed in my native country, where continent-wide developments were treated as news from nowhere; and at the publishers, Longmans, I had learned more about African educational needs and systems than the eclecticism of the BBC would have allowed; and at the Open University I had to apply myself to a methodology of distance teaching more basic and more rigorous than the Third Programme would have considered to be *troisième* (as with conscious affectation we sometimes described its style of high intelligence). I don't know whether or in what proportion I contributed to or was shaped by these phases in my life – it has simply seemed to me a continuum from my early astonishment, after arriving in England, at the quality and variety of programmes offered so freely, over the common air, by the BBC; at the pleasure of my nightly huddles with a little radio under the blankets of a freezing bed in Oxford.

What I do know is that the phase which came after all these, in which I was able to travel in Africa and Asia training people in the use of radio as a mass adult educational medium, came about through the work of Michael Young, whom I have called Mike. He is the most famous and wonderful person that I know, famous for an extraordinary number and range of social innovations, nearly all of them in some way emanating from the Institute of Community

Studies which he founded in 1953, three years after our friendship began. A mere list of the important social and educational structures which he has architected and engineered is far too long to put down here. That in which I have been most involved, at first by endless conversations and after its inception by various missions and undertakings, is the International Extension College, the IEC, which has proved as nourishing to the cause of distance education throughout the developing world as Mike's invention of the Open University has been throughout the world as a whole.

In 1980 Susanna, my eldest daughter, went to live in Central Africa as Oxfam Field Director for the region. She was the youngest Field Director Oxfam has appointed and only the third female to hold a post of that kind. It's a job which calls for particular qualities of both tenacity and adaptability, which are usually regarded as opposites and in any case – the old myth, again, about *fortitudo* as a male preserve – as requiring muscular strength and male assertiveness. The BBC, as I have said, used to make the same mistake about its foreign correspondents.

My pride in Susie's appointment just about balanced my pain and anxiety as she prepared to leave. She acquired some proficiency in the driving and repairing of heavy goods vehicles, crated up all her possessions and went out to start a new life far different from any she had known. I was relieved to hear about what was almost her first personal act in Zambia: she bought a Border puppy, Bobby. He became an enormous and beautiful dog and could, when circumstances required, behave very fiercely; but he was also a loving and humorous animal who shared and guarded her life for the four years that she was there. Jack and Ray Simons, old friends from my Communist days, lived nearby. They were glad to inherit him when Susie left Zambia, and we were glad for the safety and comfort he might bring to their long political exile from South Africa.

I longed to see Susie again and to share her knowledge of the people and the region. Planning to do just that, after early retirement from the BBC and the final parting from Le Buffaie, I was hastened in the arrangements by the IEC's request that I should to go to Zambia and train a team of officers from the Co-operative Department to make radio programmes which would encourage rural people to form co-operatives. In the early days of independence this had been a promising movement, inspired by Kenneth Kaunda and adequately funded by a copper market that was still copper-bottomed. In changed times, Kaunda invited the IEC to prepare a radio campaign to teach co-operativism to rural and mainly illiterate people.

I had visited Zambia before, for the BBC, when it was 'Northern Rhodesia' and – its black people anyway – longing to be independent. Flying over it, then as now, you notice the staggering population imbalance between the vast stretches of the African savanna, which seem almost uninhabited, and 'the line of rail', the conglomerations of settlement and development along the railtrack which snakes up from South Africa and Zimbabwe, cutting Zambia into two almost equally huge parts before it worms its way northwards into the Copperbelt and the more 'profitable' parts of what was then Zäire, that is to say the mines of the Katanga. There are villages in the country parts of Zambia, but many of them have only four or five houses. You may observe traces of more, but from the air it is hard to see if they are occupied. Looking down from the air, you could not have a clearer picture of rural decay.

But along the line of rail, the case is altered. There are European-style towns, served and provisioned by the railway – Livingstone, Kafue, Lusaka, Kabwe, Ndola, Mufulira – and these are surrounded, in most cases, by 'townships' or 'locations' to which, for living as distinct from working, the black populations used to be confined; and these, in turn, are swarmed around by squatter settlements where live thousands upon thousands of people who have left the scant livings which the land affords to try their luck in the towns and townships.

Kaunda realised that this drastic imbalance between town and country had to be addressed by his government as soon and as effectively as possible. He failed, at first, to achieve much improvement in spite of considerable effort and expenditure, not only because the copper-bottomed copper market lost its bottom, but also because the remaining rural people had not been adequately trained or prepared towards a workable or more profitable system of agriculture, in the face of the enormous changes brought about by European settlement.

I was delighted to go again to Zambia, nearly thirty years later, especially as I could stay with Susie in her little Oxfam house. The co-operative work seemed to me very important and broadcasting to tribal people was something I had not before been called upon to do. On three occasions before this assignment I had worked with Mike and with Tony Dodds, the inspiring, indefatigable Director of the International Extension College in Somalia; first in making the initial feasibility study and afterwards in helping the IEC to set up a distance education scheme for the tens of thousands of refugees who were gathered in camps throughout the country, their lives and families shattered both by war and by the terrible drought in the Ogaden.

Our purpose in that case, with the backing of the Somali government, had been to provide by tapes and self-study sheets and tutorial services – the usual means of distance education – courses which would enable these people to pass through the country's secondary education system so that they might have a chance of employment as teachers, upon release from the camps. That work was syllabus-based and naturally, since it was secondary work, it was for people literate in Somali. My job had been to train a body of subject specialists within the Somali Education Ministry, in Mogadishu, all of them experienced teachers in the ordinary face-to-face mode, to become distance specialists; to train them to produce tapes which were to be sent out to the camps where they were played to large groups of people in conjunction with the showing of any related graphics. I undertook to start the scheme not only by training but by actually producing, in Somali, the tapes that would be needed in all subjects for the first year of study. There was also a network of correspondence tutors and examiners. By the opening up of the country's education system in this way, great and homeless and fluctuating and unpredictable numbers of people can be served. This is something which conventional, school-based systems (even where they are adequate to existing needs) simply cannot do. There was an enormous response to this scheme, largely, I suppose, and sadly, because we had virtually captive audiences.

Zambia was a very different project, in its means – broadcasts, not audio-tapes – in its aims and in the kinds of audience. So I had a lot to learn. Susie and the Co-operative officers themselves helped me, all the time, to understand the problems of the different regions. In this sort of work it is essential to base all the broadcasts in the language and culture of each different group of people that you are trying to reach. So we had to prepare broadcasts, with plenty of very local material, in seven different languages, Nyanja, Bemba, Tonga, Kaonde, Lozi, Luvale and Lunda: such are the historical and linguistic circumstances of Central Africa, where differ-

Collecting material in a Zambian village

ent peoples have come together over the centuries from different directions and different cultures – as in Rwanda and Burundi the Tutsi and the Hutu have done. In Somalia there was only one language and those who speak different dialects of it can understand each other. So seven times more urgently than in Somalia, I needed in Zambia to be accompanied every working minute by interpreters.

The Co-op officers themselves, of course, spoke English perfectly, as educated Zambians do, but by definition our audiences were not educated people, not literate even in their own various languages, and remote from towns, transport and all manner of resources, and very, very poor. The Co-op officers were all, of course, conversant with Co-operative theory and practice, and were responsible for devising 'syllabuses' suitable to all the different local needs and resources. My job was to train them as broadcasters and distance teachers and interviewers, to find the ways to put it all across, on the air; and to make the first year of programmes and leave behind a team which could carry on.

In a case like this, seven different languages means seven different sets of programmes. You cannot simply prepare a basic programme and then get it severally translated. The essential part in broadcasting, of teaching by reaching, is to have programmes filled with interviews, real voices by real, local people talking about their experiences, which may then be discussed in that same language by other people who may know more about the subject and suggest new approaches and encouragements of one kind or another. Therefore, weeks before you make your programmes, you have to travel widely and choose good interviewees from local people, which means a lot of preliminary or preparatory converse with them, finding those with something interesting to say and providing for the expression of various points of view as well, of course, as getting across the essential teaching points; and you have to find local music to attract listeners and local stories to appeal to a local sense of humour. People will not listen for long without these ingredients, any more than they do on the BBC.

Michael Kittermaster and my old friend Peter Fraenkel had both worked at Zambia Broadcasting in pre-independence days and had made an admirable collection of recorded tribal music and of modern township songs. I discovered, to my surprise, though I suppose it is something well known to ethno-musicologists, that most groups of town musicians originate in the rural areas; they cannot make a living by staying 'in the bush' so they come to town, slightly urbanise the words, but on the whole keep to the village style. That, anyway, is how it was in Northern Rhodesia and in the Zambia of the early 1980s. So our research in that respect was a name for hours of very enjoyable listening and choosing in the Zambia Broadcasting record library.

The folk stories – another essential ingredient – were another source of delight. We collected dozens on our travels, in different variants. The folk hero of these regions is Kalulu the Hare (though in some of the languages he is called Nogwaja), just as in most of West Africa the hero is Anansi the Spider. These two creatures have the same rather deplorable nature – big-headed, high-handed, greedy, lazy and cunning. It is easy to find stories about how co-operation between people makes problems disappear, which was the burden of all our teaching; but I am bound to say that the means employed by Hare were almost always of dubious moral quality – and would not otherwise have been so amusing.

Village people are not simple or childlike and these stories were not exactly, or solely, used as decoys, to invite attention to the broadcasts – though entertainment is certainly a factor as this kind of non-formal programme depends upon voluntary listening. Rather, they presented wonderfully ready-made scenarios for the discussion of different aspects of Co-operation, or what my Zambian colleagues always called Co-operativism. Also, all the stories are set in a world of physical hardship: drought or sometimes flood, scarcity, hunger, fear, strife of one kind or another. To our audiences these settings did not need explanation or introduction; the need to escape perils, hardships, suffering, was neither novelty nor fairytale.

Sometimes in our preparatory meetings we told a Hare story and then invited discussion about what the point or moral of it might be – and then also recorded that discussion, which might become part of the eventual programme. It's a good antidote to the didactic approach ... One day, Kalulu and his wife, worn out with hunger and with pity for their little ones tugging at the wife's dried teats, were watching the wife of Lion resting on her side, her cubs pulling contentedly at her full breasts. Kalulu forms a plan. He goes off and cuts a hole through the trunk of a tree, a hole just wide enough to admit the passage of a thin hare. Then he goes to Lion's wife and offers her a few scabrous insults. (This is, apart from anything else, a colonial situation; the insults caused the wildest laughter, but I could not persuade anyone to translate with much particularity ...) She jumps up, spilling her cubs around, and chases the hare, who darts through the hole in the tree. Lion's wife follows but is stuck by her shoulders in the tree-hole; and Kalulu and his wife lead up their children to suck away in safety at the full breasts, and themselves take a good pull. What is the moral? someone asks. Nobody knows, apart from the too-obvious one about using your wits. Ah ... but you haven't heard the end of it. The story-teller continues: Hyena, Hare's dearest foe, sees the improvement in the health of the hare family and whines and worries until Kalulu will tell him, he thinks, the secret. Hare tells him the brilliant plan but omits to mention the size of the tree-hole. Hyena does all he was told, but this time Lion's wife can, of course, get through the hole, and soon catches Hyena and eats him.

That makes a lot of difference. It becomes obvious to one listener that the moral is 'what is good for one community may be useless or even dangerous for another' – that is the perfect English into which my interpreter puts it. No, says somebody else, what is important is to get the measurements right ... I dug a latrine pit the other day and made it too wide, and I fell in. (We have rapidly to fade the recording here, or the sound levels would explode.) Somebody else says that it shows envy to be the root of evil: you ought to work out your own solutions – the interpreter sums up a

long real-life story about some borrowed maize; and then everybody begins to agree that there ought to be a common emergency
store of maize to which everybody should contribute and nobody
would starve. It is all very useful indeed. Thank you, Kalulu.

Immersed, enmeshed, totally intrigued by the pleasure of training the knowledgeable and responsive Co-op officers through
whom I had contact with people and cultures I could not possibly
have reached by my interior resources, I paid little attention to a
message received one day in a remote village, through a passing
Oxfam worker, from the British Council in Lusaka, asking me to
get in touch with them. A few days later, in the fields outside the
village, another message, this time from the British High
Commission, asking the same thing. What is all this British stuff? I
thought. Perhaps there is something wrong with my passport? It
must wait. I found when I returned at length to Lusaka, where getting into touch could be done by telephone rather than telepathy,
that they were transmitting a request from Unesco that I should go
to Bangkok to help set up a national radio education scheme within
the Thai Ministry of Education.

I was not very willing. I would like to have stayed on there,
living with Susie in her little house, trying to improve the garden,
seeing this Co-operative thing through to a second year; and after
that of extending the distance education work which Mike and I
had begun during several visits to South Africa, which eventually
resulted in the establishment of the Ulwazi educational broadcasting unit in Johannesburg. The prospect of crossing the globe to
work with the Thai government filled me with alarm and reluctance.

So I thought out, as one does, which authoritative persons
would be most likely to give me the advice that I wished to hear,
and went to see my old friends Jack and Ray Simons. They were
both such total Africans or Africanists that I felt confident they
would not only understand but condone my reluctance to launch
forth into Asia. But they were amazed at my hesitation, when they
had heard the matter through. 'What is the matter with you, man?'

said old Jack. 'Are you getting senile, or something?' His wrinkled face and broad Cape voice were full of humour, but I could see that he felt quite stern about it. Ray was gentler but equally persuasive. So I went back through the guava bushes and the avocado pears to Susie's house, which was next door, doing what I imagined was a Thai-style dance, all angular and slow and wobbling at the neck. She got the message, glancing up through the kitchen window. Bobby rushed out with joyful barks to join the dance. That is how the longest, so far, of the alibis was decided upon.

I tried, this time, to learn something of the language before embarking on a new alibi and joined a class at the School of Oriental Studies, London University. But I had only a few weeks in London before departure and seriously underestimated the difficulty, for any European, of learning a tonal language. And Thai has even more tones than Chinese.

Imagine the unreality, in a language laboratory, of speaking into a monitoring screen which records your tones as a line of light drawing a graph, curving or upping and downing according to which of the five tones you aim to be using. One becomes miserably transfixed by it – as in hospital, if you are not too ill to see the screen tracing the aberrations of your heart. You know that it is you, or some part of you, which is controlling the line of light, but the experience is of the opposite relation. In the language laboratory the sharp, firm little line will tell you that by the tone of your vowel you have said the word for 'silk' when what you meant was 'new'; or for 'horse' when you intended 'doctor'; or 'penis' when what you had in mind was 'water buffalo'. (Europeans make that particular mistake whenever they mention the River Kwai, or its Bridge.) In hospital the little line staggering across the monitor will faithfully let you know when it has decided that you are dead.

Before my first visit to Thailand I was a complete stranger not only to the language but to the whole of the culture. At that time I had not before visited any part of Asia. Anyone of my generation would have picked up a good deal about India, at least the India of the Raj; but my awareness of more Eastern parts was very sketchy, coloured by Arthur Waley's poems from the Chinese, or the leisurely strolls I had so much enjoyed in the books about Japan by Lafcadio Hearn, and the beautiful eleventh-century Japanese novel by Lady Murasaki, *The Tale of Genji*, translated by Edward Seidensticker, in which a person's character is judged as much by the beauty of the poems which they hang upon the trees as by any part they may play in the central action.

The reality of South-East Asia, when at length I confronted it, was hard to cope with. Even in those days of the early 1980s Bangkok was an overcrowded, polluted and most confusing city. The drive from the airport was a fearful experience of the pillage of a landscape and of a city by the random and uncontrolled forces of commercialism, as (though worse every year) it remains. For several weeks I confined myself almost entirely to the enchanting small flat I had on the northern outskirts, a short walk away from the new broadcasting centre where I worked, and in the evenings to regular nightmares in the language laboratory.

My flat stood by itself, on stilts, in a jewel-like garden of tall, exotic plants and small, white plaster simulacra of Greek godesses. There was a glorious little swimmimg pool which I treasured not only for its coolth but for its extremely small size, so that by very little effort you could increase your daily number of lengths and convince yourself that you were getting nobler and fitter. I have stayed in this compound several times since that first visit; mercifully, it has not yet been swallowed by a bulldozer to make way for some huge and unattractive property speculation. It is seriously the wrong side of town from the great temples and the palace and the river and the shops and all the other sightseeing, apart from the beautiful little palace and garden of Suan Phakkad on which it almost abuts and where later on I spent many happy hours in gardening conversation with the Princess Chumbhot of Nagor Svarga. She was a good friend to me in some stressful times, and a maker

294 THE MORNING LIGHT

of magical gardens in several parts of the country.

But just because it is on the 'wrong' side of town, this compond of flats is a wonderful place in which to perform a piece of writing or reading or recovery from illness or a mixture of all. There are good little kitchens to all the flats, but if I am alone, I never cook in Thailand. Food of all kinds including quite elaborate hot meals can be bought for almost no money from the dozens of vendors who sit in the streets or pass slowly along them with their tricycles or barrows or cauldrons on wheels. Many come each day down the lane at the side of the flats and each has a distinctive cry, based upon the tones of the words describing his or her wares, so that you may know what it is, and you will go, or not go, down the steps and out of the garden to buy in the lane. Sometimes, though, the cry is that of the man with the patient female elephant, and many of the maidservants from our flats rush out with their money. This elephant, sacred like all of them, will for a small sum sniff up a little water from her master's plastic bucket, sanctify it in her long nostrils and then spray it out over you as a blessing. Or she will allow you to pass in a certain direction under her belly, which will ensure certain aspects of your love life. I saw only women paying the elephant for these services. Perhaps men need a male elephant; perhaps fully male elephants are not suitable for city work; perhaps a less than fully male elephant would not have the right powers.

Apart from mistaking the cry of the *mahout*, which I learned to recognise by the instant rushing-out of the maids, the only difficulty about this excellent system of street meals is caused by the Mynah birds. This garden, like most Thai gardens, has an aviary, and there are four or five birds of this strange and gifted kind. Beyond all parrots, the Mynah can imitate human speech, and all sounds whatever, to a deceptive perfection. In the beginning I would rush out with my money to a cry I took for 'hot broad noodles, sauce, mushrooms' or 'chicken, rice, many vegetables' or 'nice fresh mangoes cut any shape'. But ... nobody there; only one of the Mynah birds congratulating itself and its friends cackling about in mirth. They can even imitate the sound of the bell which the young man tinkles who wheels around a glass cupboard of sweet, bright desserts.

The work at the broadcasting centre was difficult in various ways, though I gradually became familiar with the Byzantine complexity of the Thai civil service. But the city as a whole seemed impossibly oppressive. For several weeks I thought I should never be able to manage the buses and concentrated instead on learning how to price-bargain with taxis even in ignorance of how far or long the journey might be. The climate in the hot season is such that the evening air – the Thais call evening 'the cold time' – is like the rising against your face of the steam from a cauldron of soup and in the noon time it is like immersion in the soup itself.

I was thankful when the work called me out of the Bangkok microclimate to visit, with Thai colleagues, distant schools and colleges; and gradually learned how to master buses, coaches and railways; and after a while vanished out of the city, alone or with friends, every weekend. Guided, very often, by Roger Welty and his incomparable and adventurous knowledge of the whole country, we went to the sea, to islands, or mountains or long drives through valleys and plains and ricefields, forests, villages, temples, shrimp farms, salt flats, often to visit the beautiful ruins of ancient cities where Siam began: Sukhothai, Phitsanulok, Kamphaeng Phet, Ayutthaya. These are among the settlements which the Thai founded, fought for and abandoned as the Burmese or the Khmer pressed onwards until Bangkok was founded, straddling the southern shore and the mouth of the great river, the Chao Phraya; saving and then rebuilding the Kingdom.

The climate you learn to endure. There are English and others who cannot but I, after all, am African, even if white, and learned quickly – and now in England often long for its extravagant heats and wets. You can talk yourself into it, too: 'if you can't deal with this climate then all South-East Asia, the Indian subcontinent, Sri Lanka, much of the East and all of the West coasts of Africa, not to mention Central and South America – then these are not for you either, nor all the wonders of their verdure and fruits and flowers.

You are like a timid, stupid butterfly in a herbaceous border, declining to visit any flower that is not a certain shade of pink.'

In any case, like the tiresome and boastful Red Queen, I could say, '*I* have known heat compared with which this is a chill.' In Somalia, working for the International Extension College, when the initial work for the Ogaden refugee radio scheme had been done, which involved much travelling, I settled down to do the training part in a very small house in Mogadishu. Only my nights had to be spent in this house, but it was so hot and airless that sleep was impossible. There was a tall, standard electric fan, but it was broken in a way which would not allow it to keep in one position, where one might have lain all night to catch the angle of its blow; instead, its whirring head swung continuously from side to side, as though looking for approval round the whole room; so you lay for a few seconds in the bliss of a lukewarm draught and for the rest of the time like a sausage sizzling under the grill of the iron roof, suffering and sweating until the slow attention of the fan should come round again. In due course I discovered that the heat further north in the Horn, in Djibouti, feels like that even when one is in the open air. In Djibouti, trying to buy a few necessities for work in the northern camps, I used to *run* from shop to shop, in case I fried in the sun. The frying would surely start, I felt, with my eyeballs since they are in a sense juicy and exposed; so I often ran rather dangerously, with almost-closed eyes.

But Thailand has not a Red Sea climate, nothing like it, and the Thais are comfort-loving people. They have a fine word, *sanuk*, which is not directly translatable. It means, depending on what you would hope to find in a certain place, whether coolth or warmth but certainly comfort, and whatever conditions would be attractive to you – it means the presence of those conditions. Because of *sanuk*, which applies also to transport, it is not at all difficult to get about Thailand, once you have learned enough of the written language to use the plethora of helpful notices. So for years now my visits there, private or contractual, have been of continuous interest and delight.

For me the essential attraction of Thailand is, as always, the plants and gardens, in the city itself and along the banks of its great river. As so often, because of my childhood, I suppose, and my Mornington garden, I cannot seem to come to the heart of a place, feel whether to accept it or not, until I have some understanding of its planting.

Even so, it is quite a challenge. For in Thailand every kind of tour is easily possible – except a gardens tour! You might inadvertently glimpse a garden while looking at the temples and palaces, markets, floating markets, weekend markets, flea markets, art galleries, posh hotels, zoos, bird sanctuaries, restaurants, floating restaurants; dining while boating, dining while watching Thai dancing; shopping, shopping while boating, elephant riding, elephant dancing; and quite a few unmentionably awful excursions, not only night-clubs and bars with girls or boys to rent but also crocodile wrestling, cockfighting and Thai boxing. But never, in fifteen years of visiting, have I come across a gardens tour! I have had to seek it all out; or have fallen in with garden lovers and garden owners, most of whom are wealthy, or royal, or both, or else atypical expatriates who have settled there.

But I did not come to know anyone with gardens in an ordinary sense for quite a time, until my friendship with Princess Chumbhot began, and with the wonderful Svasti sisters, Ning and Nunie, whose late sister, Pimsai, was a famous and influential gardener, and my great friend Noot who has shown me so many lovely Thai places, near and far. So I started by myself, when broadcasting work allowed, with the gardens of the poor. If you watch the Chao Phraya from one of the floating platforms, or set forth onto its broad and crowded waters, you will see every sign of a water-culture. Thais live as near to water as they can. All the great, ruined cities of their past have been built in the intimate embrace of a river. Rich people go to great lengths to have a lake in their

Bangkok: the gardens of the poor, in the river

garden, even if there is room for little else, and for many thousands of the poor the river itself is home. The Chao Phraya is lined down either bank, for many miles, by wooden houses on stilts which go down into the mud, and not a few families seem to live on clusters of floating logs or even on the lower girders of the four or five great modern bridges. They bath and bathe in the river, murky as it is, men, women and children; they gather and sell what grows in it, like the ubiquitous water hyacinth, and even – the poorest of the poor – what merely floats upon it: used plastic bags and bottles and all manner of urban detritus which can be reprocessed into some kind of a living.

On the western bank of the river you may most easily visit the more recognisable of the old gardens of Bangkok, the fruit, vegetable and flower farms which so copiously supply the city every morning by scores, perhaps hundreds, of boats. You will need to persuade a man with a long-tailed boat to take you there, carefully and not racing like a bat out of hell (though bats, it happens, do not roar and choke or try to overtake each other) down the broad mainstream, and then set off down side channels into the plantations of mango, bananas, jackfruit, litchi, rambutan, papaya ... If you wish to leave the boat and explore the groves, or some of the old temples which are sinking into the ooze, you will need strong shoes and bare legs, because the cultivation here is by irrigation channels from the river itself by means of very wide ditches, too wide to jump. Some of them may be crossed by springy, narrow planks, or even a single pole of bamboo, but I find it preferable to enter the ditches slowly, by foot, shin and sometimes knee, rather than by the whole body head first, as a pole-crossing invites.

I especially enjoy the orchid farms, as most people would. The famous Thai orchids are grown on shaded racks or hanging from the roofs of slatted sheds, in a very orderly manner according to the requirements of each of the many kinds. You will be drenched by the fine sprays of water that they need, and often there is ditch trouble, but there is no more colourful adventure into the exotica of the tropical plant world. For a small sum you can almost fill your boat (if you can get back to it, over the ditches, while carrying them) with armfuls of these strange creatures. In spite of their extravagant colours orchids often seem to me more like animals than plants, for in many of their outlandish forms they seem to have faces and wings, orifices, genitals even. I can understand why expeditions of this kind, the fruit and the flowers, are not offered to – or suitable for – the great masses of tourists which Thailand attracts. Their passage would endanger the crops as well as the trade.

But, even without these detours, if you keep to the main wide and crowded river and progress away from the terraces of the big hotels you will pass, down either bank, mile upon mile of the domestic gardens of the poor, and these are the real and immemorial gardens of Siam. The houses and shops and shop-houses are, as I said, built on the river itself, on stilts. There is occasionally a well-off-looking slightly larger house with a built-up and fenced-in landing stage, with a trim postbox and wooden seats and a little dog barking out its guard routines; but most of the houses are wooden, dilapidated and small, with steps leading directly down to the water from the narrow balconies with their huge clay pots waiting to catch the purer waters from the sky. At every possible point on the balcony, on the floor and window sills and hanging from the railings and the roof, there are ebullient plants in clay pots or in coconut shells, creeping ones, cascading ones, bushy and stringy ones, flowery ones, spiky ones, spiky *and* flowery ones.

These potted and hanging plants are not big enough to be thought of as edible crops, though many are used for flavouring. I discovered by such enquiries as the language barrier allowed – no English is spoken on the river banks, and my laboratory Thai is not well into intimate bodily function – that very many of them are grown for medicinal use. Thai people are not reticent about the body, and are helpfully graphic with their visual demonstrations; all the same I should be forgiven for often confusing the body-language which denotes aperients and diuretics, taenifuges, purges and diuretics; and is a woman patting and rubbing her chest signi-fying 'expectorant' or 'galactagogue'? Many of these plants are grown just for their beauty: sometimes, flung like a shawl over a corner of the roof, there is the white-pink-and-red exuberance of a Rangoon creeper, *Quisqualis indica*, which from the delicate curve of its petals the Thais call 'the fingernail plant'; or spiralling up the verticals of these shady, moist balconies are bright bougainvillea, which in land gardens will thrive only in hot places that are also light and dry. It must be that all the pots are expertly, individually tended, not least those which, like the fragrant Arabian jasmine, are essential daily decoration for the little spirit houses which stand by all the dwellings in Bangkok, rich or poor.

In the water below, on either side of the steps or in the inter-stices of the houses, wherever boats will not disturb them, there are luxuriant, floating, matted masses of the water hyacinth. On the whole this troublesome and ubiquitous plant *Eichhornia crassipes* (which with a nod to Byron's version of the *Oedipus Rex* I think of as 'Swellfoot the tyrant') – on the whole it has been a disaster in many tropical rivers in both Africa and Asia because its crass and swollen feet and endless roots clog the channels of a river and de-oxygenate standing water. But the Thais, thrifty and enterprising, have many uses for it – for flavouring a hot, sour soup, for pig feed, or compost, or dried for cigarette papers, baskets, cotton thread, garlands. Its lilac flowers are attractive but they do not make a show as expanses of many kinds of the wild water-lily will, or the sacred and beautiful stretches, in pools and ditches, of the native Lotus. But the big, green and crisp rafts of Swellfoot are encouraged to grow in the gardens of the poor along the Chao Phraya. I have read in a scientific journal that it functions as an anti-pollutant, absorbing the heavy metals present in this much-used waterway; I suppose that the very long roots and the ample storage space of its bulbous, swollen feet put it in line for that job, but I think it should not also seek part-time work as soup-sourer or anything else that is eaten.

Not all the river-dwellers grow Swellfoot. Many of them keep vigilance against it and grow, instead, masses of quite a different water plant, the water 'morning glory', *Ipomaea aquatica*, also crudely known to tourists and to colonisers in other countries, inevitably, as 'swamp cabbage'. It is a pleasant and nutritious spinach-like vegetable, rich in vitamin A. The Thais call it *phak bung*, or caterpillar plant (I don't know why). This crop is harvested and sold and eaten by rich and poor, served either by itself with a sharp sauce or as a flavouring in soups and stews. There is quite a mystery, though, about its harvesting. I once lived for a few months in a flat which looked down upon one of Bangkok's *khlongs*, or canals, a wide and pretty one, now filled in and built over by a huge parking garage for the skyscraper of 'apartments' which has replaced my modest little block. This canal appeared to be choked by *phak bung*, an almost solid mass of it; yet every morning women would come, just one or two of them, at different times, *through* it, in small rowing boats. They would harvest the plants, a patch here, a patch there, bind the bundles round with a long root, and row off again. I used to wonder: do they pull it out at random? Can anybody do it? If so, why does not everybody? Why is there not a crowd attacking the *phak bung*, in this city where even the rubbish tips and the flotsam of the river provide a livelihood?

It took me some weeks and close inspection from a boat on

which I had begged a ride to discover that, far from a random harvest, it was carefully and precisely controlled, no less than the culture of the orchids or the balcony pots of the river folk. There were slim little sticks emerging at fairly regular intervals from the green rafts of the vegetables, that I had not been able to see from my balcony above. They were upright and meaningful little sticks which must have been, somehow, bolted into the mud or else weighed down in the water, because they maintained their place and verticality even when the plash of the boat rocked the rafts of the vegetable. So, it is clear, the women knew where and how much to pick, and which patch belonged to whom and, by arrangement, when to come.

It is the same with all the waterplants round the houses on the banks of the river and in the ditches and pools and small lakes along the roads and settlements outside the city. Do not suppose they are filled with wild, unwanted plants; they are among the gardens of the poor. Their produce along with that of every other type of gardener or farmer may be seen for sale on almost every pavement of the city, a range of vegetables, stems or leaves, fruit (fresh or dried) and flowers, seeds, nuts, barks, pickles, decoctions – a range so wide I can't characterise it. It is one of the chief pleasures to be enjoyed in a city which, to so many visitors, seems merely a wilderness of urban chaos.

I feel bound to say that a large part of my pleasure in the markets and streets of Bangkok arises from my converse, limited as it is, with the street and the shop people. Many of those at the selling face, at any rate where tourists are likely to go, have a little English, but many do not. (For some reason many of the sellers of clothes in the main thoroughfare, Sukhumvit, are actually deaf mute people.) So purchases of any kind, which are always bargained for (as are the fares for boats and taxis and three-wheeled *tuk tuks*), involve a great deal of personal reciprocity, little dives

into mutuality and acquaintanceship. As I learned a little more
Thai, much of it from the street, this became more extensive. After
a few weeks I realised that the source of my pleasure lay not so
much in the language exchanges but in the fact that none of these
people, not even the most needy or anxious of them, deferred to me
as a European or wished to ingratiate themselves, or, on the other
hand, shrank from me, or appeared to dislike me. 'Thai', in Thai,
means 'free', and Thai people have always seemed to me completely
free of the ugly attitudes which, in Africa and especially South
Africa, colonialism and exploitation have bred between the races,
and which now, thank God, are diminishing.

Thailand and its armies suffered defeats in the past, but not
from Europeans. Thailand was sometimes 'occupied', but never
colonised. The street people, though they naturally want to gain as
much money as you are willing to lose, never fear to joke, or to
speak out, or to ask very direct questions, or to pour out either
praise or scorn according to how the deal is going. In Thailand I,
too, feel free. I have often reflected that the great degree of poverty
there, in spite of all the progress, was nothing to do with me and
my colonising forebears, my white skin, my mother who sacked
Lottie, my dear father who helped to mine the gold. I could face
the Thai, with no ghosts in attendance, *in* the face, as they faced
me, no more, no less directly.

What most people would consider the proper gardens of Thailand,
the ones for pleasure and for show, are, except for those which are
kept strictly private, quite easy to visit. In temple precincts you may
find fine old trees but not gardens as such, for the monks may not
dig the soil for fear of killing any living creature. Many temple
compounds are full of diseased and abandoned or feral cats and
dogs, which the monks accept and feed. The presence of these animals does not make for pleasant strolls around the enclosures.
Some of the fine modern hotels have fine modern gardens and some

have been built in what were fine *old* gardens, and they look after them well.

I once went to visit the famous Thai writer, politician, former Prime Minister, classical dance master, actor and garden maker, the late *Mom Rajavong* Kukrit Pramoj. I was taken there by Chaenchaem Bunnag, who has wonderfully translated into English Kukrit's historical novel of Siam, *Four Reigns*, which deserves a place with the great Murasaki. We were seated in a cool part of *Mom* Kukrit's famous and adventurous garden. (There had been some difficulty about where to sit because many of the garden chairs were occupied by nesting bantams.) He told me that there was no such thing as an essentially Thai garden. He said, 'We don't have a garden style. We just put together various elements we have pinched from China, from Japan, India, England, and we happen to like keeping many pets, turtles and fish and birds and so on.' He was ruthlessly insistent about this. But it seems to me, though I did not dare to contradict the master, that the borrowing of favourites is all that any garden is, and that any tradition may arise according to its consonance, when transported, with new conditions and beliefs (and incomes). This is the Darwinism of horticulture: no sense, in the real world, in calling for strict definitions. In Thailand, whether there is a 'Thai style' or not, garden after garden has the features that were also in *Mom* Kukrit's; except his training ground for the ancient Thai masked dance; strict paths around a fine, ancient lingam. To know about that, a mere gardener could not aspire.

Life in Thailand has been for me a continuously wonderful alibi. Apart from all its own and startling attractions (I have not even mentioned the extraordinary combination of great size and great delicacy in its temple architecture), there is nothing whatever in it that reminds me of Oxford which might make me long for my home; there is certainly nothing in it like South Africa except of course the enormous poverty in the midst of wealth and extravagance. So far as possible I do not even take with me to Thailand, in my head, the classical baggage which furnished my alibis in Italy. So it has been a new world. It gives me, each time anew, though on a very large scale, the excitement and encouragement I used to feel from the little 'Japanese' garden in a green oven tin which my mother gave me so long ago, and which, when I thought she had left me, I used to copy, at the McKenzies', with such pathetic and defiant persistence.

Sometimes I wonder whether the garden I have made in Oxford is another edition of that work. It is certainly based upon the Japanese style, for I saw after visiting Japan that various features, especially the copious use of stones both great and small, would solve certain problems of slope and shade, wherever grass declines to grow; and that trees and bushes should be pruned far more ruthlessly than the British care or can be bothered to do; also, Japanese plants prosper in our climate to a degree that most other 'foreigners' do not. It would be certain folly to attempt a Thai garden in the temperate, hesitant summer moistures of North Oxford; let alone in the intemperate frosts and freezes of its winters.

But plants and trees and stones are worthy and beautiful in themselves and do not need a cultural commentary or national identity. Perhaps that, after all, is what *Mom* Kukrit was insisting upon.

29 'Under the bridge'

I have found that sorrow is an effective solvent of guilt. Regret is not nearly powerful enough. In April 1994 I was teaching in Johannesburg, conducting a workshop for turning experienced black teachers into producer-teachers for (mass, we always hope) educational radio listening. April 26th arrived. It was the first day of the historic general elections, the beginning of Freedom, the first time that the entire and whole nation, including, at long last, the overwhelming majority of its people, had ever been able to vote for their representatives. The voting was to cover three days and the first day was set aside for the voting by sick and infirm people, or

A radio class in Johannesburg

the elderly, or those afflicted in other ways – including by pregnancy. On this day, of all days, I could not get in to work, to the building where we always met! I was longing to share the big day with the trainees. We had agreed to make a programme to celebrate and to commemorate it, to drive out to numerous voting stations, recording equipment at the ready, hearts and minds leaping in and out of our van.

But I could not get to work; none of us could, though many had struggled to get in from Soweto, because our work was centred in a district of Johannesburg notorious for its violence and lawlessness and which also happens to contain the headquarters of the ANC. Trouble was expected (and it came) both from the white right and from the Inkatha Freedom Party. So during the previous night, the Police had thought it wise to cordon off the whole area with huge rolls of spiked wire, 'razor wire', and to forbid entry by any means which evaded it.

Therefore I spent most of the day in my hotel room. But it happened to have a glass wall which looked out upon the voting station for central Johannesburg, at the Civic Centre. There, winding in orderly, concentric sausage-shaped circles round and round its huge concourse, a patient queue shuffled the whole day from early morning and far into the early dark of night. I watched it, and I watched the TV too, which reported widely (and very well) from every part of the country. All I had to do was to draw back the curtains from the glass wall (ten floors up in the sky) and look, from an armchair, for hour upon hour, from the window to the TV and back. What I saw was an unending stream of men and women crippled, maimed, bent, blind, aged, many on crutches, many brought by their family on boards or other makeshift stretchers, many hugely pregnant and leading tired little children. *Si lunga tratta di gente* – Eliot famously quotes from Dante's vision of Inferno, 'so long a stream of people, I had not thought death had undone so many'.

I had not ever seen so long a stream of people before; only black bus queues, like that which took Lottie slowly away from me, or queues at the Pass Office, and a particular queue, once, at the Post

Office. On one of my previous working visits to Johannesburg, during apartheid, I had to find a place where I could talk to Moses, whom we had called little Moses, since he had run away from his home in Zululand to come and join his father, the Chief, in our household, taking the place of his brother, Big Moses. Moses had heard from the servants of a family I used to know that I was 'in town, from England', and staying at a certain hotel. He waited outside its front door from early morning until late afternoon, for I was out early in Soweto, recording people before they left for work. When I returned he almost jumped out at me, on the entrance steps, and was promptly manhandled by the commissionaire who blew a police whistle and tried to push him face down in the gutter. I recognised Moses the moment he called out to me with the name they always used, for some reason: 'Iyo-Prue! Iyo-Prue!' After a chasm of thirty-five years, sight would not, for me, have been enough, for he was twice as tall as the young Moses, twice as thin; sick and shabby, a weary middle-aged man he seemed, who had been a rather rotund, shiny, smiling boy. When I had sorted things out, explained to the hotel that he was almost my oldest friend, I asked them if I could bring him in for a cup of tea. The answer, of course, was a stony and unashamed 'no'.

I longed for his news, and for news of his father, the Chief, and Zwela and Albert and the other *umfaans*! He would not have known about Lottie, but he might have known of someone who did ... But there was nowhere we could go, to talk while sitting down. I had no home there; nor, it turned out, did Moses, who was sleeping rough. John's house was miles out of town and in any case John would not have liked it – I had invited a black journalist to meet me there a few days previously, and before he arrived John – courteous, deeply embarrassed – asked me if I would mind talking to him in the kitchen since any greater show of equality, though I think he said 'familiarity', would 'upset the servants'. No cinema, no restaurant, in those apartheid days, not even a seedy teashop would have received Moses and me. There was nowhere but the Central Post Office foyer, where people sorted themselves out to

join either the short white or the long non-white queue. That is
where we went, and sat upon a window sill, eating buns and
bananas and talking until the Post Office closed its doors. Since
Lottie's roadside visit after the Dissolution, it is the only contact I
have had, in a lifetime, with the great ones of my past.

The non-white Post Office queue that wound past us as we
talked was certainly very long, even though most of the people in it
were carrying sheaves of envelopes obviously containing the business of their white masters. It was not at all as long and convoluted
as the queue for the voting; but the Post Office queue from that
sad-but-joyful day came into my mind as soon as I drew my hotel
curtains and saw, in amazement, the Voting.

In its usual cowardly way, my mind called up some literary
alibi as refuge from a painful thought or sight. *Si lunga tratta di
gente* … The shades of the men and women whom Dante and
Virgil watched queuing to catch the infernal boat to Limbo were
also physically plagued, harassed by various painful conditions and
revolting circumstances; Eliot's crowd flowing over London Bridge
was less physically, more spiritually afflicted in that wasteland; and
yet – what kind of allusion was this? It was one of sight alone, a
sort of visual trick. As I watched the voters it very soon became
apparent that *they* were not a parade of doom-stricken, miserable
shades, *they* had not trooped despairingly under an arch inscribed
'Abandon hope, all ye that enter here'. If there can be an opposite
to so complex a state of affairs, there it was, ten floors below me,
winding round the concourse of the Civic Centre. For these people,
old or afflicted, halt or blind, faint, variously burdened, were full of
joy and of a sort of wonder. They were content to wait for hours in
the strong sun, almost afraid to sit or squat – though some could
only lie or lean – in case the queue should move on without them.

Soon the TV began to interview people waiting to vote – not the
ones I could see, of course, but at different stations all over the
country. I do not think that there has been a television broadcast,
anywhere in the world, to equal it in power, revelation, joyfulness
and, at the same time, pathos – that, at any rate, was its effect

upon me and upon very many Whitefellows that I know. We understood, of course, that this was a day specifically set aside for the
infirm; all the same, the sight of this voting seemed to be a glimpse
of all our history: all the evil that had been done, all the good that
had been withheld, and also, now, all the fairness and justice that
seemed to be promised. It did not seem, on that day, to be a black
victory, though the electoral triumph of Mandela and the ANC was
never in doubt. It seemed to celebrate a victory of the spirit for
white as well as black. Anne Yates, who was with me in the ships
at Mylae – Queensfield, Wits University and Oxford, all those years
when it appeared that there could be no hope for justice or sanity
in our country – Anne called to see me that evening. She found me
exhausted by wonder and sorrow. We talked about these things as
we have done so often during our long friendship, and I was not
ashamed of my tears.

One may be deeply touched by moments of comedy, too; made
aware by the suddenness of a burst of laughter of man's inhumanity
and the price which must be paid in suffering and in collective
guilt.

Two years before Freedom I had given a workshop in Grahams-
town, in the Eastern Cape. The programmes on which I trained
people were, as usual, being put together from recordings in the
townships and squatter camps which extend round the perimeter of
this trim little town, and the subjects of the programmes were chosen, after much discussion with the inhabitants, to be of value and
interest to the poorest of the poor: garbage and sewage disposal,
clean water problems (viz dirty water problems), self-help medica-
tion, how to apply for a job, what kinds of help were to be had
from local authorities, and so on. But the theoretical discussions
and demonstrations with and for the trainees, who were all black
teachers or social workers, were held in a college in the centre of
town.

It happened that a week or so before the workshop opened a group of young boys had been discovered living under a culvert, in a ditch, on the edge of the town. They were 'street children', homeless and hungry, naked or in rags, about twelve of them. The college cleared out some storerooms in its backyard and undertook to feed and shelter the children until the social services could sort out their needs. So it was not surprising that one of the topics chosen by the trainees was 'street children'. It is a pressing national problem, and there we had on hand a group of young people to guide us.

They gave us some extremely interesting and colourful answers to the question of how, individually, they had come to be living 'under the bridge', as they always (rather affectionately) called the ditch that had been their home. I thought it strange, at the time, that they should use this very phrase, the same that John and I had always used for the hideout under the culverts in our garden. To us 'under the bridge' was a safe haven in which to hide from the occasional demands of a sheltered, comfortable, colonial life. To these children it had been a matter of life itself. (I once thought I might call this book 'Under the Bridge', because it spans the fearful contrast between the circumstances of my childhood and that of the overwhelming poor. But the phrase sounds too vague, as though one were quoting some truism about the passage of time.)

So most of these children were always somewhere nearby as, over a five-week period, the training proceeded. They seemed fascinated by what we were doing. Even when they were not being guinea-pigs for trainee radio producers, they could always hear, through the windows which opened onto their yard, whatever was going on. The rationale, organisation and financing of distance education naturally did not interest them, but when it came to radio and the making of actual tapes – music, sound effects, plays, acting, phone-ins, field expeditions, rehearsals, discussions and arguments, midnight oil, early morning oil – we were aware that their excitement almost equalled our own. They sometimes cadged lifts out to the shantytowns and squatter camps they had come from, but they were never in the way, or noisy, and (so far as we knew) they had ceased to practise, now that they had food and shelter, some of the ingenious small crimes that had kept them alive in the past.

As the end of the workshop approached we decided that, to conclude it, we would like to call a public meeting for anyone in or around the city interested to come and hear about our work and listen to the programmes we had made. We were sitting on the front steps in the sunshine discussing this, drinking Cokes and having a break, when Leon, the leading spirit from under the bridge, a lad of about thirteen, came up to us, plucked up his nerve and politely asked if he and his friends could also make a programme, and play it to 'the people'. Would we lend them the facilities? They would need, he insisted, only technical help. 'Of course, of course,' we all said, laughing; and then the young chap produced a painstakingly written cast list, and also a list of the music and sound effects they would require. The music, he said, they would sing themselves, but they would like it on a separate tape so that it could be 'fed', he said, up and down at start and finish, which made it clear that by 'fed' he meant 'faded'. The principal sound effect, apart from the coming and going of a powerful car, was more of a problem: they wanted the sounds of several people falling, and falling slowly, out of a wardrobe! We said we would try, if they would help us by doing the falling, out of whatever cupboard might be in the studio – a prospect which seemed to them delightful. It became clear that they had been working away at this play, in secret, for quite a time. There was no script, of course, since Leon could hardly write, and anyway none of the rest of the cast could read.

⌇

At our open day *Under the Bridge*, which was the name the children gave their play, took the cake, easily – even among the few whites who came. It was followed by discussions of why children

leave home, why it is so hard to get them to talk about their
parents (they prefer to say that they have none), why so few street
children were girls, what happens to destitute or runaway girls,
what kind of provision could be made for boys or girls, by what
kind of agencies, and so on. The children's play could not have
been so amusing were it not also so heartrending, a cry for love
and help from the young, desperate, resourceful dispossessed, who
were beginning to feel, probably for the first time, that someone
was listening to them.

30 From the Bee House

⟳

The Bee House is a small, old and lovely, simple house, sequestered in the depths of a large fruit farm in a huge, high valley of fruit farms, a valley which lies among the blue and sudden mountain chains of the Western Cape. It has been lent to me (for the English winters, that is to say the Cape summers) by perceptive friends who consider that I might more reliably finish this book here, quietly alone, than in the companionable maelstrom of Bangkok where I have happily wintered for the past fifteen years.

The Cape of Good Hope, which Francis Drake described as 'a most stately thing, and the fairest Cape we saw in the whole circumference of the earth', is the tip of a fairly small peninsula, as they go. Its resounding history is mainly due to its position which, as everyone knows, is at the turning point between Europe, where the ships came from, and the East, which they wanted to reach and thereafter to return from. On the way out, you turned left at the Cape; on the way home, right. The problems about following these simple directions arose from the violence of its storms and (in the days of sail) the unpredictability of its winds.

For mariners under sail the Cape was a desperately difficult place, even if the fairest on earth. Table Bay offered anchorage, but treacherously: a north-west wind was needed to get into it at all, but it is not a large bay so the same wind, coursing too strongly through the roadstead, might well blow you onto the rocks of the further shore. If the notorious south-easters were blowing, you could not get into the bay at all. All the same, it was most eagerly sought by mariners, marking as it did the turning point of their journey and profit from the sale of slaves, fresh supplies of fuel, water and food, and a few days' respite from the tyranny of the sea.

Many ships returning from the East were so eager to reach it that they mistook, for Cape Point, Cape Hangklip, which lies a few degrees to the east of it – a mistake easy to make and often made in the centuries before, in the 1760s, it became at last possible for a ship at sea to determine its longitudinal or east–west position. Turning prematurely at Cape Hangklip brought a ship not into the approaches to Table Bay but into a very much larger bay of which the Cape Peninsula forms the western boundary, effectively separating it from the longed-for anchorage and the amenities of Cape Town; so that Cape Hangklip in the beginning came to be known as Cabo Falso and the whole huge and marvellous bay False Bay, as it remains.

Within the large expanse of False Bay – Table Bay, in comparison, is a tablespoonful – there are several smaller bays for anchorage and for fisheries; in particular Simon's Town, now the base of the South African Navy. I sometimes, towards the end of the war, visited John there, he on shore leave from the navy and I on French leave from my mother. The sea nearest to the Bee House is Gordon's Bay, which used to be famous for oysters before a Dutch Governor, with amazing *hubris*, proclaimed that all pearls found in oysters belonged to the East India Company. After that it became known for whaling; now for honeymoons and holidays. The Right Whales of the Southern Ocean, those which the appalling ships of Japan and Norway have failed to slaughter, also go singing into the Bay, in the spring of the year, for honeymoon and holiday. (Right Whales were called that because they were the 'right' ones to hunt and kill, which is exactly the same crude, anthropocentric folly, even if a kinder adjective, as 'False' Bay.)

Wondrous and interesting as it is, and far easier of access than

Table Bay as it was in the days of sail, False Bay was, and is, not without its perils. It is sheltered by the mountains from the north-west winds but widely exposed to the south-easters; and before these waters were buoyed they were fraught and frightful with invisible undersea rocks. There are very many records of wrecks in the bay and against its shores. The rocks, of course, are still invisible; but I imagine so clearly, can almost hear, in the depths of night, the sobbing clangour of the bells on the buoys; it is the very sound of grief, the watery sobbing of the undersea bells of Debussy's submerged cathedral. Eliot found it, in 'The Dry Salvages', a summons for him to the certitude of Christian faith, when

> … the ground swell, that is and was from the beginning
> Clangs
> The bell.

I seem to hear the sobbing of bells at the Bee House every night in the night's silence, but for me it is a warning; its tone is unmistakably that of a desolation, not of a discovery. The power which sways the bell that I hear comes from the immense Southern Ocean, if I may for a moment reduce that measureless expanse of sea to the decades of my own life.

I seem to have come a very long way and I have tried, as everyone does, to find a purposeful peace. I have had times, sometimes quite long periods, especially in recent years in South Africa while working with Mike or teaching, of believing that I had that peace – a peace made with my childhood and the great ones of my childhood – Lottie, the Chief, Zwela, Albert, Moses – peace with history, with the British Empire and, most of all perhaps, with my mother. But in spite of all the beauty and the quietness and the interest of the Bee House and this place, it has been a restless anchorage. Perhaps anyone engaged in a conscious search for peace is always and exceptionally disturbed; and yet if peace came easily, it would almost certainly be, for me, a form of forgetfulness, Nepenthe at work, Helen's trick.

The old mariners used to refer to the vast stretches of the Southern Ocean which lie between the Cape and the Antarctic as 'the Great Fetch'. I suppose a modern and landlubber's synonym for this 'fetch' is 'catchment area', though it is a nautical term relating to the measurement of distances on the open sea, originally the length of an act of tacking. In modern usage (mine, anyway) the Great Fetch is one's past, a past which is itself set in the history of the past, reaching far, far beyond an individual's life and yet powerfully shaping it; and what the Great Fetch fetches are storms. At the Cape the storms have only the vast expanses of the Southern Ocean to encounter, and the huge waves which are there engendered are part of the storm, not a baffle or a butt to it, as islands and continents and their cliffs and coves might be. It is to the harbours and ships, the lands and farmers that the storms are fetched, to the shores of earth's 'fairest Cape' as well as to the foulest of islands, Robben Island in Table Bay.

If you look down at Robben Island from the air (which is all you could do in apartheid days if the Director of Prisons had forbidden a visit; though it has recently become a Tourist Attraction) you will notice the disgusting similarity of this pus-fringed roundish excrescence, the scab thicker towards the fleshy centre, to the sores of kwashiorkor, or yaws, on the flesh of black children, such as I several times came across in bush clinics in West Africa. It is indeed a deep and dreadful sore in the life of the nation. If it were not for the miraculous forgiveness which Mandela embodies, I would think it marked a civic wound which could turn out to be infinitely more deep and divisive than that inflicted by the so-called Boer War, which has suppurated throughout my lifetime. That was between Boer and Briton – hardly more than worn-out names, now, to the world in general. But the wounds inflicted on Robben Island are a matter to be seen in Black and White, which the world as a whole uses and understands, every day.

I can remember, when very young, sitting next to my father on a rock on the top of Table Mountain, looking at the view. I asked him what the dark, small island was, that we could see on the horizon. Robben Island was, in those days, the place where black female leprosy patients were sequestered, to die of course. (This was many years before the apartheid politicians thought, by using it as a prison for political offenders, to turn it into a bulwark of Western civilisation.) I recall the surprisingly long time it took my father to reply to my question. At length all he said was that it was where some sick people had to go before they died. Thinking to spare me the horror involved in details of the truth, for I can have been only seven or eight years old, he gave me instead an appalling symbol which always accompanies my thoughts of death. When I have been ill or depressed, through many years as a cancer patient, I have sometimes, in spite of efforts at *fortitudo*, felt my world contracting into a small, dark and dangerous island. I am at the centre of it, the ocean is closing around me, and nobody can reach me – for each one of us is at the centre of their own swallowing-up, each one alone, sinking to extinction in the endless expanses of the Great Fetch.

Something like this, according to several accounts, must be similar to what the apartheid political prisoners felt; but they felt it continuously, year after year, in their enforced and heartless, pointless, painful routines, their inward sight conditioned by the very geography of hopelessness, the small island in the limitless ocean. It must be similar to what millions of blacks feel today; they are now politically free, the first and essential condition, but still must endure what the past has left behind: poverty, educational neglect, degradation, violence, despair. These are storms of suffering which cannot be quickly calmed; lives have to be lived at their mercy, and fortitude invoked, and hope – at last a reality – looked bravely in the face.

The Bee House is about two hundred years old, they say, which makes it among the oldest of *modest* European houses in South Africa; and there remain sadly few even among great houses that

The Bee House

are older than that. It has walls as thick as those of Le Buffaie, and for the same reason – they were built of what nature, roundabout, provided: fairly large stones, roughly shaped but neatly piled and trimly buttressed. The walls of Le Buffaie were a wild display of the rich colours of rustic abandon – moss greens through viridian to the shining silver-grey of old lichen, rusty reds through ginger to scarlet, browns from umber to burnt sienna. But the walls of the Bee House are all pure white. They have been plastered and lime-washed and they have the clean, wholesome colour and inviting lumpiness of home-made biscuits; not, fortunately, the same prom-ise of a delicious and yielding crumbliness. Their thickness – in some places swelling to nearly three feet – gives them strength and stability. So far as I know, there are no gravestones piled in there, Etruscan or otherwise, though it was, in its beginnings, a place of very great stress and exhaustion, possibly death – of animals, any-way. The roof, originally of reeds, has for a long time been of cor-rugated iron painted red; it is high-pitched but ends low down above the windows – not making the house frown, exactly; it is more like the sly invitation of lowered lids. Seen from the outside, the house is like many other modest and useful buildings of this countryside and, indeed, on this farm; but it is in fact of almost unique interest.

It stands at a point on the old 'Settlers' Way', *de ou Caepse wagen-weg*, eastwards from Cape Town and after what used to be the fearsome crossing of the Hottentots Holland mountains. The old road at the very point of the Bee House front gate bends sharply, almost at a right angle – more sharply, I am sure, than spans of six or even four oxen could manage without fouling the *disselboom*. Then it continues (if the journey is east to west) to the crossing point of the Palmiet River, which flows round the bottom of the garden, thickly lined on either bank by poplars which whisper all day in breezes that I do not feel. (When the real south-easters come, I moan and shudder with them.) At this place in the 1790s a local farmer is said to have offered travellers provisions and a boat, and by 1801 there was a rough pontoon for the crossing. Seven years later, if I understand the sources correctly, a bridge was built, the first real bridge in the whole country. It cannot now be seen, though I have often hoped for a sight of its piers beneath the choking undergrowth of the strangely red water.

At this very point, it seems to me, on the old Cape Wagon Road, the early travellers, forced by the sharp angle of the road to slow down or to stop for unyoking the leading oxen, were obliged to pay a toll. And the Bee House is the old Toll House!

Sir Lowry's Pass over the mountains was opened in 1830, and that road is the basis of the modern motorway which swoops you over ridges so effortlessly that you observe the ascent only by the increasing scope and grandeur of the view down to the blue seas of False Bay. But for those men and beasts who made the early journeys over the mountains of Hottentots Holland, foraging or cattle-dealing, prospecting or escaping – nation-building, each in his way – it was a cruel and desperate procedure. William Burchell, who writes with a marvellous precision, made the crossing in 1811:

'At the first part of it the road is not very steep, but as soon as the traveller enters the hollow way of the Roode Hoogte (Red Heights) the difficulty of the ascent begins. This is a lower hill forming the foot of the mountain, and composed of a hard, barren, reddish, clayey, ferruginous earth, into which the road, towards its summit, is cut down to the depth of, perhaps, twenty feet. After this he has to climb the rocky mountain itself, and will not, without some surprise, behold loaded waggons ascending and descending so steep and frightful a road, nor will he, without a compassionate feeling for the oxen, witness their toil and labour, carried to the very utmost of their strength; sometimes encouraged by good words, at other times terrified into exertion by the blows of the shambok, the loud crack of the whip, or the whoop and noisy clamour of the boer and his Hottentots.'

These ascents and the equally difficult descents are attested by the ruts and scourings which are still to be seen if you leave the modern pass and climb to the Roode Hoogte, which used to be the only way to pass through the Kloof, the mountain cleft.

In some places the old road, where free of the mountains, was marked by the planting of extensive avenues of oaks, which are now among the oldest and grandest in Africa. The little Bee House approached by the grandest oaks of Africa? Well, we should be more particular and more honest. The Cape is renowned for its oaks, but the truth is that they don't do as well as they might. Because of the sunlight here they grow too quickly, and many of the oaks all around me, though noble and spreading and tall, are slowly dying. In the high winds only last week there was a rending, wrenching crash as the tree nearest the Bee House was reft of its largest limb, and that fell upon its neighbour, which with a similar cry lost a large branch. Upon both trunks there are gashes three or four feet long, and the dead members are lying, their leaves already browning and crisping, where one can examine the wounds; and the wood is revealed as soft, discoloured and rotten. There are many other signs of this in the rest of the trees. Because they grow too quickly they become hollow and attract fungus and disease before their time, or what their time would be if they were in their native, temperate zones of Europe.

Here, though, is the reward: of the several kinds of fungus which grow upon the ailing trees, some are huge and bright yellow-gold simulacra of the miraculous Golden Bough, the shining yellow

mistletoe which Virgil and I have seen; which I am so proud to
have seen with Virgil. Here in the Cape these strange growths,
though so different from a golden mistletoe, yet seem in the same
way to catch and absorb the sunlight which sparsely filters through
the dense green and the moving shadows. They are lambent with it,
they seem to collect it into their fungoid, brainlike convolutions
and, until the light moves or fades, they are refulgent, sullen fires of
amber and lemon, glowing in the green depths. The oaks are old
and dying but even in decay their presence is so rich an experience
that any decision to destroy them would be far, far beyond what I,
were I the owner, could contemplate.

My kitchen door is at the front of the house, facing the road. In
the mornings I throw open the top half of it (for it is the old
stable-door) to let in the light, before I can get outside to fasten
back all the shutters. Every morning what first greets me is the
sight, under the huge boughs of the oaks, of hundreds of rows of
apple trees. The early sun, so horizontal at these ends of the earth,
filters through their boughs and leaves and because the morning
dew is still upon them they are soft and shining; and so, down
upon the ground, are whatever grasses are allowed to grow
between them. The orchards are at every season lovely. There is a
presence among them of fruitful peace and fragrance and quietness.
I am reminded of how, in Umbria, Dick Sheppard loved to drive –
for he could not walk on those sudden hillsides – into the olive
groves and simply sit in the lively stillness of them, luxuriating in
the small sounds and sights and scents, the presence and companionship of the old trees, the softness of the summer air and the
warmth of it on his face.

This farm, quite unlike that at Le Buffaie (needless to say), is
also a business, a commercial matter, and a very large and successful one, employing hundreds of men and women, coloured and
African and white. I think I am reflecting on the apple trees in
order to counterbalance the depressing (it may be) effect of my
view of the old avenues of oak, the other importation from Europe
which, in contrast to the apples, has so largely failed to reach its

full glory in this country. As I write, it is the harvest season. The whole estate has gone into overdrive to get the fruit in during the exact period when each of the dozens of varieties are at their individual right time for picking, refrigeration, labelling, packing, dispatch to abroad – where in Oxford, I often buy them. A friend who came the other day said he had recently bought some in Moscow.

I do not often go into the offices, so I don't see the coloured and African folk there who are being brought in to the management, but many times a day I wave, in the country custom, to the men who are driving great tractors down the oak avenues, pulling crate upon crate which the pickers have filled. There have been, in the past, great iniquities in this country, especially in the vineyards. My friend's grandfather, who first acquired this farm, had all the vines rooted out and replaced by apples, as he refused to join or to countenance the evil system of paying the workers, in part, by 'tots' – that is, a measure of the strong spirits which the grape can produce, upon which many workers became, as was intended, dependent. But I live closely with the men's wives and families; we visit, house to house, and I enjoy attending church with them. The Afrikaans in which the services are conducted presents, to me, a barrier as impassable as my unbelief; but I enjoy what I see of their reactions to the news which is given out of absent members, sick or in trouble, and the custom of kissing and embracing, at the appropriate time in the service, anyone whom you can reach over the pews.

Last year, at the kitchen door of the Bee House, admiring the early morning trees, I heard a song approaching down the avenue towards me, men's voices singing very musically, a song very stirring, a marching rhythm. When they came at length into view I saw they were labourers and were indeed marching, many of them with rakes and spades and such things over their shoulders, carried like rifles. I thought: what a disciplined workforce, turning out to start the working day like this!! When they were close enough, only a few feet away, where the road turns round its right angle, I waved at them and smiled in a congratulatory way. They didn't break their step but most of them forgot about their 'rifles' and waved their implements courteously in my direction, or else their free hand, or both at once, and continued their singing through their smiles. The next day I learned that it had been a Union demo, a big, militant demand, not just from this farm, but regionally organised, for improved conditions. So I set this down, too.

I've not been able to trace that there was a period when the oxen which drew the wagons were supplanted by mules, who are so sure-footed and often used in other countries for mountain work, but the people who passed into the Overberg were always carrying very heavy loads; often, as in the case of the trekboers, they were removing their lives to elsewhere, carrying their entire material substance; and I suppose that the quarters of a mule are not as strong as those of the ox, and repute has mules twice as stubborn. Perhaps mules would have died rather than climbed the Roode Hoogte. (My knowledge of mules, I confess, is based upon their haulage, in Homer, of the princess Nausicaa's laundry wagon down the cliffs to the beach where they found the exhausted Odysseus. Why was the royal dirty washing so heavy, I used to wonder, as to need mules – you may recall that I was a laundry expert – even on the outward journey when it would have been dry? If it had been the royal sewage, in a big tubular tank like the 'donkey' carts, I would have understood.)

But later on, when carriages came to take the place of wagons, the draught oxen were certainly replaced by horses. The Bee House became a post house where you could change or provender your team, if necessary staying the night yourself, after the long, high haul into the blessed country of the Overberg – or, conversely, before the long high haul which took you to the urban rewards of Cape Town. Stalls, at this period, were provided for the horses down each side of the main room of the old building, a large and airy space which is now the living room. Danie du Toit, who still lives on the farm, tells me that his father remembered the time when these stalls served as sleeping cubicles for the young women and girls who were the pickers and packers when the extensive fruit farming in this district began in the 1930s, for the toll-house-turned-post-house became their dormitory. It was considered a great refinement for the girls to have the privacy afforded by cubicles, even if the wooden part-walls had been designed to prevent you biting your neighbour's neck or pinching his fodder. My bedroom (though none of this is 'mine') was added on to provide quarters for the overseer of the girls. The first girls and women, I am told, were whites, Europeans, and travelled round the country in groups at the picking seasons. Coloured pickers and packers came later. White or coloured, it was supposed that the women needed nightly overseeing and I have many times wondered about the function of a small, now filled-up, hole in the bedroom, in the thickest part of the common wall. I want to believe it was what church historians so beautifully call a 'squinch', through which a medieval preacher might keep, for whatever reason, an eye on his flock.

After that, as the fruit industry developed, the labourers both coloured and black began to have their own family settlements on the farm, which have become the trim villages of today, with several types of housing and clinics and schools and shops and a library. What, then, happened to the Bee House? That is when it *became* the 'Bee House'. Orchards need bees, and the old house, no longer a dormitory, was used for storing hives and all the other aids that beekeepers need: wax, I suppose, and frames and smokers and gloves and veils. I don't know why their stuff needed so much and such high-quality rooming; but then my knowledge of bees, you may recall, is founded upon Virgil, *Georgics IV*; and he was not explicit about technical aids. (The only one I can recall is that of clashing cymbals to attract and muster the bees, a fact accidentally discovered, he says, by the mother of Jupiter when she was hiding her infant son in a cave to prevent his father, Saturn, from eating him. The cymbals were primarily used to disguise, with their noise, the child's crying but also attracted a swarm of bees, which usefully provided honey. Virgil doesn't go so far as to recommend cymbals, though. He puts more weight on the organic method of providing any passing bees with the scent (he says) of yellow flowers, to muster them. Jupiter and Saturn, cymbals, and all that ... well, he must have acknowledged, as some of us have to, that he was too easily carried away by the pursuit of classical allusions.)

All the same, knowing nothing, I love to think of all the bee equipment – of each trade, as Gerard Hopkins says, its gear and tackle and trim. But these days, the big fruit farms round here don't keep their own bees. Like the former bands of pickers and packers, the modern bees are itinerant. They come, always by night, tucked up in their hives, in big vans. Before they want to rise, their hives are placed in the orchards wherever they are needed. The eager bees emerge, do a day's pollination work, for the farmer knows to a nicety when they will be most effective; go back, tired and laden; when in the hive they are locked up again and taken away, again at night, to some other stand, some other customer. I find it a heart-breaking thought, because here I am in a little house where the very walls tell me that it used to be women, not bees, carted around like this. *They* can't have been fooled into not minding.

When my friends decided to enlarge and recondition the Bee House, making it into the lovely yet simple dwelling that it is today, they kept its latest name Curiously, it is still redolent of honey. They laid down floors and put in doors and windows and shutters, and covered the huge, high ceiling, all with beautiful yellow timbers of Oregon pine. When the sun shines onto the floor or reflects off the walls and illumines the great ship-like arch of the wooden ceil-ing, the whole house fills with a honey-coloured light and the old place is suffused by a deep sweetness. I sense a sadness, too, when I think of the exhausted travellers and hard-driven beasts and the herded and spied-upon girl packers. Lucretius, seduced, challenged and maddened all his life by the evidence of the senses, remarks on several occasions that honey is both sweet and bitter; and tries, of course, to account for it.

You have been expecting, in this final chapter, should you have got so far, that I would redeem the undertaking I rather faintly gave about saying how South Africa appears to me, since I have felt able to return and to compare the now with the then. Well, all this Table Bay and False Bay, fair winds and foul, blue calms and undersea rocks, small island and Great Fetch, wagon road and motorway, oxen-horse-and-mule, rotten oak and golden fungus, exploited girls and migrant bees, labour disputes-and-cheerful waves, sweet and bitter – all the Bee House stuff – what do you *think* I have been writing about? Evolution, of course, human, historical evolution. It is all going on, nothing can stop the pressures and the conflicts. The political revolution, which most find glorious and some find a disaster and everyone, I believe, an experience of Open Mind surgery, cannot stop it. Change, and effort, waste and decay, beauty and cruelty, innovation and adaptation, suffering and alienation – now, here is a problem; am I in a position to write, after 'alienation', 'reconciliation'? Nobody can today refer to South Africa without being asked for an instant opinion on Archbishop Tutu's Truth and Reconciliation Commission.

I have tried, I've made an honest attempt to develop an opinion on this important matter. I have, as I've said, visited South Africa several times since 'Freedom', as well as enjoying these lovely summers in the Bee House. I've acquired strong feelings; are they 'opinions'? The things that have struck me, sometimes nearly struck me dumb with sorrow and with rage, dismay, disbelief, do indeed seem to relate to matters of truth and reconciliation. I feel almost reverential towards Archbishop Tutu, as I do towards President Mandela, and I can see why each of them places such faith in the work of the Commission. If I do too, it is largely because of my faith in them.

Let me tell you of my 'honest attempt'. In the loft of the Bee House there are many wooden shelves along the length of the walls. I suppose that at one time they were meant for fodder or tackle, bee equipment, or more lately for apples. Each day I read most of the newspapers, which are kindly brought down to me

from the estate office, and from them I cut out all reports which
bear upon anything to do with the Commission: the terrible confes-
sions which come before it, and visits they pay, and exhumations
which they order of murdered bodies, the opinions of others about
their work, and so on. Then, in the evenings, I attempt to classify
the cuttings and I put them in different, labelled piles upon the
shelves. It is a hopeless way to start the night; gives me very bad
dreams; but you cannot say that – in my limited way – I have not
tried.

I'm afraid, however, that I do not wish to write about any of the
topics filling and piling upon the shelves. I know that much of the
alarm which they suggest is warranted. In particular, nobody was
prepared for the revelations which have poured forth about the corruption and brutality among sections of the Security Police and the
former Defence Force, and the Freedom movements themselves; or,
beyond that, for the rise in the incidence of all kinds of crime and
violence in the townships, suburbs and cities. I am among those
who think that all this evil was bred by the evil of apartheid, or the
centuries of selfish, blind and brutal attitudes before that which led
to apartheid and to the exploitation and impoverishment of the
black nations, the basic inequity and frequent iniquity of the society
into which I was born. And behind and above all that, there is the
vast movement, all over Africa, of country people abandoning an
impoverished landscape and surging towards the towns, and the
social disasters of these economic forces for both town and country.

What is also clear to many, since the voting-out of apartheid, is
that once an imposed and unnatural system of control has been by
decree abolished there will for a time be all kinds of licence and
chaos. In Britain people still think uneasily about the terrible violence which succeeded the (right and inevitable) granting of independence to India: the ravages of Partition and the birth of
Pakistan – and, now, after more than fifty years of their separation,
the muscling up of these two nations against each other with preparations for nuclear conflict. And right into the time that I am writing, the collapse of the Soviet Union into major secessions, united

only by increasing poverty and the crime it breeds; and the continuing tragedy of the savage rivalries in what was Yugoslavia. In the even poorer countries of Africa where military takeovers have for so long nullified any democratic process, and everyone except the military is so poor and so defenceless, the consequences have been even more horrifying.

I would not like all that to be taken as 'opinion' since it is merely a set of common observations. What is vital – here is an opinion – is that this violence and corruption should not be *all* that is happening: that wherever it is possible the truth of these evils shall be established, whether by Commission or, after its writ is run, by the courts. The case for the establishment of truth is plain, and South Africa in this regard has emerged a leader, a star among the nations – after all that time as a polecat! There are no doubts about the need for establishing 'Truth' and I think that ordinary, solo people and not just commissions should reach out for it.

'Reconciliation' is much more difficult. I suppose that word was chosen because 'forgiveness' sounds at once too churchy and too, somehow, amateur. Also, in a multiracial state, 'reconciliation' has suspiciously facile, correct political overtones. All the same, to many people what it primarily means *is*, in fact, 'forgiveness', and they do not see how to do it. I do not know what it might mean, to a Christian or anyone else, to 'forgive' a crime of the repulsive enormity of some which are now revealed, even if the dead were quite unknown to you. I do not believe I have ever forgiven, or even tried to forgive, the young braves of the Ossewa-Brandwag for their brutal attempt to murder my beloved. Surely it is most unlikely that any civilised person will 'forgive' the men who murdered Steve Biko; and there were so many other thousands of victims.

The problem about 'forgiveness', for non-believers anyway, is not that it is difficult but that it is impossible. In my experience, if the hurt, sorrow and anger persist, then to 'forgive' the perpetrator would be a denial of the hurt, and therefore an untruth. And if the hurt itself has vanished, passed into numbness or amnesia, a person might wonder what they are said to be 'forgiving'. An insentient or

unconscious person cannot be said to 'forgive', any more than can
the dead. The attempt to forgive is like sending a canary down a
mine to test for the presence of poisonous gases. If the poison, the
pain, is still there – why, then the sweet bird dies.

And yet reconciliation is most certainly a political and moral
necessity, and problems about forgiveness seem to cloud the issue. I
support the Commission's work entirely, whatever they meant or
didn't mean. I think, and it seems to me that most of the world
thinks, that its establishment really was a very great achievement,
in fame and glory less only than the triumph of political freedom
itself after so long and deadly a struggle. I feel little patience with
the people who phone in to phone-ins about the Commission saying, 'Why are they stirring up all this past trouble?' or 'Why is it so
many *whites* are had up?' or even 'It only goes to show us up in
front of the world'! There are even some Whitefellows that I know,
educated people who wouldn't use such crude and ill-motivated
words, who seem not to feel the historical necessity for the Commission. They pick holes in its procedures, deny its results and its
merits; they even grumble about the expense.

Here, in the Bee House, I am very far from the texts of Greece
and Rome which have so often shown me the way of things, and
I'm surrounded, instead, night after night, by all these newspaper
cuttings which tell of cold murders and hot murders and group
murders and, inevitably, of murders of all kinds to come, unless the
Commission and the politicians can find us some way out of this
dire history. Here in the Bee House, I am afraid of facing it all; but
also afraid of escapist delusions, so I try to resist the solace of
ancient reflections.

And fail. I find it impossible to forget the savage history of the
House of Atreus, the storyline of the soap-opera of a great part of
Greek tragedy, which underlies and conditions our own. The great
Greek dramatists of the fifth century BC gave the story their pas-
sionately enquiring attention, from the ghastly banquet at which
Atreus served his brother the flesh of his own sons, through genera-
tions of retributive murder, to the agonised, unwilling murder by

Orestes of his own mother as a necessary vengeance, he believed, for her murder of his father Agamemnon. The need for vengeance which dictates the murders of a blood feud is different in kind, and in scale more limited, than today's terrible factional and tribal wars of Central Africa or the interracial conflicts and animosities of the South. But the agonies which it presents to the captive minds of individuals are the same: the violent, irrational and insistent demands of the Furies within our blood; and also, in our saner moments, the search, established for centuries by the dark brooding of the Greek choruses, for an end to the cycles of suffering, hatred and murder. But until at the end the goddess, Pallas Athene herself, steps in, taming the fearful, vengeful Furies and establishing from among the citizens of Athens the rational authority of the court of the Areopagus, there is no solution, no release from the cycles of violence and retaliation; and without the acceptance of judgments, no possibilities of forgiveness.

Classical readers will have to put up with this extreme compression (of, in particular, the trilogy of plays by Aeschylus, the *Oresteia*) which nightly floods into my mind as I brood upon the historical chain of aggression, exploitation, vengeance and blood-based racial division in South Africa, and upon the establishment, after centuries of strife, of the Truth and Reconciliation Commission. It is true that the Commission has been instituted to last not for ever but for a limited period; but there are, all the same, striking correspondences with the mythological account Aeschylus gives of the founding of the Areopagus, not least the fact that both tribunals are composed from citizens of the country itself. When NATO or the United Nations is driven to intervene in the bloody affairs of Eastern Europe and elsewhere it is inevitable that the warring factions should bitterly resent the fact that war criminals and human rights violators may be referred to an international court – which they regard, of course, as lying at the heart of the international enemy, the intruder, the vociferous critic. There could not possibly be a greater advantage for a nation struggling to be born than its ability to require that suspect citizens should stand before a tribunal of their own countrymen, a tribunal established and protected by their own elected government.

I've discovered that a small reason why I support the Commission is that it helps me forward with my own attempt to arrive at a peace through understanding; understanding even what has seemed to me most hopeless. If you don't know what happened, to whom, why, who did it or caused it to be done, either in your own or in the country's history, then there is naturally no understanding it. Without that, no peace; without peace, no desire to be reconciled. 'Forgiveness' has a spiritual dimension which is hard to demand of most people. In history, the challenge arises from the forces which shaped apartheid, and those forces that were destructive in colonialism, and so on backwards to the first dangerous landfalls at the Cape. How is one supposed to 'forgive' history? 'Understanding' is at least within reach – if one can find a way through one's own, personal electric fences and other fortifications.

I think of Hilda – Hilda Kuper who so long ago at Wits shared with me an anthropologist's way of looking at human division and diversity. During her final illness in Los Angeles, I spent with her as much time as I could. (She asked me, one sad day, to write on her behalf to many of her closest friends – scattered, in the way of old Whitefellows, over all the continents – to say 'goodbye' and to thank them for their love.) If she were with me now, I would say, 'What I think about peace and understanding is: can I be sure it's not just a way of making a scapegoat out of history? Doesn't one have to blame someone, or something?' Even if history were conceived to cover the whole of human affairs, beginning in the primeval ooze, I am sure Hilda would not be at all discouraged, and that she would simply point to the processes: 'This is how that or this came about' and (though her sweet brown eyes might be sad) she would continue, 'What on earth have scapegoats got to do with it?' 'But what about guilt, Hilda?' I might say. 'How shall we ease our pain? Don't we need someone to be guilty, even if it is ourselves? From the prophets of the Old Testament to the clerics of today, isn't this idea of "guilt" too useful to be surrendered? Also –

if you wish guilt to be detached from the violence of endless retri-
bution, then isn't 'forgiveness' your last card?' I am sure that Hilda
would laugh, and taking her cue from the mention of cards, would
dismissively, though kindly, agree; for she would understand that I
was not so much defending the mysteries of forgiveness as trying to
praise the need, in some people, to bestow it. (Anybody can understand the comfort of receiving it.) Hilda would laugh and say, perhaps, 'We are, I suppose, to play this word-game for ever!' What
she would mean is that it is not definitions that matter; it is the
fairness of honest intentions and open minds, minds lacking a narrow (even if millions-wide) self-interest; or if they have it, being
aware of it, weighing it in every balance that life presents, and
being willing, if all else fails, to accept open-mind surgery.

It could well be that I have this difficulty about the nature of
forgiveness because I have not been hurt *enough*. I have not suffered any personal violence, let alone the agonies and atrocities
which came before the Truth Commission. I have not spent twenty-
seven years in prison, or any; I have spent only about a quarter of
my life in South Africa, facing or not facing its problems. It is part
of the meaning of Mandela that because he has endured so much
and knowing himself to be free of guilt, he has had the spiritual
power to forgive.

As for *being* forgiven: criminals or deluded and unthinking people might in these latter days like to think they have been forgiven;
but Reconciliation more reliably depends upon understanding; and
the same goes for understanding oneself, to be rid of guilt. If these
are opinions, I confess to having them. They feel more like feelings.
I feel that the coming of universal political freedom, fought for by
generations of Africans, initiated by an Afrikaner government and
supported by so many Afrikaners (in the end by the Broederbond
itself!) as well as English, and the work of the Commission, have
set me free from the shame and depression I used to feel at the
nationhood into which I was born.

In trying over the past few years to understand where I came
from, I have at last lost my haunting sense of guilt. Not about my

mother, perhaps. I did not love her enough; I loved her only when
she pleased me, and I did not understand her at all. That is infantile
behaviour. My usual excuses are that I was too young, and crushed
by my father's death, before I could understand how much she did
for me or meant to me. But about South Africa, almost certainly,
the guilt and shame which drove me away, and to the edge of
despair, have left me, even though it is apparent that the wounds
inflicted over centuries of rivalry, exploitation, every kind of conflict will take as long again to heal.

Sometimes at the Bee House I walk out of the house at night to
stand on a lawn silver with the moonlight on the dew, and look at
the sky. I feel again something of the astonishment of my first sight
of the stars, when my father took me in his arms to carry me to the
car while I was hiding the granadilla pips in my appendix; and I
feel the fear, too, the old terror of the view from below. But in these
extreme southern latitudes, in country places, the air is so clear that
one seems almost amongst the stars, because some are much nearer
than others. In fact, one seems to be standing on one of them; must
be; in fact ... is. The realisation comes rather slowly. It is suddenly
evident that one is part of all this, has a place in it – standing
room, anyway. Here one can sense the distances between the stars,
huge drifts of deepest black (Lucretius calls them 'the caverns of the
sky') between and behind the swathes of light, the prickly constella-
tions, the magnificent bright loners, the large, lazy, liquid nearers.
And the spaces between them that are not so dark – Hopkins's
'lovely-asunder starlight' – in places other than the southernmost
Cape (so far as I know) you can get no sense of that. It is not at all
like T.E. Hulme's celebrated description of 'the old moth-eaten
blanket of the sky', which sees all the stars as the same kind of hole
in a fusty, woolly, material. The clarity of this extreme air, I suppose, reveals all the whelming immensity and random beauty, the
magnificent, frightening, unimaginable distances.

This very week the Comet Hyakutake appeared and for three days I have alarmed myself to rise before dawn in order to thrill with fear at the sight of the fuzzy big moon of it and its monstrous tail. 'Last passed the earth 15,000 years ago,' the radio said, as though it were a statistic from the weather forecast. As I watch its astonishing, fiery progress I wonder: am I, is anybody, safe from this powerful, mindless phenomenal thing with (heretofore) regular habits? Or from whatever else might come at me from above, onto the silver lawn? Or from the Great Fetch of the past; coming at this privileged, fortunate person, who bolted in distress from a lover, a mother and a whole huge country, all of them also in distress; and who in spite of this defection was rewarded by a wonderful marriage, long and faithful friendships, incredibly interesting jobs, loving and gifted children; and who is able to return to the beloved country at the dawn of its freedom?

What personal, tiny questions! Monstrously small. And I seemed, on the silver lawn, to be addressing them to the immeasurable, endless universe! What is more, they would give the universe a far too rosy, a less than truthful impression of my life. The universe should not forget that from childhood onwards I have many times had to beg help from *fortitudo*, which has nothing to do with any network of stars.

This morning, as I turned to go back into the house, after what is billed as the last (for some time) of Hyakutake's special appearances, I told myself that all I – or anyone – can do is to make an effort to understand what we can, to endure what we cannot, and to attempt to improve the pitifully small part that we can reach. None of this, not any part of it, can be done without love and understanding; understanding not only of people whom we know – 'people like us', same ideas, same background, same colour – and not only of those who live now but of those who long ago had their world destroyed and whose children are trying to shape a fairer model of it; and understanding, too, those who fear that the great achievements of their immigrant forebears will be forgotten or wasted. We need as well, and as always, fortitude; of the quality and perhaps the desperate inventiveness of *Welwitschia mirabilis*, of which, if it had a mind, you might say it knew that without it there would be no future.

In my own case, the attempt at understanding is often a failure; even so, it usually picks up heart, driven by an awareness of all that – in spite of my early desertion – I owe to this beautiful, difficult country; and to those people, white and black, who gave my life, in the clear, bright light of its morning, all that I have most enjoyed and valued.